Bridge from Saigon

Bridge from Saigon

*A Viet-American Memoir
of Family and Mind*

HOANGMAI H. PHAM

McFarland & Company, Inc., Publishers
Jefferson, North Carolina

"Hearts and Bones"
Words and Music by Paul Simon
Copyright © 1982 Sony Music Publishing (U.S.) LLC
Copyright Renewed
All Rights Administered by Sony Music Publishing (U.S.) LLC,
424 Church Street, Suite 1200, Nashville, TN 37219
International Copyright Secured All Rights Reserved
Reprinted by Permission of Hal Leonard LLC

ISBN (print) 978-1-4766-9849-6
ISBN (ebook) 978-1-4766-5745-5

LIBRARY OF CONGRESS CATALOGING DATA ARE AVAILABLE

© 2026 Hoangmai H. Pham. All rights reserved

No part of this book may be reproduced or transmitted in any form or by any means, electronic or mechanical, including photocopying or recording, or by any information storage and retrieval system, without permission in writing from the publisher.

Front cover image: Riding with my cousin, Sử. Ho Chi Minh City, 1997; background *Matte Blue, No Purple*, acrylic and paper on canvas (Hoangmai H. Pham artist).

Printed in the United States of America

McFarland & Company, Inc., Publishers
Box 611, Jefferson, North Carolina 28640
www.mcfarlandpub.com

For my parents and grandparents

Acknowledgments

This book is my offering to ancestors whose unwavering life force made it possible for me to become an American, and to people who have loved me here, who helped me flourish as the kind of immigrant intensely committed to making the country ever better.

I'm indebted to the Diasporic Vietnamese Artists Network (*diaCRITICS*) and *Immigrant Report* for publishing earlier versions of several chapters.

Many friends and coaches laid kind but keen eyes on earlier drafts to distill what was worth keeping, especially Dorothy Bukantz, Rich Baron, Emily Anthony, Marion Roach Smith, and Sue Katz Miller. My parents, aunts and uncles, and Faye and Dan Ross offered memories of events outside the view of my child eyes. Renee Brachfeld taught me how to tell these stories out loud and hear them deeply. Jan Herman and Karen Branan's convictions in, and advocacy for the book made it inevitable. I could not have created this without the open-spirited support of my husband, David Roodman, who patiently tracked down original documents and checked on my progress while impatiently waving away all my doubts about investing in this fifteen-year project; and my therapist, Blue, who saved my life.

Table of Contents

Acknowledgments   vi
Cast of Characters   ix
Preface   1

Part 1—Alien Princess

Origin	3	Contact	51
Calamity	4	Blind Sight	53
Running Sài Gòn	7	Kitchen	56
Day, Night, Week, Month	15	Bà Ngoại (Grandmother)	59
Gap	19	Boy	62
Hear, Say	21	Wall	66
Alien	24	Teacher	68
Passing	29	Cook	72
Bridge	32	Rooms	75
Michael	34	Label	77
Red	37	Carpenter	79
Rich	39	Altar	84
Stranded	43	Memorial	88
Vigil	47	Clock	92
Talking Cure	49		

Part 2—Native

Homegoing	97	Legend	123
Nhà (House)	101	Generation	125
Hear, Say	104	Book	127
Mirror, Door, Whore	107	Allegiance	131
Newsman	111	Hustle	133
Trail	117	Flow	137
Seed	119	Her and Him	139
Missive	121	Brood	144

Hạnh Phúc (Blessed Happiness)	146	Quê Hương (Ancestral Land)	151
Monkey	148	Shield and Sword	154

Part 3—Remains

Un-Altered	157	Numb	186
Seven	160	Tree	188
Little Girls	163	Pieces	191
Cells	166	Michaela	194
Art	169	Well	199
Tango	174	Preparation	202
Eight	178	Tiger	204
Rain	181	Lioness	206
Smash	183	Storm	209

Part 4—Harvest

Thrill	213	Offering	226
Trace	219	Legacy	230
Bah.... Bah.... BS	221	Beloved	233
Chosen	223		

Index 237

Cast of Characters

Family

Oldest Generation	Bà Ngoại	Maternal grandmother (Lê Thị Cạnh)
	Ông Ngoại	Maternal grandfather (Nguyễn Đức Kính)
	Ông Nội	Paternal grandfather (Phạm Hữu Sán)
Immediate Family	Mẹ	Mother (Nguyễn Thị Anh)
	Bố	Father (Phạm Hữu Bính)
	Ân	Oldest brother
	Chương	Second older brother
	Tuấn	Younger brother
	David	Husband
	Benjamin	Older child
	Alex	Younger child
Other Relatives	Anh Sử	Cousin in Sàigòn (my father's nephew)
	Bác Chỉnh	Aunt in north Việt Nam (my father's oldest sister)
	Bác Vượng	Second cousin in Sàigòn (my mother's cousin)
	Chị Hảo	Cousin in Hanoi (my father's niece)
	Cậu Hải	Uncle (my mother's younger brother)
	Bác Sơn	Uncle (my mother's older brother)
	Bác Tân	Uncle helping us escape (my mother's brother-in-law)

Inner Characters

Baby	My toddler self
Eight	My eight-year-old self, the most troubled little girl
Four	My four-year-old self

Cast of Characters

	Michael	Most important friend whom I met at age eight
	Seven	My seven-year-old self
	Teen	My sixteen-year-old-self
Others		
	Blue	Therapist
	Carpenter	High school teacher
	Dan & Faye Ross	American couple who sponsored our family's immigration
	Danny Zemel	First rabbi
	Hương	Alley neighbor when I returned to Sàigòn in adulthood
	Peter	Colleague
	Phoebe	Girlfriend

Preface

I can honestly say this book began taking form when I was eight years old. That's when I started crafting my own internal, dark and exuberant stories, the meaning of which I didn't understand until decades later. Over the rest of childhood and young adulthood, I instinctively collected and researched other stories—about family, Việt Nam, my own mental health and spiritual journeys—without any ambition that they would coalesce one day into a memoir. War refugees like my parents don't want to talk about what they've left behind. I stubbornly pried from anybody who might know anything tidbits of insights, gossip, and secrets you'll find in the following pages. I triangulated different versions of "truth" across oral history, my own observations, scholarly books, and original documents from a century ago. That drive to unify my present and future with the past felt lonely and mysteriously alienating at times, but it paved a path to this manuscript. I want to leave you in awe of the immense sacrifices immigrants are willing to overcome for a chance at a better life, and the depth of human resilience made possible by good genes, imagination, and the strength of a family's collective will to thrive that reaches through generations like a gift delivered with an outstretched arm.

Part One—Alien Princess

Origin

I was named the morning the Tết Offensive began. My father already had two sons and yearned for a girl. In January of 1968, when I was just a spinal cord with appendages in my mother's womb, he stopped by one of Sài Gòn's street markets awash in flowers and prepared foods for the upcoming lunar new year holiday of Tết. He carried home several three-foot-long apricot tree branches to put in a tall ceramic vase. He made a public vow—by the first morning of Tết, the buds would bloom, they would be yellow to assure I'd be born a girl, and he would name me Hoàng Mai—Yellow Apricot Blossom. But on Tết eve, the tight green buds were stubbornly closed and he panicked.

As my great-aunt tells it, when he thought no one was watching, my father dumped an entire bottle of aspirin into the vase water. The next morning, Việt Cộng guerrillas stormed gates at the U.S. Embassy. As gunfire from their tactical and public relations coup sputtered on newsreels to be sent around the world, the stressed apricot branches bent to his will and relented, blooming yellow. Four months later, I was born into my sunny fate.

Calamity

Thirty-eight years later, I was a naturalized U.S. citizen with degrees from Harvard and Johns Hopkins and other markers of the model minority. Yet desperation enveloped me in oxygen-deprived delirium and fear. Each night over a monthslong downward spiral, my reserve of control ran out a few minutes earlier than the night before. That October afternoon before my husband David got home, I just managed to reach our back gate after work when blood vessels constricted in my temples, gut, and wrists. My fingers shook and my eyes slid in and out of focus. I sent our seven- and four-year-old kids to the basement for a video and sat on steps one floor above in the dark, clinging to the railing, my nails digging into my palm. With the other hand, I dialed the first girlfriend's number I could remember.

The wisdom of panic attacks is that they force you to ask for help.

"Phoebe, I think I'm going to die."

"Call David now," she said, "and then call me right back." The next day, she coaxed her therapist to give me references. The therapist I chose was willing to be aggressive. He sat forward, his questions giving an impression of the tiny, repetitive dissecting strokes of a scalpel debriding rotten tissue. He wasn't deterred by what wincing they might induce.

"Please," I begged him, "give me a toolkit. I really need a toolkit to get through the day before we fix anything else." He tilted his chin up and signaled with the look of a first responder facing an accident victim who asks for a cup of tea as blood gushes from her head wound.

"Sure," he promised in a deliberate tone, "we can do that."

I call him Blue.

* * *

It's unseemly for good Asian girls to want to be "in the room where it happens" unless they're supporting someone more important. I was unlike most of my medical school classmates and my oldest brother, Ân. They dreamed of private practice as front-line doctors and live for daily touch with patients. I came into my early career loving big abstractions like how health care markets and political systems work. I dreamt of leaving a mark on the grand stage of American health care policy. But I hadn't gone to a top-tier medical school. I felt uncomfortable in the traditional academic settings where most physicians with policy expertise seemed to land. Wielding influence was a hazy, distant goal for me the way of princes and lucky lottery tickets, not something to speak out loud or plan for.

Snatched straight out of training, I was instead hired into a well-regarded research group in Washington, D.C. I racked up a string of respectable publications at a modest pace that left me energy to tend to our kids, Benjamin and Alexander, who were barely in grade school by then. I wasn't particularly confident about my career trajectory, but I stood out among my colleagues as the only physician on a hallway of social scientists who brought a more rounded clinical perspective. My lateral thinking style attracted researchers from other organizations who wanted to partner with me. That mix was fertile ground for interesting projects. After just a few years, my breakout moment came.

My main collaborator, Peter, observed that where other people are afraid to color outside lines, I'm unconstrained by conventional wisdom. I simply cannot not see the box. I led a straightforward but unconventional analysis that struck a controversial chord because it implied that trendy new policies were unlikely to work. It was my first taste of serving up inconvenient truths. I was caught off guard by the strong (positive and negative) reactions that people in the industry and government audiences had to it. That the study finally got accepted to the country's most selective medical journal after six months of scrutiny felt sweet, but exhausting and anti-climactic.

"No, no," Peter corrected me, "Your life is about to change dramatically—for the better."

Several months after the article's release, speaking invitations came one after another. With little experience standing at a podium, I defaulted to illustrating research by telling stories and asking provocative questions. My newly discovered gift for bringing home for audiences the personal meaning of numbers on a chart earned me even more credibility in policy discussions despite my outsider status as often the youngest and only woman of color in the room. "You have a fresh voice," someone pointed out. Foundations and national policy groups asked me to write white papers. Ivy League researchers offered to include me on their grant proposals. Then one day, a company executive asked what my ambitions were. "You are a rock star, and we should think about how you get to the next level." Headhunters and universities called to recruit. A Harvard professor offered to nominate me for an award. Wherever the policy conversation turned, it seemed, I had the relevant perspective.

"Isn't this fun?" Peter asked on a call. I glared at the receiver, not explaining to him that my neck and shoulders cramped from stress and only unflexed in sleep. I startled at every ring of the phone and began closing my office door out of habit because when palpitations struck, I needed to lie down on the floor with lights off.

Soon, those palpitations surged daily. No one had prepared me for this assault of attention, but neither did I understand exactly what my distress was about. A friend told me to Google something called the "imposter syndrome." I recognized myself in the Wikipedia description but was utterly unconvinced I *wasn't* an imposter. That circular conversation spun at the base of my brain while I multi-tasked between parenting and work. My poor sleep fractured into no sleep, which only grew worse after months of taking Lunesta, little pills the promising color of a blue moon that forced my eyes closed but did nothing to snuff out synapses gone wild. Five days of low-dose Ativan, I thought wishfully, that's all it would take to readjust.

"What do you think?" I asked a doctor friend visiting for dinner.

She watched me bounce from exhilaration to despondency and switch direction three more times before dessert, then pursed her lips. "Maybe you should try talk therapy first?"

I searched desperately for a staircase back down to professional anonymity, but it didn't exist. I stood stranded and paralyzed, stretched to the breaking point between two irreconcilable selves—the unthreatening ingénue and the bulldozer personality that might burst out any second, alienating everyone and bringing about my doom.

Running Sài Gòn

In Việt Nam, I was too busy to care what I wore. In one photograph on the banks of a waterway, I was three, sitting with my older brother Chương on a bench, feet bouncing in the air and nearly falling off with laughter. In pictures from every year of my early childhood I posed in a different outfit to celebrate the lunar new year. Each was custom-sewn to match those worn by one set of girl cousins or another: red polyester with blue polka-dotted patch pockets and puff sleeves one year, yellow pantsuit another year with large white daisy appliques. My younger self was usually turning this way or that, looking at something besides the camera, smiling or laughing.

I ran everywhere, oblivious to the care my mother took to stock my wardrobe with the most expensive dresses and shoes. As soon as school

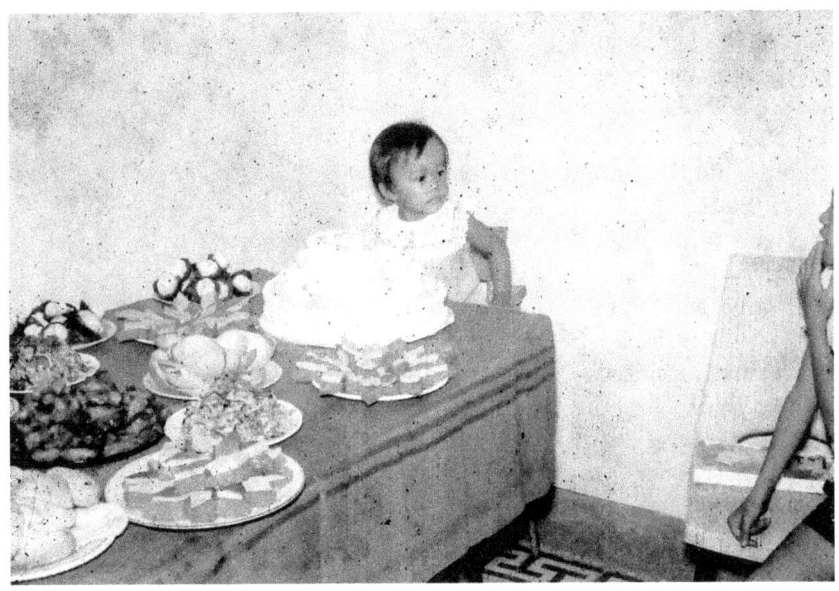

My second birthday, Sài Gòn, 1970.

dismissed at midday, someone drove me home where I leapt out of uniform and into loose and cottony house clothes, the cheap ones we slept in. I loved how light they were on my limbs and didn't get in my way. I'd run to my best friend Châu's house, down to the intersection and after a left turn. Without anything to alert her, Châu's mother was often waiting in their foyer, cheerfully calling out my name and greeting me with a chair to sit in while she readied a basin and washed my feet, dusty and hot from the journey. Or I'd run across the road to the neighbor's gate. I could tell they were richer than us because they rarely mingled with other families on the street, and their house was set back much farther from the road. Too often for my mother's comfort, I climbed the fence to reach fruits growing in their yard and only got caught once in a while.

I ran out our gate and in the opposite direction away from the intersection, where the world grew gradually more exotic. Houses turned to cramped lunch places where customers squatted on small plastic chairs, palm readers, a pharmacy and herbal shop, and stores with meats hanging in the door frame. The walkable street narrowed ominously and became dense with beggars—a blind man, a cripple, a leper with only one eye visible, a man sitting with a long pipe and glazed eyes, old people with black teeth from the betel they chewed and spat out. Steaming meat broth, incense, and the faint stench of garbage all marbled together. Soon I couldn't hear the crisp Vietnamese of my parents anymore, just the syrupy, guttural drawl of southern accents. Street people called to me, reaching out gingerly with gnarled fingers. There I stopped and waited for the growing fascination to turn to palpitations.

My mother with Ân and Chương, Đà Lạt, 1967.

Running Sài Gòn 9

With my brothers Ân (left) and Chương (right), Sài Gòn, 1970.

With my brother Chương, Sài Gòn, 1972.

And then I'd run home. Ân and Chương always seemed to be waiting for me. Had they been watching? It was a couple of hours before my father would come home on his baby-blue moped and scoop me up onto the tippy front of his seat for a spin down the street and back.

Ân was seven years older than me, and Chương six. They made me run for their own amusement or because it was a more reliable way to keep me constructively occupied than leaving me with our housekeeper. They devised treasure hunts, with clues and instructions written on

At the zoo in Sài Gòn, 1972.

Celebrating Tết at home: Dan Ross (left), my father, my brother Ân, my mother, and my brother Chương, Sài Gòn, 1970.

small scraps of paper they folded and tucked into odd corners: solve an arithmetic problem, then take that many steps left, then right, look up, down, jump—they stood back and laughed as I scooted around, in and out of the house, down the alley, up the street, until I solved the mystery and ended at the hiding place of a small packet of treats—dried shrimp or cuttlefish, three candies, sweet and salty dried plums, a homemade toy. As long as I didn't stain my clothes, my mother didn't care.

One afternoon at six years old, I ran later than usual, following a dog or another interesting animal down the alley framing one side of our house. Other houses cast shadows and made hollow echoes of even my light footsteps. I thought this was where the bread cart must've come each morning, hawking crispy, hot baguettes. The light changed pink-orange and I guessed my brothers were sitting down to dinner. But the alley kept stretching away and bending enticingly. Just ten more feet…. Then around the next bend a man stood blocking the alley. He was my father's height, wearing green and brown with a round helmet obscuring his eyes, a thick belt with packets of something attached, and holding a long gun diagonally across his chest. The soldier didn't scold but led me back to my house where my mother had me lie face down and whipped me with chopsticks for disobeying curfew, until my father came at my screams and swooped me up in his arms. Other days the *thwump-thwump-thwump* of a helicopter's propellers beat overhead, but they receded quickly before I could grow curious enough to ask an adult about them, and street sounds swelled again.

Some afternoons and weekends a parent or aunt or uncle would drive me on a motorbike to a cousin's house. Some days they were cousins on my father's side—older like Ân and Chương, with fine, sculpted features. They called me Mai Đen—Black Mai— because of my careless,

With my cousins (from left): Luân, Vân Giao, Quỳnh Giao, Khánh Giao, Sài Gòn, 1972.

unladylike tan. I bossed them around, ate snacks and watched my aunt chop meat in the kitchen, hoping to catch a spare morsel now and then, and then someone brought me home. Some days they were cousins on my mother's side. Three sisters, just older than me. Their bedroom looked out onto a dark courtyard crisscrossed with lines of hanging laundry. We lay in the bed they shared as they taught me songs and we played pretend games.

Once or twice a month, we piled in our red sedan and drove to my grandmother's (Bà Ngoại) house. She was my mother's mother. We headed to the city's edge, down a long dirt road. There was a cemetery along the way, and I held my breath and ducked my head down beneath the rim of the car's windows until we passed.

At the zoo with my mother and my brother Tuấn, Sài Gòn, 1973.

At a corner where the road turned, we pulled up to Bà Ngoại's gate. My mother nudged as I lingered outside the car, looking at women squatting on the other side of the road next to large cauldrons of steaming soup with floating knuckles of gelatinous meat.

"Those are human fingers!" my great-aunt whispered to me with a straight face, "That's what happens to children who run away from home and get lost!" I scooted inside the gate.

My grandmother's house was yellow and elegant. The black iron gate opened inward onto a patio and garden where banana plants and short palms swayed high above my head. Each Tết, we took family photos on the patio. Beyond lay her living room, with a sofa children were not supposed to sit on and polished chairs of carved tropical wood. Small bowls on a table with inlaid mother-of-pearl offered roasted pumpkin seeds, crystallized papaya and coconut.

Bà Ngoại was always sedate and immaculate in an áo giài dress, a

Family gathering for Tết at my grandmother's house (left to right): Uncle Sơn, cousin Trương, Aunt Nhung, cousin Luân, Bà Ngoại, Uncle Vân, great-aunt Liên, my brother Ân, Aunt Bình, cousin Tháng, my brother Chương, and my mother, Sài Gòn, 1971.

strand of pearls at her throat. She was not beautiful, but looked like Buddha, her face unfurrowed and her standing body the shape of an almond with its thin hair in a bun at the top, round tummy in the middle and small feet. We children swarmed all over her house until after dinner when we drove home.

In summertime we drove farther to a crowded beach where we changed into bathing suits and sat in a row on towels while my mother futilely smeared Vaseline over our limbs, backs, and faces as sunscreen. We spent the day running in and out of saltwater foam and picnicking. A day or two later, we would sit in a line, railroad style, and take turns peeling sunburnt skin off each other's backs. We had contests to see who could get the largest piece.

A single large room on our second floor held two beds and a black and white television. There was usually news on TV for half the day that we children never listened to; and static the other half of the day. One bed was for Ân and Chương, the other for me to share with my baby brother, Tuấn, and our housekeeper. Each bed had a canopy from which mosquito netting hung, curtaining everything inside behind white gauze. The bed had plenty of room to roll around in, and two pillows—one rectangle for my head, and one hot dog pillow the length of my body, to wrap my arms and legs around. Baby sucked on the corner of his pillow.

Ân and Chương were often busy in their bed long after we dozed off. Sometimes, after our housekeeper fell asleep, one of them would sneak over to my bed and beckon with a crook of his finger. I ducked under the mosquito netting and tip-toed with him back to their bed. The floor was enormously wide and the room black. They put me between them, propped up on pillows. Ahead of my knees, they hung a bed sheet as projection screen. They switched on a flashlight behind it and began the show. They took turns making hand shadows—a herd of galloping horses, swooping birds of prey, rabbits and barking dogs, two boxers sparring—and narrating the improbable story lines. Shadows growled, and the screen stretched to the periphery of my vision. I was breathless. When the show was over, I'd beg for more and get a short encore. Then their hands tired and I obediently tiptoed back to my bed.

In the mornings before breakfast, I opened doors from our bedroom to the balcony, and went outside to watch the neighborhood wake up, careful to rub crud from my eyes. My great aunt also told me those were flies' eggs, and if I didn't clean them out maggots would grow on my face.

The only place I never ran was at school. The headmistress at our private school was tall with a small bun at the nape of her neck. We called her Madame and were terrified of her. I wore short-sleeved dress uniforms. Everyone got into trouble eventually and the teacher meted out swift discipline. Sometimes it was a ruler on my hand, sometimes I had to kneel on the floor next to my desk. I was content being a good student, not the best, not the worst. I learned how to write in cursive the Vietnamese way, with a "p" that didn't close at the bottom but instead looked like a long-legged "n."

"What did your parents tell you about the war?" Blue asked.

I looked at him blankly.

"You saw a soldier in the alley. You broke curfew," he nudged.

"But then he took me home and everything was fine," I said. I didn't understand what Blue wanted.

"What did you think the helicopters were doing overhead? Did you hear reports about the fighting on television?" he pressed.

I shook my head. I was sure my vocabulary didn't include such things. They didn't teach about current events or history in first grade, and neither did my parents. Whatever intuition or anxieties they might have had about the tenuousness of our life in Sài Gòn never filtered down through my hazy happiness.

Day, Night, Week, Month

Blue told me most people experience a singular life stream, a narrative that may skid forwards and backwards, but hews to one line with a connected beginning, middle, and end. Even if images from a few hours, days, or months fade, there aren't skeins of film shaved off the top and bottom, discarded and coiling on the floor. For most people, it's one long story where I had only scattered frames, in a roughly appropriate sequence but with missing lengths of context.

What I kept of my last day in Việt Nam was this.

I came back to our house at midday from school to eat lunch and nap. In the early afternoon, I ran out front at the high-pitched trill of my father's Vespa but he didn't cut the engine or dismount. Instead, my mother got on her motorcycle and they both rode off, turning in different directions at the end of the block. Our housekeeper brushed me back inside.

In late afternoon, both parents returned. They told us to change back into street clothes. Someone—was it my father?—drove us and suitcases to a waiting bus. Nearly all my mother's siblings were there with their children and my grandmother, but not my father's relatives. The bus lurched through rush hour traffic toward the airfield. On the city's edge, brakes hissed and it came to a slow stop. A soldier was just outside. I felt adults on the bus simultaneously tense their backs and relax muscles in their faces. The soldier waved us through, and the bus jolted and accelerated again.

Many families had come to the airport. We slept overnight in tents. At dawn, we climbed into the hull of an olive-colored cargo plane, small bodies and luggage filling the belly of a mother shark. I couldn't tell what flag it had painted on it. I was suddenly the only one standing with the others making a lumpy carpet around me. I was bewildered by the sudden severing from our home life, the vast unknowing of what was to come, the lack of explanation from adults around me.

A man wheeled away the steel staircase as the hatch began closing. I felt my grandmother gently tugging me to the floor, folding her arm around my waist. The engine's hum vibrated across my skull as the orange of Sài Gòn's dawn slowly narrowed from the vertically oblong rectangle of the doorway, to a horizontal rectangle, to a slit, and then blinked to black. I fell asleep.

Less than a normal sleep cycle later, we disembarked in a place that was hot but dry. There were no trees and the ground was unpaved. We got on another plane and flew to a second place, just as hot. In the dust, families sorted themselves and their piles of valises and duffel bags into little clumps. There were now hundreds of people and I concentrated to track my parents by their trouser legs. There was a steady hum of voices without shouting or laughter, but I felt oddly comforted by the mass of bodies all sharing an adventure. My parents took turns standing in line. There were many lines in succession that ended at long foldable tables where men in uniforms sat with piles of folders. They were light skinned and had wrist watches with large faces.

By the end of that day or the next, we had an assigned tent. It was olive like the cargo plane, without walls. Underneath were a few dozen cots laid in a parquet pattern. I sat on one near our luggage and wondered why our tent was filled with strangers and not my aunts and uncles. The blankets they gave us were gray, thick, and scratchy. Warm cross winds blew through.

My relatives were in nearby tents. They told my parents what numbers they had, my parents whispered theirs back. One aunt said she could make her telephone call tomorrow. They shared sightings of co-workers and neighbors. Someone had given us bags of fruit and cans of food, which didn't taste bad. I went by myself to my uncle Hải's tent and found their cluster of cots. I sat on one and reached for a cracker in an open box, then got up again because my aunt had an unfriendly look on her face. Maybe she was tired and thinking of something else; maybe she didn't want me sitting on their cots. I retreated to look for Ân and Chương.

Within a few days we took a much longer flight and landed in a different place. Here there were thousands of Vietnamese and the sky seemed farther away. Instead of tents, there were rows of wooden one-room barracks, raised on stilts so their floors hit at the level of my neck. There were a few communal buildings. One was a mess hall, where two long lines snaked through three times a day. The food was prepared hot and not in cans. No one noticed when I snuck back into line for second helpings of powdered scrambled eggs. The eggy taste was instantly familiar but I had never seen them in this cloud-like form before; they were comfortingly mushy and had a clean, sunny taste, slightly sweet. Another building served as a gathering place where children came in the morning for games or lessons, and families congregated in afternoons or evenings for Catholic services led by a Vietnamese priest. Loudspeakers perched on poles around camp, barking announcements in Vietnamese. The place was large enough that I never saw its boundaries, or if there were fences. Its breadth meant that no sound seemed large except when loudspeakers went off.

Adults stood in lines to collect new numbers. My mother's twin sister and her family were also there, a few rows of barracks away from us, but not all our relatives had arrived from the first place. I spent time chasing around with my cousins and other kids, or sat near the barracks, sneaking underneath their stilts to squat in the shade.

One late afternoon, I stood with my mother in front of the church-y building. Adults crowded around. They each looked as if they had dropped something and watched it break. They were eerily quiet for such a large group. I clutched my mother's pants, buried in the sea of legs, and heard the loudspeaker crackle. It wasn't the priest this time. A different Vietnamese voice began to speak for longer than usual. There were murmurs but most mouths in the audience were silent or moving soundlessly. I asked my mother what the man was saying. She leaned and told me with no more expression than her usual furrow above the nose bridge, "Sài Gòn bị mất rồi." Sài Gòn is lost. "Việt Cộng have the city."

Years later when my father took us to parades commemorating its anniversary, I would realize that announcement happened on April 30, 1975. We had hopscotched from Sài Gòn to Manilla, Guam, and finally Fort Chaffee in Arkansas. In adulthood when I traveled back to Sài Gòn, a relative would explain it had been eight days since we fled.

We landed in one final place where a tall, thin pale woman greeted us. She had short brown hair and a wide smile. My parents were glad to see her. Our tribe had mysteriously dwindled down to just the six of us. My grandmother had gone with an aunt or uncle. This place wasn't as hot or dry as the first two places, with sky punctured by very tall buildings and paved ground everywhere instead of dust. There were no mopeds revving or weaving in and out, just cars swooshing forwards, politely obeying lines on the road.

At the end of a long drive, we pulled up aside a boxy stone house on a silent street lined by trees with canopies six times as wide as palms. The house had three doors—one to a room at one end with walls of windows, one at the other end opening onto a grassy yard. The third was in the middle, behind an arched gate. Faye Ross opened it and we inched into the beige foyer of her house. We were the first Vietnamese refugee family to arrive in the West Mt. Airy neighborhood of Philadelphia. It was the middle of May, three weeks after we left, and two weeks before my seventh birthday.

I didn't know back then that our evacuation was part of "black ops" coordinated by a small band of American military and diplomatic staff. The boat- and airlifts operated without permission and possibly against orders of the then American Ambassador, Graham Martin, who resisted starting formal evacuations until the last few days of the war lest they set off panic in South Việt Nam, as if tens of thousands hadn't already begun frantically looking for escape routes months before. Black ops officers understood what would happen under Communist rule to Vietnamese associated with Americans and improvised a flotilla of commercial and military cargo planes to shuttle between Tân Sơn Nhất Airport and Guam as quickly as possible. They had no travel papers or visas to issue. They just spread word among Vietnamese staff to gather their families, including my uncle Tân, who triggered our group departure.

The cargo flights were a relatively efficient transfer of bodies, until North Vietnamese pocked the airport with bomb craters in the last week of April, days after our plane took off.

Gap

When our children were small, I was wistful about how hard it would be for them to remember their babyhood, all those precious hours we lavished attention on every inch of them. We cradled and bounced them to every kind of music. We nuzzled their perfect noses, cheeks, hands and bellies (Hapa babies—those of any Asian parentage—are gorgeous). We ooh'ed and ahh'ed when Alexander showed us small finds on walks like a special leaf or pebble, or when Benjamin built an impossible marble chute. I conjured games with them—using chalk to draw a neighborhood map on the patio, with lots of roads and parking spaces for vehicle-obsessed Benjamin to steer matchbox cars down; or covering the kitchen counter with crafting materials and implements so process-loving Alexander could experiment with pipe cleaners and stickers. At bedtime, David and I took turns lying down in their beds to giggle in the dark, recall with them what happened that day, stare at glow-in-the-dark stars on the ceiling, and listen for their breathing to slow.

Infants have only crude tools to chisel with; their neural substrate is limited and they spend most of their lives sleeping, shut off from external stimuli. They also don't have the ability to encode memories in a way their language-based adult selves can interpret easily. They know in their bones when they are loved or threatened but their adult selves will be too dim and limited to recall it with words.

In my early days with Blue, I puzzled about the conditions required for me to bind the sensory and emotional assaults of long ago to the present. Did my child-self build language in layers, gradually securing a memory fossil record as the sediment deepened? What about the seismic interruptions in my life, the onslaught of new grammar and alien idioms, and blankness where words could not keep up with what my heart felt? Did the sediment shift and settle misaligned, or did it not settle at all?

At my exclusive school in Sài Gòn, education was trilingual. In first grade, I learned to write Vietnamese, to pronounce a handful of English nouns, and recite common phrases in French. I sat sentry at our front door (I am told), refusing entry or exit until the traveler offered a greeting in

French. I spoke my demands loudly using the Franco-Indochine creole for piano, clothing, vehicles, zoo animals, cà phê (coffee), bơ (butter), and other favorite foodstuffs. I knew most of the designations for "other" in Vietnamese, the honorifics that root every person to their proper place in the Confucian hierarchy, and hence situate me in mine, like:

> Cô—aunt younger than my parent, wife of an uncle younger than my parent, Miss
> Bà—woman of my grandparents' generation, Madam
> Ông—man of my grandparents' generation, Sir
> Chú—uncle younger than my parent, husband of an aunt younger than my parent, Mister
> Bác—aunt or uncle older than my parent, Sir or Madam older than my parent but younger than my grandparents
> Cậu—my mother's younger brother

But I had no access to or use at that age for a broad vocabulary of emotions. I was adored and happy and my feelings were concentrated at the contented end of the spectrum. When we left Việt Nam, this emotional muteness diminished one source of stress for my parents, because I could report little and asked few questions.

We had barely sorted ourselves in the Rosses' attic bedrooms and learned to navigate the house that May, when my father walked me one morning to a large building ten blocks or so away. It was made of red brick and windows the height of small trees, looming atop three dozen concrete steps from the sidewalk. Inside its double-wide front doors, children—very dark and very light—most bigger than me, pounded their feet across green diamond tile floors.

Suddenly my father was gone. I stood affixed in the first-floor hallway of Henry H. Houston Elementary School. Bodies passed in every direction and the din of their spoken gibberish was deafening.

The panic swelled so quickly I couldn't name it. Through my sobbing and terror, a man's hands reached down to cup under my arms. His skin was pink and he made soft and soothing shushing noises. Mr. Kligerer, a first-grade teacher, lifted me to let my head fall on his shoulder and carried me down the length of one hallway after another, long after all the children disappeared into rooms, until I was spent and quiet. After two more weeks like this before school ended in June, I didn't want to leave the Rosses' house if I didn't have to.

Hear, Say

In the mornings that first summer with the Rosses, we assembled in turns around their small kitchen table. Unlike in Sài Gòn, only grownups got to drink coffee here. Someone put a bowl in front of me and a tiny glass of orange juice. Into the bowl they poured nuggets of something light and crispy, with a stream of milk following on top and denting a small well in the bowl's contents. It remained a mystery why the wet came on the dry and then the rush to eat cereal quickly before everything got mushy.

My father planned a routine for me. After breakfast, either he, Ân or Chương, would lead me into the sun porch. I sat cross-legged on the carpet while they set out pencils and index cards, some with clearly printed letters and some blank. English nouns were easy—brother, mother, father, sister, school, book, house. Verbs seemed redundant, changing their endings depending on who and how many people were doing the action and when it happened. I thought Vietnamese verbs were much more solid—they stood their ground regardless of time context or the trivial people involved. I found other patterns on my own: "—er" means "person who does that," as in teach*er*, bak*er*, rid*er*. I recited speaking drills and wrote vocabulary on blank index cards. I got in trouble over the use of relational adjectives—Chương pointed to himself and I responded, "Chương is my younger brother," because he was younger than Ân. Chương scolded me and indignantly crossed out my sentence with his pencil.

We'd take a short break for lunch and then go back at it. By mid-afternoon, everyone was exhausted, and we'd pack up. At night, I sat in pajamas next to Faye's husband, Dan, with his toddler son Kevin and Tuấn on his other side. We read *Go, Dog, Go* and other board books.

Linguists break the process of second language acquisition into several coarse phases. First there is the "silent" phase, a time of language shock when the learner speaks little if at all to others, but may be engaging in "private speech," self-talk as a rehearsal for an eventual public exchange. But this theory about sequential structures tells me little about how a child, in particular, understands the onslaught of newness or even the goal of speaking, if no one explains and negotiates it with her. Am I learning English to find playmates? To please my parents? So school is less terrifying? Or is it to ask for help? I had stopped hoping that we would return home to Sài Gòn. Lack of explanation from my parents just reinforced the void behind us. I took from their stoicism that it wasn't my place to mourn what we had lost and besides, there was no one to show me how.

There was nowhere to go but forward. I have no memory of teetering between English and Vietnamese. I simply put the Vietnamese aside when not speaking with my parents, coding thoughts into pictures and an inter-language now lost to memory. Neither did I engage in trial and error like substituting "I don't," "I won't," "I did not," or "I hadn't" if one didn't seem to work; I would speak it perfectly or not at all because that was what my parents expected.

One afternoon that first summer, Faye walked me across Lincoln Drive to the Alt family's house. Letitia was my age, Stephen two years older. They tossed a ball between them and then to me. They bantered until Letitia said she didn't like this or that.

"How come?" Stephen asked. The phrase echoed in my head. *How come?* I watched his round mouth wrap around the schwa vowel of "come" and replayed the motion in my mind, translating it for my tongue and facial muscles. How. Come. *How* did it *come* to be? How come = why. I waited until a pause in the conversation

Nine years old, after my bicycle accident, Philadelphia, 1977.

seemed appropriate, my heart beating insistently.

"How come?" I piped up and got an appropriate response from Letitia as immediate reinforcement.

In September, my parents sent me to second grade with perfect English and no accent. If teachers had been worried about what to do for the first Asian immigrant student in the school, they seemed to take for granted that I didn't need any help at all.

Young children acquire new languages much more easily and are less likely to have residual accents than adults, but it doesn't tend to happen in one summer. I didn't have a choice.

The Ross family (left to right): Faye, David, Kevin, Eric, Dan, 1971.

Alien

My parents found jobs before our first winter in Philadelphia. Dan helped my mother get a secretarial position at an insurance company. A few months later, my father started teaching school as he had in Sài Gòn. They both commuted downtown.

That fall, a friend of Dan's offered to rent one of his properties to my parents and we moved two blocks south to our own house on Glen Echo Road. At first the little stone row houses with their concrete stoops seemed to stick out in a land of colonials, but later I realized it was the colonials that were unusual. Park land was the economic compass. Houses and properties expanded as you neared any entrance to Wissahickon Creek, the shoe-lace of green winding for miles from tony Chestnut Hill in the north down to where water spills into the Schuykill River and flows downtown. Our new house was a good mile from the nearest park entrance. When we arrived, we were among only two or three non–Black families on the block.

Faye didn't watch me after school anymore. I walked home by myself and would sit on the front steps, waving back if other girls passing by waved at me. Kelly was in my class and vouched for me. Her hair was cut close to her head, with just one layer of tight curls covering her brown scalp. She and her girlfriends would sit above me on our steps and coo at my long, straight hair, limp and slick. They'd pick up a strip and divide it in three. I liked the pull on my scalp, the harder the better. When the cornrow was done, they'd let it go and squeal in surprise as it fell apart. Three or four attempts later the thrill would finally be gone and they'd leave.

The neighborhood was safe. Otherwise, my parents wouldn't have let me walk to school by myself. Everything was a similar shade of a color I couldn't name. Stone facades on houses and the mottled bark of oak trees were all the color of cement sidewalks. Trees didn't stay green year-round. When they lost their leaves, the entire landscape was desiccated, washed in cement color. There were no street people and almost no stores. The only food scent came from an occasional banana peel on the ground. Faint car exhaust was the strongest detectable smell. The only sounds when I walked were birds and automobile hum.

Closer to school, larger houses were set back behind hedges just taller than my head. I could walk several blocks before seeing anyone. The few people climbed into cars, too busy to talk or wave. More activity lurked near the railroad tracks, but commuters walked briskly, their eyes down. Across the foot bridge, children spilled out of buses and cars from different directions to stream into school.

My classmates were curious about me. Some pointed. I had different skin from them but no accent and soon they seemed to forget that I was new and didn't know everything. I tracked how dark kids played with other dark kids and light kids played with other light kids. Sometimes I tried to play with one group, sometimes the other, my medium skin tone and ability to alter my speech ever so slightly to match their different accents somehow moderating the divide and allowing me to ping-pong between groups.

Sometimes I sat on the stone border of the schoolyard to take it all in. One light skinned boy hit a fuzzy yellow ball with his hand against a wall, let it bounce, and then leapt aside so the next boy could hit it. I found a ball and practiced at home for a week against the outside wall of our basement, before stepping forward one day at school and asking to play. I tried not to ask too many questions to avoid reminding them that I was different and didn't know everything. They asked me none.

One day in second grade I wrote in cursive with the letter p in Vietnamese style, its bottom curving out and open like a long-legged n. Miss Fink didn't know what to do. She wasn't asking anyone to write in cursive. She told me to close the loop on the p. Another day she asked everyone to tell a story about their summer. My legs grew tight. When she called my name, something snapped inside and I bolted from my seat. We were both surprised when I ran under her desk and stayed there, but she didn't disturb me and let me come out on my own when the bell rang for recess.

On another day, we were told we would plant flowers by the new playground. Teachers gave us each three of what looked like small onions. Someone had already troweled out several rows of holes so the hillside looked pocked from a horde of groundhogs. "Put one bulb in each hole with the roots down." I squatted and stared at the onions. One end was pointy, the other scruffy. I fingered the entire surface for clues. Everyone else had deposited their bulbs and were already pushing soil back into their holes. I decided to spread my bets, planting one onion with the point down, one with the point up, and one on its side. I tipped in soil over each and patted it firmly, heart pounding, before anyone could see.

In December, a snowstorm was supposed to start in mid-morning. Everyone in class was excited except me. "She's never seen snow before!" When early flakes began falling, Miss Fink let the other kids steer me to the window. I sat in a chair looking out with them standing behind, watching me. After a while, they took me outside and repeated the observation as I held out one hand and watch a few flakes land and melt. It was white and cold and wet, just as promised. I tried to muster some surprise and enthusiasm because they were watching. We went back to class.

Every Wednesday, eight or ten kids left class. They were the smartest ones, sitting in the Purple reading group while I was only in Yellow. They spent the day somewhere else with a different teacher, then came back on Thursday. I felt smaller watching them leave. The class was less interesting when they were gone and they looked bouncier when they returned.

Halfway through the year, my teacher handed me a hall pass and told me to walk to a room near the principal's office. A man wearing glasses closed the door on the two of us. He wasn't a teacher. He told me we were going to play games and answer some questions, then he put little red and white blocks on the table before flipping over a large card with a red and white pattern on it.

"Can you make that for me?" he asked as he watched the second hand on his watch. After we finished pattern cards, he showed me pictures and asked what I thought was happening in each scene. He told me series of numbers and letters and had me repeat them back to him. Then he asked simple questions, the last of which was,

"Who is Benjamin Franklin?"

I smiled a big smile. "He invented electricity!" I answered triumphantly.

The man smiled in turn and told me to go back to class. I waited for news of how I did on the man's tests, but no one told me. When the semester ended, it seemed I wasn't smart enough to go with the Wednesday group. I thought about that failure all summer. I asked Ân and Chương what they thought went wrong, and they laughed, explaining that Benjamin Franklin didn't *invent* electricity; he *discovered* it! I was sure I'd never be able to fix this mistake, but at the beginning of third grade, without any more testing or explanation, my teacher sent me to join the Wednesday group. It was my favorite day each week. We had assignments like creating a new arctic mammal or seeing how many uses of a light bulb we could imagine in three minutes.

Striving to get into the Wednesday "Academically Talented" group was the first time I recall feeling a *need* to be among the best at something, driven by fear of the abyss of being average, like treading a wide sea to reach land. It made me ravenously curious about anything new to learn, but also self-conscious in waves of anxiety.

Some days I caught up to my classmate Heather Egan after school and we crossed the railroad bridge together to walk on the west side. The path was obscured by a jumble of vines. She told me a flowering vine was honeysuckle. "This is how you do it." She picked off one white flower, held the narrow foot and pinched off its tip. A slim stamen stuck out there at the new orifice. She raised it and tilted her head back, tugging gently on the slim thread until a drop of sweet dew formed at the end and dripped into her mouth. The nectar was delicious but I felt a cringe of indecency; it was like taking the dress off of a fairy.

Heather explained what it meant that her parents were divorced. Their house was always messy, as if someone had taken the wrapper off a crayon and smeared its side all over the boundaries my mother would have imposed. An electric river rock tumbler hummed in one corner, shoes and socks lay scattered on the living room floor, cats roamed freely, even on the kitchen counter covered with half-made sandwiches, a canister of granola, and paper scraps with poetry and shopping lists scrawled on them. Heather was a serious ballet dancer and could run long distances faster than any other girl in our grade. She tossed a football through a tire swing with her brother. They politely included me, but I learned to not follow her home more than once every other week because she wanted time to play with other friends.

Most days I walked home by myself. Tuấn was still in daycare and Ân and Chương were not back from school yet. In good weather, I walked along our side yard to the alley, down the alley to Lincoln Drive, and back around the block to the front of the house.

I looked for interesting things on the ground. If it was soft from rain, I went into our small yard. Its front sloped toward the street, shielded by a privet hedge. I'd look for a flat rock and strong sticks to dig a hole. It was more important that the hole be wide than deep. I'd bring out a bowl of water from the kitchen and with dirt piled on the hole's edge, I'd make dumplings, wetting soil to make sludge, then scooping some into a large maple leaf. I wrapped it the way my mother folded rice paper to make spring rolls and then skewered each package with a twig to secure it. The dumplings then went into the hole, along with crumpled leaves, and water to finish my witches' brew. When my legs were tired from squatting to stir and stir, I'd go inside and watch Electric Company and Sesame Street, and then a show about people stranded on an island, before my brothers came home. I liked it that on TV everyone's emotions were exaggerated; they broadened my range of emotions.

Every few weeks, I grew more adventurous and walked farther from our house. I watched Matthew MacGregor walk down Allens Lane after school and followed to see where his house was. The homes and yards were so large there that each block had only two or three properties.

Across the lane grownups in running shoes disappeared into Wissahickon Creek. The path narrowed and sloped steeply. I leaned my weight back on my heels and slid down, to see where the water ran. I sat on a large rock jutting into the trickling water and dropped in leaves and twigs to watch them float downstream. No one saw or bothered me.

"Did you leave any marks on the path, Mai?" Blue asked.

"What do you mean? No. I left things just the way I found them."

"You wouldn't have left marks on the concrete sidewalks, but I was hoping you at least left footprints in the dirt, or scratched it with a stick. But you walked all those places and left no trace and no witnesses. Hours and hours you walked...."

I rummaged deep to feel something—anything—to report to him. "What happens to a life that is unobserved?" I asked instead.

"Typically, one of two things...." he said in the slow way he used to titrate my responses when he dosed out important information, "Either a person retreats into grandiose beliefs about the value of that life, or she comes to believe the life is not worth observing."

Passing

The Rosses had taken me to Lovett Memorial Library once. One day after school in second grade, I recreated the route in my head based on my new starting point at school—left to Mt. Airy Avenue, east to Sedgwick, jog right then left, then uphill to the cobblestones of Germantown Avenue. It took fifteen minutes each way on short legs. The first day I overshot the first turn and headed back home, careful not to ask strangers for directions so I wouldn't have to answer questions they might ask.

I made it on my second attempt. I looked straight ahead and quietly made my way upstairs to the children's section where I scanned the long room. Where to start?

"Do you need help?" a librarian asked. I shook my head so she would leave me alone in my confusion. The books would tell me what I needed to know, and they wouldn't ask me questions or react to my alien-ness.

"A" seemed a good place to start. I stared at the spines. Abbott, Adler, … look like you know what you're doing! There were so many Louisa May Alcott books that they took up their own row. I knelt and loosed one from the crowded shelf. Yellowed plastic crackled when I split open its covers. I read jacket blurbs about girls triumphing over tragedy, someone rescuing an orphan ugly duckling who turns into a swan. These books were thick and smelled different from those above and below, like old perfume and dusty, velvet curtains. They smelled like they would teach and watch over me. *Little Women* came home with me the first day, then all the others, sometimes two or three at a time. When I finished Alcott, I moved to the next "A" book if it had the right smell or color. When I finished "A" I moved onto "B." In tenth grade, at the library near our final house in Philadelphia, I read two Isaac Bashevis Singer anthologies to finish "S," and then walked away, having learned all I wanted to from the library.

I was the first Asian child to ever enroll at Henry H. Houston Elementary. Over the next two decades, Cambodian, Laotian and Vietnamese families would fill in crevices of Chinatown and South Philly then trade up to row houses in Northeast neighborhoods. But inside the city, few other refugee families would creep as far north and west as ours did, with horse country just a few miles beyond. The Vietnamese professional class, my parents' friends, decamped to far suburbs instead.

I developed the Rosses' faultless Midwestern English and a steady competence in school. Perhaps exposure to Vietnamese tones had nurtured neural wiring my schoolmates didn't seem to have or want to use, allowing me to map and mimic all their varied speech patterns, from Kelly Green's drawl and seesaw rhythm to Eric Olsen's terse, clipped vowels and Ilana Cohen's lush consonants. I slipped in and out of this group and that one, a lingual Zelig, sounding just enough like each pack to stay and take note of their habits. In this way, I learned that to look chipper and confident I should walk on the balls of my feet with my toes pointing out like Heather did, or carry a book under one arm like Jennifer Highland, to whip out and read under a tree when there were no games to join.

But other things remained out of reach. How to host a birthday party when my parents couldn't invent treasure hunts with clever clues in English and my friends wouldn't take to the dried squid my family considered a treat. Where to get the funky thrift store clothes Christina Clawson wore. How to put French braids in my stubbornly slippery hair. Who to go to when darkness and depression set in and I couldn't name them out loud in either language at home.

People offered to help with things I could figure out for myself, like finding library books, but not with the many things I couldn't figure out.

(from left) Chương, me, my mother, Tuấn, and Ân, in front of our house on Glen Echo Road, Philadelphia, 1976.

"I could walk for miles alone and no one stopped me to ask if there was anything they could help with," I complained to Blue.

They still don't, I pointed out to him bitterly. My colleagues took little notice of my spiraling anxiety as the career successes piled on.

"Is it possible," he asked, "it didn't occur to anyone that you needed help?"

"How can that be? I was seven. I was tiny."

"Is it possible," Blue tried again, "that things would have been much easier for you if you hadn't passed so well for normal with things like finding library books?"

Bridge

I craved human connections outside of school to fill the many hours of silence, but found actual engagement with other people frightening.

"Were there places you walked every day?" Blue wanted to know.

"Sure. Up Lincoln Drive, toward the railroad tracks, up the path alongside them, across the foot bridge, back up Allens Lane to school."

"How did you feel going that way?"

I paused. "I'm small. It was a lot of ground to cover, and I was small. The trees were tall, and I had to concentrate on getting there on time. There were honeysuckles growing west of the tracks. I always looked forward to how they smell, like Red Riding Hood going to Grandma's house."

"Take me there," he nudged.

"I'm leaving school, and right at that corner where the path slopes down to the bridge, a lot of kids turn to go another way. But I have to cross the foot bridge. There's a car bridge, too, but the sidewalk there is very narrow and cars whiz by so fast…. The path down to the tracks is asphalt and I'm storing a mental map of all the cracks in it. I'm at the bottom of the foot bridge. I have to adjust my stride to climb the steps because they're each only four or five inches high and slope down in the middle." Like old glass sagging down a window.

"What do the steps look like?" Blue asked.

"They're wood. Old, rotted wood. I can't tell what color the paint used to be. There's peeling paint everywhere. I'm at the top step. I'm on the landing and turn left to the part that goes over the tracks. It … it slopes up, it arches up to the center. The walls are moldy and there's graffiti and bird shit everywhere."

My tongue slowed, to make certain I wasn't lying to him. I was confused. Why was I reliving and describing to Blue such a different bridge from the one I remembered? I knew the bridge was bright and yellow and smelled like pine sap and sweat in summer. But there it hung insistently in the air between Blue's chest and me, rank and contoured in shadows.

"There's no safe place to touch. There're just different colored patches of mold."

I described the scene—Wedges of sunlight streamed through jagged openings high up on the walls. The openings were too high for me to look through, but just wide enough for birds to fly in and drop their shit. The only light bounced off high reaches of wall on the other side; it was dark where my feet were. Bird wings fluttered in the rafters, a squirrel scurried. My little legs grew heavy. One foot slipped slightly on something wet and my legs tensed to keep balance. The floor rose, up and up toward the top of the arch in the bridge's center. I put another foot forward. Someone tall rushed by and made the floorboards shake. I wasn't afraid of the man but his vibrations wouldn't stop. More grown-ups rushed in the other direction and the entire bridge oscillated. The floor heaved up in a slow flick like a floppy banana peel, and the opening on the other end receded…. I desperately wanted someone to reach down and pick me up, to lift my feet off the rotted wood.

"I can't do this!" I cried out in panic, "Oh God! This is where I still *live*."

Even in adulthood, my feet were still paralyzed at the top of the bridge's arch, left to navigate an alien land alone.

"I know, Mai." Blue let me cry until the hour ended.

Michael

"Real isn't how you are made," said the Skin Horse. "It's a thing that happens to you. When a child loves you for a long, long time, not just to play with, but REALLY loves you, then you become Real. It doesn't happen all at once.... Generally, by the time you are Real, most of your hair has been loved off, and your eyes drop out and you get loose in the joints and very shabby...."
—Margery Williams, *The Velveteen Rabbit*

I was eight when, in the dark of the ceiling's vault above my bed at night, figures appeared for the first time, leaping and tumbling through the air. A pack of them flew in skintight superhero outfits that shielded them from the crushing vacuum and radiation of space. They moved in wide silent arcs, one colored red, another yellow, purple, blue. In flawless choreography, this one pulled the next forward with an invisible torque as her somersault ended and his began. Their bodies were trim without curves; ten, eleven years old, just older than me. Perfection. Untouchable. When they leapt too far away to see, I fell asleep.

I didn't tell anyone about them because I knew no one else could see them or was supposed to.

This experience was different from typical imagining. In our Wednesday classes, the teacher would tell us to imagine walking on Mars, by willfully creating the scene and inventing sights and sensations. What I began to experience that night in bed was not a deliberate, willful exercise. It was closer to receiving characters and narratives that inserted themselves into my consciousness. They were the willful ones, commanding my attention. They had their own truth.

On bad nights, a different vision replaced the young Space Flyers. Now I hovered alone in the void of space. Straight ahead, a small pinprick of color slowly enlarged. It was a mass, smooth but misshapen, like a giant blood cell dented and diseased. Its density was enormous and wildly out of proportion to its size, enough to warp the space around it. It hurtled forward in slow motion, end over end, toward me. I was a line almost without dimension, a whisper, with less matter than a chopstick or a wire. Space wind barely bent around me. I shifted left, then right, but when I looked again, the mass had adjusted course to find me. When it was too close for me to see its outer edges, my breath froze in my chest. In the very last second before impact, my little line of a body instinctively flicked and deflected the hurtling mass ever so slightly onto a new path. By the time I straightened and whirled around, it had already turned and was coming back toward me.

I told no one about the Space Flyers. But one day when recess began, I told my third-grade teacher about the hurtling red mass and asked her what she thought of it and the thin line.

Ms. Blount took a minute to regain composure before answering, "Maybe it means no matter how daunting something seems, Mai, you can overcome it in the end."

I went out to the school yard to get in a game of pick-up wall ball with Ms. Blount's reaction stinging in my head, a reminder to not share too much about my inner life because I was already different in too many other ways. I knew I had overcome nothing. The space mass had overcome me and would come back for more. It was the shape of my anxieties lurking in the dark, pouncing whenever I dared let down my guard.

At age eight or nine, I gradually became aware of an invisible friend, a boy always a bit older than me. Unlike a neighborhood playmate, he didn't appear fully formed. He evolved from the Space Flyers. His story and the world he lived in emerged over many years, refined while I lay in bed, rode in our station wagon during family vacations, sat in classrooms. Rarely, he might appear in an actual night dream. Occasionally a new detail about my friend would be so striking, I could record where I was and what was happening in external reality when it appeared, but more often than not, I experienced overlapping waves of new awareness, not singular incidents.

I wrote down this version of Michael's story when I met Blue. By then, my mental editing had stopped because he and his history had reached their underlying truth. Earlier versions of him are barely visible now, like under-layers of paint on a finished canvas. Italics here and in the rest of the book mark what happens in the world Michael inhabited, and what I experienced there.

In 1965 or so, a young diplomat of vague royal ancestry came from Eastern Europe to America. During lunch hours, he escaped the embassy compound to wander through museums and gardens. In a sculpture gallery one day, he almost tripped over a woman sitting on the floor with her legs inconsiderately extended, camouflaged against the walls in white pants and blouse. She was sketching a wire sculpture and looked up when he interrupted her line of sight. She was tanned and glowing, dark hair flowing to her waist. Her eyes were hazel and unnervingly still and wide. She smiled and apologized. He stopped to talk.

They took car trips into the countryside. At night, he played clarinet for her and gently twisted her hair while she talked to their dinner guests. Six months later, they were married. That he claimed no religion of his own made the Jewish ceremony easier to negotiate.

The baby was born a year later.

When Michael was four years old, they moved back to his father's baroque capital in Europe. They lived in a house not far from his grandparents. Michael's mother spoke to him in English and Hebrew to help retain his native tongues. At his eye level, she stuck small squares of paper on objects around the house, some with their English names, some with their Hebrew names. They made a treasure hunt of it. She strolled with him around cobblestone streets and rode trolleys. They bought vegetables and bread, plus a stale loaf to crumble for geese on the river.

After dinner, they would answer the doorbell once and leave the lock open as visitors came. There was a physicist and sociology professors, an older man who told long stories, and artists who hovered around his mother. But the musicians were Michael's favorite. They coaxed his father to bring out the clarinet. Someone sat down at the piano with Michael in his lap and played with arms spread and fingers bouncing up and down the keys on either side of Michael's waist. On weekends, grandparents and an uncle who didn't seem comfortable came for supper, and the adults talked late while Michael fell asleep upstairs.

When Michael was nine, his parents dropped him off one morning for piano lessons at his teacher's house and then went off arm in arm for a stroll. When they hadn't returned several hours later, his piano teacher called the house. The housekeeper came to bring him home. At nightfall, she called his grandparents and together they alerted the police. Officers came and took notes but made no promises. The housekeeper helped Michael into bed.

On the second day, the housekeeper walked Michael to school. When he came home, the police had returned and so had his grandparents. They found his parents' bodies floating in the river, not far from one another, with no sign of trauma. The bun of his mother's hair was still intact. On the fifth day, Michael counted hats in church at the memorial service and walked with his grandmother in the funeral procession. On the seventh day, he arrived on the front stoop of his uncle's townhouse. He had with him two valises, a box of school books, and his father's clarinet. Inside the case, wrapped in the scrap of leather his father used to clean the instrument, still supple and fragrant from linseed oil, was his mother's wedding ring.

Red

In our new house, I shared a bedroom with Tuấn, our beds tucked into opposite corners. He slept in footed pajamas inside a well, a fortress he meticulously built of stuffed animals. Various cotton and velveteen species mounded around the oval border with him curled up inside, pulling a blanket over them all. He chewed on the nose and ears of his favorite mouse until it was crushed and matted grey with saliva. I kept more order in my bed.

The first year in that house, at age seven turning eight, I woke often in the middle of the night and let my eyes wander the room's walls and listened for Tuấn's breathing, then fell back asleep. But one night I woke and couldn't fall back asleep. Something was making light outside the room, a light I didn't like. I slipped out into the hallway. Now I had to escape. I turned to face down the stairs and stopped cold.

On the stairs too far away to touch me yet was an enormous Red Ball. It blocked the entire passageway and quivered ever so slightly, menacing me. It reminded me of the hurtling mass in Space. I sat down on the top step and whimpered, keeping my eyes open through tears to keep the ball in sight. My mother woke at my noise and came to sit beside me.

"What's the matter?" She asked.

I blubbered about the Red Ball and pointed to it, but when she turned her head, neither of us could see it.

The red of my dreams was not a daylight color. In daylight, red is bold and substantial. It boils and gleams. It's touchable, on the petal of a tulip bloom, a warm brick wall, the polished hood of a sports car. But in my dreams and Michael's world, red was not touchable. It had presence but no mass. Its internal glow pulsed and emitted heat beyond its blurred edges, until it was ambient.

The Red Ball never appeared again, but it wedged open a crack and made way for other night reds to seep through.

The danger of the reds I saw at night was not fast and furious, like a fire engine or flashing siren. Night reds were dead and still, stalking and threatening to swallow me.

The most ominous red was in Michael's uncle's house, its top story always dark, bathed in red light that defined a round disk on the floor, projected from some ceiling corner. Michael was only with his uncle in the red attic, and when he was in the disk of light, he felt neither warm nor cold, as if the red was calibrated to his skin temperature.

Rich

Rich first came into being as I walked to and from school in third grade or waiting for sleep at night. As with Michael, his story settled over many years.

Rich's house was a grand and welcoming stone manor with three fireplaces. Every room had large, soft furniture. By the grand piano were music stands and instruments—fiddles, a cello and bass viola, guitars, a banjo, penny whistles, a trumpet, and various drums. Things my parents' house did not have.

Outside was a barn with horses and a large garden. Woods stretched beyond. Walking paths led down to a creek, which widened and deepened just enough to swim in.

Rich was married and had young kids. He had lots of visitors, like Michael's parents when they lived in America. There were diplomats, scientists, and an occasional military officer with a message to deliver, but mostly, there were musicians. They sometimes came to take a break from tours or just to crash. After a communal meal, they lit the fireplace and pushed back chairs, and anyone who could claim an instrument jammed into the night.

The year I found his house, Rich got permission to adopt Michael from his uncle and bring him to America. Rich showed Michael to a small bedroom with one door to the hallway and another to Rich's bedroom. A small desk faced out the window. The bureau had a neat pile of new clothes on it, and a framed photograph of Rich standing between Michael's parents from a long time ago, because his mother was cradling a baby. Michael unpacked his valise. He put his father's clarinet case on the bookcase, and swapped his coat, heavy boots, and sweater for jeans and a flannel shirt. He sat down on the bed and recognized the blanket spread on it, from his parents' house. It smelled familiar.

For days, he wandered around the house, suppressing his startle reflex whenever someone appeared. Rich's kids showed him secret doors and passageways and let him pick a horse, which he already knew how to mount and ride. His English was serviceable so they taught him slang. It was hardest for him to get used to the light, which was clear and sharp, so different from the *glowing, hazy red light in his uncle's house. Even at night under dim incandescents, something about the house made it impossible to hide anything. He could clearly see dents in the baseboard of his room while lying under the bed covers. He didn't realize the adults could see him in just as much detail.*

It was early summer, several months before school. He learned to make breakfast for himself. Each morning he did chores in the garden or barn. He played music with visitors when they came. His body healed from some deep and unknown injury, and straightened to normal pre-teen form, and if he didn't laugh too often he at least smiled, and looked at peace.

But at night he shrank. After lying awake for many nights in the dark, he developed a habit of turning on the desk lamp before getting in bed. But the lamp only made the walls glow red and the shadows immense. He curled under the covers, wallowing in a pool of shame and dread. It stalked him in the dark, more solid than everything he could see in daylight. It filled the air above his bed until the density bore his body down into the mattress foam and he could feel vague outlines of bedsprings in his ribs. His heart didn't palpitate because panic is a waste if you aren't going to flee.

One night, he rose and stood still for a minute because his legs were stiff from lying the fetal position. He opened the door to Rich's room and saw their two forms in bed, and an armchair by the window. He closed the door on the shame behind him, dragged his blanket to the armchair and nested there. He tried not to fall asleep.

He was too tired to hear Rich's alarm clock. Rich's wife stroked his arm and pointed to the chair. Rich carried Michael, still asleep, back to his own bed. He asked about it casually in the afternoon, but Michael just mumbled that he couldn't sleep in his room. All day, he scooted from one room to another with the last person leaving.

The next night Michael crept next door at midnight and leapt quietly into Rich's bed, huddling between their two pairs of legs. Rich woke in the dark when the boy was fast asleep. Rich pulled him under the covers, and woke him up the next morning to break Michael's grip on the front of Rich's pajamas.

On the fourth morning, Rich asked questions as gently as he could. Does something in his room scare him? Does he have trouble falling asleep? Does the room remind him of something bad? Michael's eyes flickered and Rich's tone grew sharper. What bad things happened? Michael avoided Rich's face. He kept his jaws rigid and counted the seconds until Rich gave up.

The following night, Michael pushed back his covers as soon as lights in the rest of the house were out. He pulled out his backpack and placed a rolled-up sweater in the bottom then his father's clarinet on top. The little pocket money he had and a Swiss army knife went into his jean pockets.

He pushed the blinds aside. Moon shadows marked distant trees and telephone poles; he could barely make out the textural contrast of asphalt next to grass. His chest felt cold, like the first minute in space, the sharp freeze stretching away in every direction, hissing in lonely doom as body tissues begin their small explosions in the vacuum.

He backed away from the window and thought about Rich's toddlers and how many questions they asked in a day, and their weight in his lap. In a week Rich would want him to start school. He would wear a backpack like this one, go to class, and then bike home, just like everyone else. But the longer he tried to focus on the vision of that routine, the more frequently the interruptions came.

Flash. He was awash in red like the inside of his eyelids. Knots in the wooden floor of his uncle's attic rubbed against his bare knees and hands that pressed into the floor because there was nowhere else to go. The red light cast shadows under his torso. It glowed where the body of a large beast was slowly receding from behind him as the pressure on his knees and hands eased, then faded to black at the perimeters of the room.

He shivered and his eyes blurred. He had enough English now to tell anyone who might ask what happened, and his chest caved at the prospect of not being able to act normal anymore. It was time to leave.

He thought he could hold his breath until he was clear of the house, but he was so focused on making his boot steps quiet he didn't notice light under the study door until it was too late and a floorboard creaked. Rich opened the door, flooding the stair landing with light, and took in the boy's gear in one swift glance. Michael looked around Rich to the stairs beyond and made a calculation, panic and shame in his throat. He leapt forward and to the side. But Rich's left arm stretched across the path and bent him in the middle, and the right arm pulled his struggling legs tight to Rich's body. His face was drenched in tears. Rich crouched down on the rug and held him tight until the sobs had dwindled to loud mouth breathing. Rich asked a very few questions to confirm his suspicions about the rape. Rich channeled his rage into his jawline, so Michael wouldn't see it. I am behind Michael's eyes as he falls asleep in Rich's lap.

"How did it feel when Rich finds out?" Blue asks.

"It feels *sooo* good to Michael, and to me; orgasmic even. He rushes from utter despair to total safety. It's this huge release. I replayed that scene over and over, just to get to that feeling. I couldn't wait to get into bed to see it each night. The worse my day had been, the more I wanted that scene. I lingered on it. It was my go-to fix. I craved that orgasmic feeling."

"Anytime? Anywhere, Mai?" he asked.

"No, just at night. In the dark. I have to be alone to feel it." Years after this conversation, when both Blue and I agreed my recovery was as complete as I needed it to be, I recognized what it was Michael felt just before Rich's revelation. It was shame, a deeply red rush that swelled and peaked as Rich's understanding crept closer to the truth. I used Michael, subjected him to that scorching over and over again, just to get to the healing climax. The aftermath and its calm made it possible for me to fall asleep.

"But why did *you* need that climax, Mai?" Blue asked.

I was stumped. "Because then I knew that Rich knew something bad had happened, and that made Michael safe.... Because then there's nothing left to worry about hiding; secrets can be exhausting to keep.... Because that's just the natural end to the story...."

Blue let his skepticism hang silently between us and patiently waited as I spun in the blind alley.

Stranded

Ân and Chương no longer waited for me after school or watched over my play. An acquaintance of Dan's sat on the Board of Chestnut Hill Academy, an exclusive private boys' prep school, and arranged scholarships for my brothers. It's possible no one thought the local public high school was a viable option for them, or someone was sensitive enough to think teenage boys would need even more support to adapt than a first grader.

I lost my brothers' watchfulness, their engineering my play. They left the house earlier than I did each morning and came home later. As they got older, sometimes they didn't get home until dark, usually separately, because of different sports practices after school. They disappeared into their bedroom and emerged only when dinner was ready. They didn't invite me to their school events and I didn't invite them to mine.

We ate mutely. My parents didn't ask what happened at school, and we didn't offer. I was somewhat relieved, because my Vietnamese wasn't sophisticated enough to explain anything meaningful, and English didn't feel right or welcome at the dining table. But the daily routine lowered a dome of isolation around each of us. Our dinner soundtrack was network news and commercials booming from the television, and my parents occasionally talking about this or that relative, or arguing over what not to spend money on.

After dinner and on weekends, Ân and Chương would take over the TV. When there weren't sports on, they let me channel surf to sitcoms but drifted out of the room if I landed on anything on public television.

The summer after we moved to Glen Echo Road, my parents packed us into the station wagon for a weekend trip. We rode silently past grimy oil refineries bordering the airport, across a bridge into Delaware, down I-95 past towns with low rises and half-starved trees. I closed my eyes and leaned into the seat cushion to calm car sickness. On the other side of Baltimore Harbor Tunnel in Maryland, we careened around the D.C. beltway then abruptly climbed steep hills into a middle class subdivision. My mother's twin sister and another aunt and their families had been sponsored by a church group here. We would reunite with my older girl cousins for the first time since leaving Sài Gòn.

Two or three times a year, when Maryland relatives would make the reverse trek in our direction, I would bookend the reunion with tingling anticipation, and then a mixture of relief and loss when it was over and cars repacked with children for the ride home.

My cousins had an entirely different bedroom inventory than mine: Barbie dolls and their wardrobes, make-up kits, teen magazines and a few years later, their own drivers' licenses and credit cards. We laughed easily in the beginning, pre-pubertal years. When I slept over at their house, we made snacks by cutting up green mangos and dipping them in an absurd amount of nước mắm (fish sauce), made sludgy with sugar. As teenagers, they gave me facial make-overs and put rollers in my hair. They took me to prowl long corridors in malls; I marveled at the volume of their purchases. When they snuck us out at night to local dances with Vietnamese kids and an occasional white face, I let someone tug my hand back and forth in a stiff cha-cha-cha, then hid in a corner with a cup of punch until they were ready to leave near midnight.

In between visits, my experience of them was static. We didn't trade phone calls or letters. I reverted to my bookworm habits, jeans and T-shirts, and could no longer see the glamorous possibilities for my high forehead, oily skin, and vague eyebrows. Once, I begged my parents for a sister, sobbing in desperation, but also afraid of what she would be like.

* * *

In the late 1970s, Mt. Airy was a neighborhood proudly straddling many divides—wealthy professionals in parkside Tudors and Colonials mixed with middle class Black families and blue-collar Irish and Eastern European ones; synagogues and churches of every denomination speckling the area every few blocks; WASP-y families who crossed the city boundary to shop for preppy clothes or kitchenware in Chestnut Hill, and hippies who kept afloat a thrift store and a shop on Germantown Avenue selling tiny wind chimes, incense, and geodes. Allens Lane Arts Center offered scholarships for kids who couldn't afford ballet and ceramics classes. And a woman who hired me to babysit her toddler explained that our block once had only white families on it, but changed its complexion as neighbors exerted peer pressure on homeowners to sell to minority families.

Schools were troubled, the trolley often near empty, cultural misunderstandings flared not infrequently, and housing values stagnated for decades. But this unassuming community infused in my bones an expectation of grit, that honest people could wrestle with and own the discomfort of living with others not like them, even if they didn't probe too much. They didn't think twice about making space for me.

Our family outgrew the row house on Glen Echo Road by the end of sixth grade. Most of the basement floor space was claimed by barbells and the weight lifting bench that An and Chuong used to train for their wrestling team. It was becoming awkward for me to share a room with Tuấn, and my parents had saved enough money to aspire to a place with a yard.

In late May, the Rosses followed us in their car south along Wissahickon Creek, to an intersection where two avenues rolled downhill to collide, with six crisscrossing bus lines meeting a park. Caddy corner to the park was a stone colonial with cream trim and a sun porch, edged by a driveway and a sloping yard with oak trees, azalea and lilac bushes. Inside, beige wall-to wall-carpeting ran from the kitchen upstairs to the second floor. Dan raised an eyebrow when he took it all in; it looked just like his house. We left most of our old furniture in Mt. Airy for bargain hunters and the garbage collector.

From our new house, I commuted by car downtown in the mornings with my parents and Tuấn to a middle school my father had pulled strings to get us into. It was racially and economically diverse, with more upper-middle-class families than Henry Houston. After school, Tuấn and I took a long bus ride home.

A typical family reunion in Silver Spring, Maryland, 1980. From left: me, Aunt Khuê, Tuấn, cousin Tháng, Uncle Tân, cousins Minh, Vân Giao, Trường, Khánh Giao and Quỳnh Giao, my mother, Aunt Bình, my father, cousin Thuận.

On a long, timid walk around our new neighborhood, I found a small library in an old stone church building. If I wanted to get to Wissahickon park, I'd now have to walk over a mile along a five-lane avenue where I rarely saw other kids. Everyone else headed to the park drove. In Mt. Airy, even when my afternoons passed in loneliness, the proximity of the Rosses and my classmates and foot traffic in the park had cocooned me in a safe and familiar sense of place. I had lost even that.

Vigil

Near the end of my first American summer, I had working English under my belt but not yet used it in any public, spontaneous way. My priority was to just focus on answering questions when school started again, not starting conversations. That could come later.

In August, I stood in front of the Rosses' gate one morning with my mother. A girl my size came walking down Lincoln Drive, crossing over toward us. She was with her mother, both wearing identical bobbed helmets of straight, light brown hair. She looked familiar.

"Hi!" She waved and smiled, showing a neat, narrow gap between her front teeth.

I recognized Alison Kukulka from three weeks of first grade but didn't tell my mother. I thought I smiled but no sound came out. My mother jabbed me in the back and raised her hand to wave back with a bright smile. Fifteen silent seconds until they passed. "She said hello and you can't even wave back or say anything. Such a simple thing. That was rude and stupid." She repeated this to my father and my brothers but not to the Rosses. She knew better than to share that side of her to anyone outside the family.

She likewise monitored and calibrated my possessions. She thought my backpack was too full and heavy; no one needed all those books at the same time. She counted new scuffs on my shoes the day they appeared. One day in fourth grade I tore across the school playground in wild zig-zags and didn't notice until recess ended that my bracelet was gone; my birthday bracelet in delicate gold tone with "Gemini" inscribed in cursive. My heart sank with disappointment but palpitated in anticipation of her scolding; she noticed the minute she came in the house. She didn't seem to see as sharply around my brothers.

In our second house, she was a night crawler, patrolling the second floor as if scouting enemies along a dangerous perimeter. For many years, my parents slept in separate rooms. "His snoring is too loud," she said, so she slept in the room next to mine. In the small hours, her socked feet creaked first in her bedroom, then on floorboards beneath the hall carpeting, then into my room. She creaked in the dark around my bed, the ironing table, the desk and dresser, carefully repositioning a folded shirt, an open notebook, a jewelry box. I mapped her movements by radar. She pat-pat-patted my comforter, smoothing out dents from my feet in the far corner and straightening the undersheet into a crisp border over my neck. I lay stiller than still, eyes closed, breathing deeply in a faux sleep rhythm. If I sank into the mattress I could barely feel her hands through the comforter and the added buffer of my inert body.

As my mother trolled my bedroom, I floated back to Rich's house.

There, I could slip into another dimension where furniture melted away and all colors swirled to a deep scarlet. In this plane his house had only one room, filled from wall to wall with a giant, round bed, tufted in soft velvet and scattered with body sized pillows and throws. The whole family slept on this bed in a spoke pattern, each burrowing into his or her pocket of mattress around the perimeter. That way, they could all keep watch for one another.

My mother patrolled the house in waking hours too. She handled family finances, poring over savings, checking accounts, and receipts neatly packed in an accordion folder. She picked up wisps of lint and straightened sofa pillows. If a book was left open, she closed and moved it to an acceptable spot on a table. Because she wiped the kitchen floor with a rag every day and checked on knick-knacks on the shelves regularly, she could document changes in our habits, like if someone started to wear new shoes that left different tread marks. She mentally logged who ate which foodstuffs and how quickly, so she could tell me how to adjust our grocery list. On weekends, she had me dust and vacuum but trailed behind to pounce on bits of dirt I missed.

She patrolled me, too. Like the insistent blink of a hazard light, she marked with a scowl and complaint whenever a new pimple appeared or if I scratched at an old one, if I wore the same outfit two days in a row, if my hair was not combed or was covering my eyes. Why couldn't I be more like my girl cousins? She put a bottle of astringent on my bureau for oily patches on my face, and moisturizer for snake skin on my hands and knees. She claimed to have never had these problems as a girl. She worried that reading so much would make me anti-social, that I didn't smile enough, and was too rude or too soft when I did speak. But mostly she was wounded and coldly angry that I didn't help her run the house unless ordered to.

Whenever she barked an order, I had to leave something I was doing with Michael.

To Americans and Vietnamese guests, she presented a cheerful, gracious generosity. But my mother's face was nearly always furrowed when guests were not in the house. Even her slumber was disturbed by watchful worries. She had little reserve left to see or worry about the things that worried me.

Talking Cure

Rich spent a few days nursing regrets. If he had been more aggressive with the State Department, could the adoption have happened faster? If he had pressed Michael's grandmother for direct contact with the boy sooner, what would he have learned about the uncle's house? But he veered back to the present and the task ahead.

He sat down with Michael and explained what was about to happen. A visitor came the next morning. He was middle-aged and kind looking. His eyes were deep set as if to protect them from what they saw. He offered his right hand to Michael and said hello in a deep voice. He carried notebook and pen in his left hand.

Rich steered them through a secret door into a narrow, carpeted office with a skylight. The visitor sat in an armchair; Rich and Michael on the sofa opposite. There were paper and crayons, blocks and dolls on the table between them. Once Michael settled and answered questions spontaneously, Rich slipped out the door.

The visitor and Michael sat together for an hour that day, and again two days later, their conversation often cut off by rips of terror when Michael seemed to flee out of his skin while glued to the sofa. That was all I could see; something shielded the room's walls to keep my eyes and ears from penetrating them. After three weeks, the visitor took Rich aside. "I don't think this is going to work unless you come in with him." From then on, Rich joined each session.

Michael became strong enough to start school. After a year of sessions, the visitor gave him a farewell hug. Michael would grow six feet tall and brilliant, as he was meant to.

"Where would a child get the notion of how psychotherapy works?" I asked Blue.

I didn't know what a psychologist was until eighth grade, and then only that they were sometimes professors who did experiments. They didn't appear in my library books. In high school, Jenny Highland said her mother was a psychotherapist with patients who didn't function quite right. And here I was, only finally understanding in middle age how the talking cure actually works. How did Rich and Michael figure it out so long ago? What else did they know that I didn't?

"I find it remarkable, too," Blue confessed, "that you intuited what Michael needed."

Thinking about blond, blue-eyed Rich rescuing Michael and staying by him as long as was needed, I drifted back to the present and Blue's narrow, carpeted office. My eyes swept over the rug beneath my boots, the brown sofa, slanted light from an eastern window, the sound proofed office door, notepad in his lap, and in his arm chair, the lanky, comfortable man with blond curls and blue eyes gazing back at me in this secret healing space.

"You can understand my confusion?"

Blue nodded.

Contact

When I was ten and Michael not quite starting junior high, he decided to spend summer at home rather than at sleep away camps. He loved to garden. Each morning, he irrigated the beds, then teased weeds out from softened soil. Rich sometimes came to help, and they kneeled back-to-back in the vegetable rows in silent companionship.

Then on a Monday, Michael heard a different sound, something more than hooting from mourning doves. It was my voice. It was familiar and so immediately responsive to his every thought that at first, neither one of us realized there was an Other. His hands paused and touched down on his thighs, and he raised his face to the wind, but the sound wasn't flying out there. It was within.

His face flushed in recognition, and warmth simultaneously rushed my chest. I was no longer observing him from above. I could now swing from behind to in front of his eyes with a wish, or stand in both places at once.

Rich noticed the break in Michael's movements. I hear her, Michael said. He settled back on his haunches with a new solidity and resumed weeding. Rich knew the explanation would come later, and sensed Michael had found something belonging to him and lost long ago.

"How did it feel to have him recognize your existence?" Blue asked.

"It felt perfectly natural, like it was meant to be," I answered. I hadn't been trying to hide from him.

"Tell me more about Michael," Blue said. He meant it.

I eyed his frame. "Your height, six feet tall."

"What does he look like?"

"Just short of GQ," I shot back. Blue smiled appreciatively. "Wavy auburn hair, gray eyes. He wears glasses but not all the time, wide cheekbones."

"How is he like you?"

"He is nothing like me."

I explained to Blue—

Michael commanded every room he enters without arrogance. People instantly trust and respect him. He never needed to shout. He was strong but not overbuilt, and moved crisply, efficiently. When he rode horses, mounting them like a pommel in mid-canter, I could see the gymnastic form he inherited from the Space Flyers. I sometimes glimpsed him striding across a lawn at Harvard, his graduation gown billowing around him on each side. He was the kind of person who would see a problem and fix it before other people noticed. The air around him was warm and quiet, slightly sunny and sad, such that small children wandered up to investigate. He let them play with his fingers and pull on his pant leg before he absent-mindedly reached to chuck them under the chin or pull them onto his lap. Most people told him their secrets if given the chance. I never saw him angry except once, when he thought my life was in danger and broke down the door of a burning building to carry me out. His hands were always quietly busy, whittling wood, cooking, playing music, reaching for my face or to rest on the high of my back to reassure me.

He was all the things I couldn't be in my mother's house.

Back in Blue's office, my eyes widened.

"Would you like to meet him?" I asked.

"With you? I think that would be fascinating, and an honor," he responded with no note of alarm. "How do you imagine it would happen?"

Michael stood downstairs on the front stoop of Blue's building, in a leather jacket and jeans. He dialed Blue's security code and upstairs, Blue pressed a button to open the door, but Michael wouldn't go in.

"You have to go down to meet him," I explained to Blue. "He won't come up."

"Why?" Blue asked.

"Because he doesn't belong in here." Michael wasn't a pathology anymore; he didn't need to be in the healing room.

Then I saw myself and Blue walking downstairs in our jackets, and watched him shake hands with Michael. They let me move ahead a few paces, leading us past the corner café, the comfort shoe boutique, and Blue's favorite music shop. Out the corner of my eye and in reflections in store fronts we passed, I saw them talking just far enough behind to muffle their words.

Blinking slowly brought me back to Blue's sofa.

"Someday," I told him.

Blind Sight

Everything was wrong with my eyesight. By nine years of age, untreated astigmatism and farsightedness made my eyes cross. I got my first pair of glasses the same month I rode a runaway bicycle down a hill at my cousin's house that sloped at thirty degrees toward a six-lane highway. Unaccustomed to the torque required to make pedal brakes work at that speed, I steered the bike into a tree, which snapped my free fall as well as my front tooth and enough blood vessels to coat my face and shirt in red. In the months before a dentist could put on a crown over the jagged remains of my tooth, the crossed eyes, black triangle in my mouth, and hexagonal eyeglass frames that kept slipping off my flat nose bridge induced a Cubist sensation of my own face. My eyes seemed to migrate asymmetrically, not fully under my control, their muscles rehearsing new tasks under the discipline of the lenses.

"Wonder Woman!" the school photographer shouted, so I would smile for a yearbook picture.

Unbeknownst to me, I was also colorblind. Despite regular eye exams, a couple of eye surgeries, and the phalanx of visual tests accompanying them, no one shared this diagnosis with me. Hence the maddening sense of incompetence when I couldn't find enough birds teasing with their chirping in tree canopies to earn a bird watching badge in Girl Scouts. And the inexplicable headache that muddy colors—ochres, tans, mauves—gave me when other people cooed over them. The substantial fraction of the world presenting itself in small pixels, in orange next to Kelly green, blues next to purples, or pastel shades, was elusive and mysterious. I hated pale pink roses because they looked gray.

Sometimes I chose not to care, squinting to deliberately blur it all and wallow in an impressionist view of life. Other times I faked it, guessing and using color labels that other people suggested. "I don't think I see things the way other people see them," I confided to my high school boyfriend.

For this and other reasons, my mother didn't wait for me to choose my own clothes. From puberty on, she strode through my closet and bureau and then her own each night, piecing together a suitable outfit she laid on my bed. If I dared to ignore it in the morning, she tailed me through breakfast, berating me for ingratitude and lack of judgment.

"What's the matter with you that you don't like this one? It's perfect and you look good in that color."

My father didn't like the results. "You're making her look like an old woman." But he didn't fully trust me to decide for myself.

My torso was long on top of short legs with aggressively robust calves, topped by a short neck and a head that looked too wide from the front and too flat from the side. Since there was nothing to like about my proportions or appearance, I sank into faded, ripped jeans and flannel shirts when I could get away with it. There was no romance; the jeans weren't tight or sexy and the flannel evoked truck driver rather than Gap dancers. For emphasis, I sometimes added a baseball cap. It all looked like a puddle of brown to me anyway.

Everyone gave me clothes. I inherited hand-me-downs from cousins, from Faye, my mother.

"You're so lucky to get all these good things," my mother said. She bragged to her sisters about the effort she made to dress me.

I had trouble judging the value of things I hadn't spent money on or time choosing, just accepting that sometimes we wear colors that make our eyes hurt, because they're good clothes someone gave to us. It was normal to be uncomfortable with the color over your own skin.

"I'm feeling pretty ragged," I told Blue. I needn't have. He could see me slumped on the sofa, eyes brittle from lack of sleep and crying, my left hand massaging tense muscles behind my collarbone. "Someone asked me to write a white paper but it's a last minute thing, so I've only got two weeks to pull it together."

"Why don't you turn them down? I have no doubt you can do that charmingly."

"Because the last time I tried to, I had horrific neck spasms for half a day."

"And they eventually stopped, right? The point is each time you say no, it'll be a little bit easier." He was utterly unconvincing.

He tried a different tack. "Maybe you need a break. How about a staycation? What would you do if you could do anything?"

I thought about my bucket list. "I'd like to go to Tibet." Tibet had long lured me with its vivid tangerine oranges of monks' robes and poppies, open skies, cold mountain air. Orange is complex and irreverent and glorious, the opposite of staid and reliable navy blue. My inner turmoil seemed like a raging battle between orange and navy blue.

"What would Tibet look like?" he asked.

What kind of slacking at work could I get away with? "Maybe insist on a month to write that white paper rather than just two weeks. Maybe stop taking calls and just work from home part-time for a week."

He inhaled sharply, incredulous and exasperated. "Mai, that's the *worst* Tibet I've ever heard of! What about a spa treatment? Or going to a country B&B?"

Not really believing this would work, but hating to disappoint him, I tried again. "Maybe turn down the white paper and take the whole week off. Go window shopping on U Street? There are lovely shoe boutiques and little bakeries there. I saw a pair of orange boots recently … maybe even *three* pairs of shoes?"

He approvingly wrote me a prescription to buy as many new shoes as I wanted.

Kitchen

Coming home from middle school on a typical day, I hopped out of dry radiator heat on the 32 bus and crossed Henry Avenue, climbed our front steps, around the side yard, and unlocked the back door. I was the first one home. After dropping my backpack and having a cold drink, I confronted the refrigerator.

I tried to remember her instructions. Two thick lengths of fatty pork thawing in a plastic bowl, onions, garlic, fish sauce, soy sauce, and something else, what? On a split cutting board, I carefully chopped the onion and dumped it in the bowl. I smashed the garlic with the side of the cleaver as she did it, picked out the papery peel, and chopped the flesh. I doused the bowl with a liberal amount of soy and fish sauce and then massaged the half-frozen meat until my fingertips were numb. What was missing? Not salt; the sauces are salty. Lemongrass? I sprinkled in a fistful. I dabbed the marinade with my pinky and tasted it. Edible. My father came home and went upstairs to change. I turned on sitcoms while he puttered in shorts and polo shirt, my eye wandering up to the wall clock every fifteen minutes. At some point my brothers came in and disappeared to their rooms. At five o'clock, I went back to the kitchen, measured out three cups of rice and added water to the 3.5 mark because she wanted it cooked more moist than American rice, then pressed the cooker's "on" button. I put a rack in a long cake pan and arranged the meat on top. It went in the oven.

My mother hopped off a different bus at 5:30 p.m. I heard the click-clack of her footsteps, close together, half the length of my stride, straining in heels under the weight of her handbag. I turned off the TV and moved to the living room with a book.

"Mai đâu (where are you)? Get in here!"

I was careful to clear my face of expression as I stepped into the kitchen.

"Did you put ANY sugar in the meat?"

Sugar.

"It's inedible. Stupid. Now I have to fix it."

She had me stand there to watch her mix four soup spoons of honey into water and soy sauce, and coat the meat. She put another cutting board and a head of broccoli in front of me.

"I ask you to do two things for dinner and I have to fix everything."

I cut the broccoli into florets and dumped them in a pot and left the kitchen.

Michael was waiting for me. We took a spin at the skating rink and then a slow walk through the woods to finish with cocoa at Rich's house. He smoothed the hair back from my forehead and held my hand as we crunched through an icy veneer of snow on the path, far away from Henry Avenue.

My mother noticed not at all. She retold my offense to everyone at the dinner table but they were all listening to the blaring tickety-tack of local news, eyes tracking food from the table to their chopstick ends, to their bowl, then up to the television in the corner of the room.

Kitchens were rehearsal halls. There was dinner to prepare every evening, school lunches to pack, dishes to wash, appliances to clean. She showed me how to soak bowlfuls of sticky rice and dried yellow split beans, swirling in food coloring and setting them under lids overnight until they doubled in volume and turned a brilliant red-orange, ready for steaming. I arranged plates of lettuce, cucumber, and herbs for weekend lunches, careful after one scolding to snip off only the tender leaves of mint at the tip of each branch. When we washed dishes together, she didn't trust me with the soaping—she scrubbed harder and longer—so I stood at the rinsing sink and ended the assembly line by arranging each dish as she preferred in the dish rack.

Some weekends Vietnamese guests came, and the kitchen became a stage. I learned the rhythm for welcoming and showing them to the living room, answering questions and smiling modestly while they cooed as my parents bragged about their children. Then I ducked away to find trays she liked to use, good glasses trimmed in gold tone. It was important to offer both warm and cold drinks. While the kettle heated, we filled the caddy with jasmine tea and loaded a tray with cookies and fruit. They cooed again as I bent at the knees and maneuvered the tray onto the coffee table. My parents' guests met me, but rarely my brothers.

My skin prickled with yearning for my own kitchen. When I finally got it in adulthood in our Manhattan apartment—our first home as a married couple, I obsessed over a nostalgic vision of Americana—rustic apple pies and country oatmeal—and adventures with foreign cuisines, anything Mediterranean or that required fresh basil. David once watched me sleepwalk, barely conscious post-call and naked, from the bedroom to the refrigerator to check if custard filling in a tart had firmed up.

When we began house hunting, I agreed to buy David's first choice of house when he promised to give me a new kitchen within three years.

The old one had four entryways, no counters, and an oven that became a health hazard when a gas line leaked and we couldn't fix it because the 1970's parts were no longer available. Renovate we did.

In my redone kitchen, as my first year with Blue drew to its end, I would swing from the steel sink to the range, moving homemade pizzas onto the counter. I shifted pork from the freezer to fridge to thaw and moved riper tomatoes to the front of refrigerator shelves. I made dinners and school lunches and birthday cupcakes while the kids finished art projects on the pine floor. I had a rotating menu but was careful to insert something completely new at least once a month.

When all the prep was done and the bowls and plates were full, I took my place standing on one side of the counter where we usually eat, watching David's and the kids' forks fly, ready to pounce when Alexander raised his hand to his throat in a gesture for "Water!"

"Sit down!" David pleaded. I stared at him, unable to comprehend how or why to do that, or why he was so exasperated. It was easier to reach something they needed if I stood.

Blue explained, in the slow words necessary to introduce a foreign concept, "You are so far at that end of the spectrum, worrying about meeting other people's needs ... that if you worked *really* hard and became what would feel to you like a flaming narcissist, you might just approximate normal."

Bà Ngoại
(Grandmother)

I was eleven before I knew her name—Lê Thị Cạnh. We called her Bà Ngoại—Bà for female of the grandparents' generation, and ngoại of the maternal line, the "outside family" that has to earn acceptance by the "inside," nội, village of the father.

She puttered around the edges of my childhood. She never had a home of her own in America, instead rotating from one aunt or uncle's house to another, spending a few months each in Florida, Texas, Maryland, New Jersey, or Pennsylvania, so as not to wear out her welcome. Some houses she rarely went to. She was as ngoại as ngoại could be.

Having few living expenses, she spent her Social Security checks on graduation and birthday gifts for grandchildren. She spent her days taking slow walks, gardening, or nannying my younger cousins. She claimed to not speak English, but watched soap operas most afternoons, ankles crossed with her tiny body barely denting the sofa, crocheting or knitting as the dialogue and commercials droned on. She could relay the latest storyline from any of the shows, but only in Vietnamese.

When she was in my mother's house, she helped more with cooking than my mother sometimes wanted. She stood silent whenever my mother lit into me but might say something quiet out of my hearing range later, enough to calm the mother.

Bà Ngoại was my only living forbearer, the one I didn't have to conjure.

When I was six, I had no grandfathers. My world in Sài Gòn was managed by my mother and her siblings, and Bà Ngoại was the matriarch of it all. I marveled at the parthenogenic power of her small round belly.

In America, I became aware of grandfather ghosts when we had reunions with my mother's siblings, eavesdropping as the grown-ups chatted late at night during card games while we children lay like so many sardines on bedsheets spread on the living room floor. Occasionally their talk settled on something precious and lost, someone they variably referred to as "Chú (uncle)" or "Ông (old man)," and their voices would lower and soften. But then they stopped talking, or turned the conversation, and left the ghost undisturbed.

I connected faces to those ghosts at the altar table. In my parents' house like most Vietnamese homes, there was a quiet place called a *bàn thờ*—a place of offering where we practiced ancestor worship. Sideboard, mantel, or bedroom bureau; it didn't matter. It might be permanent or portable but always had incense sprigs propped up in raw rice in a teacup-sized vessel, photographs of the dead laid out or hung on the wall above, and banquet food piled on mismatched china when needed, then put away.

We made offerings to the wandering and apparently starved ghosts of ancestors on their death anniversaries. Told by my parents to pay my respects to these dead relatives several times a year, with little else explained to me, I stood balancing incense between my hands, and helplessly turned my eyes downward toward the photos, aware my Vietnamese was insufficient to reassure them, and uncertain if they understood my English thoughts.

Photographs were precious enough to take up limited space in the emergency luggage my parents packed in January of 1975 in anticipation of fleeing Việt Nam, months before they actually found a way to get us out. For weeks the suitcases hid in a secret crawl space, then in the trunk of our car, ready for any opportunity. Photos nestled among a few changes of clothes, birth certificates, school diplomas, proof of employment, and dog tags on chains to later hang on each of us children, engraved with our names and instructions in slightly imperfect English for contacting Dan Ross should we get lost. There were color photos of Ân, Chương, and me with our scouting troops, posed before scenic backgrounds at the zoo, by water in the resort town of Đà Lạt. Black and white photos of my debonair parents—him walking a bicycle with hair slicked off a high forehead, a tilted Hollywood head shot of her in a wavy Bouvier do, full lips and cheekbones, looking barely Asian and vaguely like Anne Frank.

And then, a separate pile of photographs of the dead—the paternal grandfather in mandarin headdress and black robe with dark, bottomless eyes; the maternal grandfather in modern blazer and tie, the film overexposed and faded so his hair looked blond; grandaunts whose names I didn't know; but no photos of the paternal grandmother, which made my father so sad my mother forbade us from asking about it.

My grandmother kept no photographs on her bàn thờ, not even of her lost husband, as if that gesture was too painful to make. She set up a table in her bedroom when she came to our house, usually low to the floor near where she sat to pray. She arranged on it a bit of silk, incense, bronze boxes and a Buddha statue, and off to one side, a small drum and prayer books.

She had remained Buddhist when my parents converted to Catholicism. An hour or more each day, she sat cross legged and chanted in the bastardized Sanskrit passed down from Indian missionaries to their Vietnamese converts, accompanying herself with a steady rhythm on the drum. It was gibberish to me but sounded unbearably sad.

    I sat outside her bedroom door, secretly listening to the sedative white noise. I wondered if they channeled for her the mysterious things she had lost, right into the second story of our house. The syncopated rhythm of her nasal mutterings seemed to open floodgates to an overwhelming grief as much mine as hers. She was never surprised to find me outside her door. We barely spoke during her visits, hobbled by our half languages.

Boy

My one high school boyfriend was an accident—a trumpet player whose sister sat next to me in the flute section in summer camp orchestra and brought him along when we walked between classes. He was blonde and kind, more talented at composing than performing, especially when nervousness brought on the slight tremor in his hands. Our conversations relapsed into geeky analysis of his name (John Thomas) and why baselines were more fun to play than melodies (I moonlighted as a bassoonist and tenor saxophonist whenever our band director needed me to). It was a relief to get home from our dates and stop performing. I felt guilty when he gifted me his guitar at graduation, along with a hand-notated original jazz suite for bassoon.

Freshman year of college, I fell into a relationship with my first and only Vietnamese boyfriend, who must have chosen me through a process of elimination after considering what Việt women on campus were passably pretty and not taken. He was only two years older but much more of my parents' generation. He was cheerful but traditional, speaking English with a thick accent, keeping American friends at a distance with an easy laugh, envying his older brother for landing a Vietnamese girlfriend no mother could object to, who was beautiful, unobtrusive, and supportive. He was my attempt at compromise with my parents. We disappointed my mother by not lasting through the summer.

A year later, a white, skinny boy appeared. He smiled long smiles, his voice was elusively reassuring, and his wide, open expression reminded me of Mt. Airy. There was something so instantly familiar about David that he was the first person I could make understand about Michael.

"There's something strange about me you should know...." is how I introduced the topic. David was completely unfazed and listened whenever I shared something new that Michael did or described a scene in my inner world just as he would to my telling him about an outing with a real girlfriend. He only asked reasonable questions, like whether I thought other people could see Michael, or if I thought I could touch him like the beds in our dorms.

He played a Joplin tango on piano for me in the empty dining hall at midnight and took me to an animation festival in an old theater where I was mortified when he took off his sandals and put bare feet up on the seat in front. He wore ratty, faded clothes with no sense of style. A mathematician, his eyes lit up when tutoring me in multivariate calculus, approving when I asked about abstractions. He held me tightly as I sobbed after reading Maxine Hong Kingston's *Woman Warrior* for a class in Asian American literature, when I couldn't explain why the book undid me. He revealed an easy feminism and insistent, Talmudic need to dissect anything that seemed facile or said with too much confidence. He knew everything, and his hands and feet were just right. His family was vaguely Jewish and had less money than mine. The picture on his state ID card was elfin, and everyone treated him that way, men and women alike.

That summer my mother shook off David like an inconvenience. She kept asking friends to introduce me to their Vietnamese sons, to whom I had nothing to say. My aunts fretted with her. Bà Ngoại also met David briefly, but she didn't fret.

A couple of summers later, I came home for a short break during one of Bà Ngoại's stays at my parents' house. I lay on the carpet in the sun porch while she crocheted in the recliner above me, her slippered feet crossed at the ankles and not quite touching the floor. This was my usual silent companionship with her, and I almost dozed to sleep. Without warning, she started to tell a story. At the time, I didn't have enough Vietnamese to catch all the nuances, but this became my best understanding of it after she repeated it several times over the years.

When she was barely a teenager, Bà Ngoại's father sent her from the countryside into Hà Nội for schooling, because she was so smart he didn't know what else to do with her. For a girl, this was almost unheard of in early twentieth-century Việt Nam.

On campus, she watched a confident young man leading a demonstration against French rule. Nguyễn Đức Kính was driven and righteous in a way she had never known. She helped him hand out nationalist leaflets and listened, enraptured, to his speeches.

"He was...." and here she used a Vietnamese word I didn't know. She put down her yarn at my quizzical look and gently waved her hand in my direction. "Like David," she explained, "he didn't need very much."

Not long after they met, French authorities made one of many sweeps for revolutionaries, and this young man was caught and sent to prison where he was recruited into the Vietnamese Communist Party. For months, Bà Ngoại prepared care packages for him. She wrote letters to sustain him, and he replied in poems. When he was finally released during a rare amnesty, they quickly conspired. They bedecked her in fake gold jewelry borrowed from a friend and rode back to her village so Kính could ask Bà Ngoại's father for her hand. Their first child, my uncle Sơn, was born soon after. Ông Ngoại (grandfather), she said, did a lot of different things to support the family, but he never stopped working for the Party.

Her story leapt ahead seventeen years, to just a few days after her seventh child was born. Kính's comrades came to tell him of orders to "march into the mountains," a euphemism for facing a death squad. They promised that if he went quietly, they wouldn't harm Bà Ngoại or his children.

Ông Ngoại went home and resolutely removed all his guns from the house as my grandmother frantically protested.

"We could run away," she begged him.

"How could we run away, with all these children?" He hushed her with his logic.

She watched him leave the next day, walking between armed men who used to be their friends. They kept him in a makeshift holding room for several days where my grandmother visited and he tried to reassure her. Then the French parachuted into the region and ground fighting made it impossible for my grandmother to maintain contact.

He disappeared in a vapor the way of ghosts. He was thirty-nine years old and my mother barely eleven. When Bà Ngoại managed to find his old comrades again, they met her questions with stony silence. In the void and haze, theories and dreams and illusions swirled about what happened. Did his friends kill him in a party purge because they thought his opium addiction made him vulnerable to French cooptation? Was he an outright traitor? Did the French capture and kill him as he fought?

In desperation, my grandmother wrote to Trần Huy Liệu, the Party's famed propaganda minister, who was a close friend of my grandfather's and at that moment, by Hồ Chí Minh's side near the Chinese border. Liệu denied any detailed knowledge of such local Party activities, but his response was ominous—"dữ nhiều lành ít"—more likely something nasty rather than good happened.

To my questions about why they wanted to kill him, she said only that she had asked the same thing. She begged Party officials for any shred of information.

"You were his friends! Tell me where he is. Give me his body!"

They had nothing to say, but a few weeks later, a soldier knocked. He slipped into her hand a piece of folded paper with script she recognized. A poem, from him, written just before he died and passed to the soldier with a request to deliver it to Bà Ngoại as one last favor. When I asked her to tell this story again several years later, she recited his farewell poem from memory, without tears, in a voice with the timbre and rhythm of an anguished and angry train. My aunt and uncle translated it into English.

A Final Farewell

The rose petals fall on the veranda
Or is it my soul torn up because of you?
We have not savored our tender love
Yet we endure our despair again.
I am ensnared in the perils,
But once committed, I must step further.
In this dangerous situation
Why should I dwell on my own existence?
I have determination in my heart
to pay my debt to the nation.
Although the tiger has fallen into the trap,
My love, have no distress because of me.
My body may someday become dust
But my soul will be at peace forever.

In one gesture, Bà Ngoại had anointed my beloved, added flesh to my grandfather's ghostly frame, and hinted I had something important to inherit, to grow into. But sharing it left her spent, and I didn't have enough Vietnamese to ask the remainder of my questions or understand what answers she might offer. We lapsed back into soft silence in the afternoon sun.

Wall

That anyone would, unprompted, gift me with family history as Bà Ngoại did was unheard of. There were no innocent questions in my parents' house. Allowed questions were practical—What time will the guests arrive? Where will we go on vacation? Of my father, I could also ask about the world and expect a wandering treatise in response—Why is there an Israeli-Palestinian conflict? What was so great about John F. Kennedy?

But questions about life before Philadelphia, where the edges of family were beyond my mother's siblings and their children, about Việt Nam or what my parents brought of it to America, were met with a sudden agitation from my father, a sharp burst of argument between my parents, or silence stretching away from the conversation. In our house, the war was crated and warehoused. If we wanted to learn about it, we were on our own and could count on them hindering us however they could if they knew we were looking. It was as if my parents had confined their children and the things they needed to sustain us under the protective glare of a streetlamp, and surrounded the circular light cone with sentinels to hiss us back from the dark if we dared to stray.

So I collected clues whenever they were dropped and hoarded them for future sense making. I noted postmarks on thin blue air-mail envelopes with handwritten letters, some from Hồ Chí Minh City, some from other places in Việt Nam I didn't recognize, and a rare one from Canada or France. I saw how my parents receive envelopes from Việt Nam with silence and anxious faces, but the ones from Canada with smiles; how my father's investment in any piece of art Chương made was so out of proportion to the time my brother spent making it; how sometimes when they argued and my mother sniped about some former female student of my father's, he would bark at her and they would silently retreat to their respective corners; and my father's unpredictable paranoia that someone was cheating him—a waiter paying attention to another table first, or someone cutting in line.

Mail went in the opposite direction too. I helped my parents pack small boxes with bottles of Tylenol and vitamins to send to both north and south Việt Nam. They sent cash by wire, each transfer padded with something extra to bribe government officials. It seemed my father was responsible for supplying material goods for the entire extended family.

I pored over family albums looking for clues to relationships between the characters and where scenes landed in time and place. If I caught my parents in a relaxed mood, I might point to a photo and ask, Who is this? If the person was alive, they told me where they were living. If not, they murmured and turned the page. One weekend, prowling through the oldest pictures, a small color photo slipped into my lap. It was a stray, not fastened under the sticky plastic cover. It looked a bit like my father, I thought, in combat fatigues and helmet, a gun in his hand. But I wasn't sure.

"When were you in the army?" I asked casually.

"I was never in the army!" He denied it in an almost angry voice, and when I went back to find the proof, the photo was gone.

In high school, American history class ended around the Cuban missile crisis and world history class, having started with ancient civilizations, only got as far as World War II. The world conspired to keep me from unearthing the Việt Nam war. I learned to be afraid to ask. The wall my parents erected to repel any curiosity about our past stood fast, too tall for me to climb, unmoving when I pounded my fists on it.

Teacher

The first thing I knew about my father was that he was a teacher. He was a teacher in Sài Gòn, a teacher within months of arriving in Philadelphia, a teacher until he retired. In a photograph from the early 1980s, he stands in front of the blackboard in a powder blue suit with wide lapels, black hair slicked back from bald spot, eyes and face wide open, gesturing with his left hand to the intensely orange persimmon held up in his right hand. It was a class of English as a second language (ESL)—what he spent most of his time teaching in the U.S., the type of class where a teacher could demonstrate vocabulary with a fruit so strange to native English speakers and so familiar to Asian students.

He was scornful of the teachers' union that represented him. When I was in junior high, Philadelphia teachers went on strike three years in a row, delaying for weeks the start of school. My father was furious. Not only was he idled against his will and better judgment (he didn't think most of his colleagues deserved higher salaries and benefits), but neither were his two younger children getting an education. On that he was wrong. One evening deep into a strike he came home from a union meeting with a face full of fury, tumult, and fear.

"What happened, Bố?" I asked. He stood up during the meeting to urge them to end the strike, lecturing that their demands were unreasonable and enough was enough.

"Do you know what it's like to stand up and be booed by a thousand people?" he asked.

No, I thought, I don't, but it seemed worth doing. I imagined the thrill and adrenaline of righteously staring down a thousand shouters.

He had a different reaction when it was my turn to stand up. When I was newspaper editor in high school and wanted to devote a special issue to stories of refugee boat children, I showed him the layout mock-up.

"Be careful," he said ominously, "Politics is dangerous." Really? I thought…. At a high school newspaper?

He was equally uninterested when during medical school I organized a teach-in with police officers, social workers, and pediatricians for us to learn how to detect and report child and sexual abuse. The event consumed me and was attended by over three hundred people. He asked me nothing about it. A few weeks later, he took some of my conference brochures to use as scrap paper.

In the ghetto high school where he taught a rapidly growing number of children from Laos, Việt Nam, and Cambodia, my father was proxy priest, social worker, and family attorney. In 1975 and again as the first waves of boat people arrived in the 1980s, I spent weekends helping him organize used household items and clothes into shopping bags, then tagging along in the station wagon down to South and West Philly and awkwardly helping him drop the bundles at homes of newly arrived families. He helped the parents with legal paperwork and tracked the progress of kids having the roughest transitions, usually teenage boys. At night, he did extra tutoring. He would help establish the Vietnamese Association. And when we visited the Vietnamese congregation every third Sunday or so, the priest greeted him at the door with both hands and walked us to the front pew of honor.

Around American acquaintances he didn't seem professorial, and they wouldn't have guessed his stature in the Vietnamese community. He had lost some hearing from bombing during the war, my mother said, and so spoke a little too loudly with unpredictable bursts of laughter. I compensated by speaking softly around guests. He couldn't be casual with small talk, too eager to find a laugh line or quickly change the topic to things he was more comfortable with. But he heard everything said around him and took note of small gestures and expressions. I could see his flickers of reaction.

He rarely lost his temper or raised his voice at us kids. Instead, some unnamed distress translated into abrupt loss of his smile, tense pacing around the discolored beige carpet, and long stares to shadows he was intent on keeping buried like something locked in the cupboard.

His waking life was punctuated by startling impulses. In the middle of pacing, he would occasionally shout "Ping-y!," a nonsense word, loud enough to make me jump, and then resume his stare. His acting out resulted in our discovering one day that an entire nine-foot lilac bush in the garden was chopped to its roots, or that an impulsive purchase of a large copper fish sculpture hung in the dining room. These sudden gestures drove my mother to exasperated fits, but we children learned to suppress our reactions and duck until the storm passed.

My parents and many of their Vietnamese friends had a deep prejudice against Black Americans, although they considered anyone not Vietnamese an Other. On Glen Echo Road, my father had a long running dispute with our Black neighbors, who complained about our pet guinea pigs straying over to eat their grass. My father felt unfairly accused, that their lawn was never as well kept as ours. I couldn't understand why something so small as the condition of a lawn made him so defensive and angry. Yet when I turned nine, he decided it would be good for me to sing in a choir. He prodded me to sing at the Vietnamese congregation but gave up because I couldn't read the lyrics fast enough to keep up, and I had nothing to say to the other kids when the singing stopped. So instead he walked me a few blocks from our house to a small Baptist church and left me there with six little Black girls and the choir director. I lasted one whole season.

My father was a staunch Republican, virulently anti-Communist and like many Vietnamese Americans of his generation, would have voted eight times for Reagan if allowed. American colleagues and friends assumed this was because his family had suffered at Communist hands, the details of which he didn't share with us kids. But he was conservative through and through. He loved Jeffersonian democracy and opportunity for self-betterment, not the welfare state. His faith in the meritocracy was unshakable; if he resented any bias he experienced as a minority teacher, he was confident he would conquer the system in the end.

His Catholicism deepened over time, long after he gave up bringing his teenage children to services. He fretted over David's imperfections but never questioned that he was my true life mate. My parents got used to David's ease with our relatives, his knack for fixing electronic things for them and lack of consternation when they slipped between English and Vietnamese (David said it sounded like so many ducks quacking), his genuine appetite for anything my mother cooked, the way I curled up next to him. Yet on my wedding morning, Bố wandered around his bedroom where I was putting on makeup and waiting for my mother to pin on a traditional bridal headdress of coiled pink brocade, and nervously fiddled with the bedding.

"At least I had you baptized," he said half out loud, "so I know you won't go to hell." He meant, for marrying a Jew.

He didn't interfere when my mother ordered me, but not my brothers, to help with grocery shopping, cleaning the house, or laundry. I could feel him agreeing with her shrill anxiety that I couldn't keep up with my girl cousins' sense of fashion, and was devolving into a sad, unpolished and introverted shadow.

Yet he would allow nothing to stand in the way of his daughter's learning. In third grade, when I refused to accept on faith that any number divided into zero equals zero, he sat down after dinner to show me the proof, the eraser tip on his pencil waving hypnotically above the paper with little flourishes, refusing to deny me any part of the logic. When I started asking more questions than he could answer, he bought a used set of encyclopedias. He made sure I got dance and flute lessons and my summers were filled with art and music camps. He indulged my whim for an expensive Vietnamese zither and stopped my mother if she complained about my reading. And when I opened the acceptance letter from Harvard, he decided in that moment to pay whatever was necessary (several times more than he had to pay for my brothers' college educations) to get me four years in Cambridge.

If these contradictions were apparent to my father, he was still perplexed and occasionally dismayed that I was developing distasteful reflexes—in my nerdiness, my growing sense that you couldn't avoid politics if you wanted to make lasting change in the world, my questioning of authority and tradition—as if he had had no hand in it. To be a true teacher demands constant discipline. Lessons drip off you with each flick of the wrist or turn of the head, and children watch and listen for them all day long.

Cook

The labial word "*Mẹ*" (pronounced may-ah) is Vietnamese for mother, first formed by lips pressing softly together around a nipple, or just before crying for help. It is the sound of a child enveloping a morsel and gently sweeping it down to where it will nourish.

I watched the endless hours Benjamin hung on my breast with his pursed sucking creating a second dimple in his cheek, his one exposed eye staring unblinkingly up to keep me in sight and his thighs and knees folded into my belly, shuddering contentedly under my stroking fingertips. When he sat in a high chair and took his first spoonful of butternut squash mush, I marveled at how, up until that moment, every cell but one in his body had come through me.

My mother didn't nurse her children, having proudly been able to afford the fancy foreign-made baby formula my father bought at the commissary on the U.S. Army base where he worked part time. But as soon as we moved to solid food, she ruled everything that fed us. Our housekeeper in Sài Gòn was sous chef, going to market and doing prep, but Mẹ picked the menus, applied the heat, judged when the seasoning was right.

Rice and stir fry, clear-broth soups, and pungent meats punctuated our days at lunch and dinner. On holidays symmetrically arranged plates of sticky red xôi gấp (rice) fragrant with coconut milk, roast chicken, lemongrass pork skewers, and shredded papaya salad covered the long dining table. I learned when to lunge with chopsticks for choice pieces of squid or beef in the hotpot, just as they finished blanching. And on Sunday mornings, she spooned sweetened condensed milk into my short cup of dense cà phê (coffee) and showed me how to swirl the concoction from black-brown to the au lait color of her skin, then twist off a crispy chewy hunk of warm baguette to dunk in it.

The few months we spent in the Rosses' house must have been torture for her. Faye and her mother experimented by putting out different foodstuffs each night for dinner, buffet style, and noting what we preferred to eat. A large baked fish was more popular than dry white rice. For my mother, the ingredients were unfamiliar, the range of what the American palate could tolerate numbingly narrow—no chili, tamarind, fish sauce, or shrimp paste.

Once in our own row house, my mother turned the Formica'd galley kitchen into a laboratory, skeptically but gamely co-opting 1970s staples like Minute-steaks and instant pudding into her own inventions. She gradually incorporated interpretations of spaghetti and meatballs, sloppy Joe, and steak frites into a steady dinner rotation, along with her core repertoire of rice meals. To this day, any of her children will exit a highway at ten o'clock in the morning for fried chicken; good or bad—it doesn't matter—we're forever chasing the memory of weighty drumsticks seasoned with nothing but salt and pepper and fried in light batter just to the point where the moist muscle groups come apart in the mouth on their own.

My mother was a fierce hunter gatherer. She brought me grocery shopping to push the cart and pull boxed goods off shelves as she selected them. She sniffed produce, tsk'd tsk'd and frowned disapproval on under-ripe fruit, and outsmarted anybody daring to offer a discount. In South Philly, she didn't bother being polite to the Italian street vendors, demanding they reach in to trade out individual crabs she considered lethargic before she would pay for the bushel. They learned to fear her.

For years, she sat in the car on her way to work along Schuykill River Drive, clucking her tongue at the waste of all those Canada geese freely congregating along the banks.

"Who would miss one?" she'd say. We did briefly have a white duck waddling and quacking in the basement one weekend, but it mysteriously disappeared just before my parents hosted friends to dinner.

My mother could make a meal from the most barren landscape. On vacation at the Maryland shore, I sat under an umbrella and grew bored watching her wade in ankle deep sea water, the woven brim of her hat obscuring her face and intentions. When she emerged an hour or so later, she carried a pail full of inch-wide snails dug out of the tidal pool floor with her feet. Back in our rented condo, she steamed them and gave us each a safety pin (from where I don't know) to spike and gently twist the meat out of its shell to douse with salt-and-peppered lemon juice.

Food was a weapon and a shield. It both fed and alleviated her litany of anxieties. It crept into her conversation many days before a party. As the time drew near she would itemize out loud bargains she had found, her timetable for cooking, and her reasons for doing it this way or that. She keenly observed and kept tight memory of her eaters' likes and dislikes, so she could choreograph elaborate efficiencies like when to scoop out vegetables from a simmering broth because of Ân's aversion to onions or how much of precious braised oxtails to set aside for me to snack on without skimping on portions for bowls of phở soup for the rest of the family.

When American guests arrived, she arbitrarily interrupted conversation to explain the menu or ask what they thought of an appetizer, not waiting for a response before moving on and leaving me awkwardly steering talk back to anything else. She judged her grandchildren by what she offered that they dared to refuse. When I arrived late to a family gathering, she pounced with a full plate of everything and tense instructions about what to eat first, second, third. Her conversation perseverated on the contents of a meal until she had chewed its fibers to a pulp.

In her kitchen, there were never trials of Mediterranean cuisines or Mexican food, no interest in French technique or the Great Chefs specials I watched on public television before there was a Food Network, and no one else who could be trusted with producing an entire meal. My brothers rarely set foot in it except to raid the refrigerator. I watched her pickle carrots and radishes, turn cabbage into sheer cobwebs to toss in vinegary fish sauce for a summer salad.

On weekends while we slept late, she woke at dawn and began checking on marinated meat or yellow peas that soaked overnight. She chopped vegetables and ground pork for spring rolls. I eventually came downstairs, obediently sat in front of giant mixing bowls of flavored meat, reached for a moistened sheet of rice paper she had spread on towels, and began rolling then sealing spring rolls with beaten egg. Frying revealed which rolls were mine and not hers, when sloppily tucked corners of rice paper unfurled in the bubbling oil to cause minor imperfections. I learned how to execute the second half of many Vietnamese dishes.

Her children are now all adventurous gourmands, driven by an imperative to not waste eating on food that is not at its best. We all live in our kitchens and collect restaurant experiences. Ân went so far as to marry a chef.

When my children were small, once a week, Bố and Mẹ picked them up after school and brought them back to our house. My father played with the kids, but in her nervousness, Mẹ cleaned my house, did our laundry, and glared at Benjamin and Alexander until they bathed. She handed them each a pouch of contraband treats—juice boxes, Pringles, Girl Scout cookies, apple slices, curated to a balance of crunchy, salty, sweet, and something to wash it down. She was often gone by the time I arrived, having just skirted the periphery of my weekly life. On the counter, she left Tupperware full of fresh fried rice, stewed stuffed tomatoes, eggy noodles with fat shrimp and wilted onions, cut fruit, and broccoli steamed al dente to see us through to the weekend, relieving just enough stress for me to enjoy cooking then.

Rooms

My childhood was a marathon of transits between rooms representing different versions of myself. In one room, I followed my mother's housekeeping instructions, wandered the neighborhood alone, or sat expressionless in front of the TV. In this room I barely spoke, my family and relatives looking on with pity and perplexity. *There, Michael would whisk me far away for a horseback ride or hold me on the sofa.* In another room, I envied schoolmates for their easy hipness, gossiped on the phone with my few girlfriends for hours, gorged on ice cream and pickles, and read prim Dorothy Sayers mysteries. *Here, Michael conducted an orchestra and figure skated like an Olympian.* In a third room, I slummed it with older kids at city summer camps, survived a hold-up at gun point during my midnight shift at a gas station convenience store, and trash talked on the volleyball court after school. *In this room, Michael seduced me with a barefoot dance to "Brown-Eyed Girl."*

In the fourth room, I reunited with girls from my elementary school when we all entered ninth grade at the premier Philadelphia High School for Girls. They were curvier now and more confident. I had become a faint memory to them. I slipped back into competing with the Highland twins for everything. I alternated between Sarah's flannel shirts and trucker boots, and Jenny's tartan plaid skirts. When she came to school one day in a periwinkle wool cape, I asked my mother to help me find black wool to make one of my own, lined in sky blue satin. I gunned to edit the newspaper when Jenny ran the literary magazine. I managed the jazz band when Sarah managed marching band. I tracked their grades against my own. We graduated first, second, and third (I was third) in our class.

In a generation before the arms race of pre-college extracurricular activities, I hadn't planned my high school resume of awards and scholarships, hobbies, and high test scores. I didn't understand enough to be as excited as other people were when I got into Harvard, and I thought Yale was in California. I had applied to both only because the Highland twins had.

"Why the Highlands, Mai?" Blue asked.

"Because they were so happy and confident. Their parents were so certain of everything. And because if I didn't do well, I wouldn't survive."

"Really? Why wouldn't you survive? Lots of other kids survive without besting Highland girls."

I thought a minute about how to make him understand the existential nature of the threat.

"This had nothing to do with my parents. Nobody pushed me to do things. I didn't need to be better than them. I just needed to be as good, or almost as good. If I fell out of that stratum, I could never become what Michael was."

"And why was it important to become what Michael was?"

"Because that was the only hope I had…." My voice trailed off. The abyss beyond that cliff was unthinkable. Michael was a prince, by birth and the way the world anointed him. I had to believe there was a path for me back to being a princess, a room in which I could reclaim what I had in Sài Gòn.

Label

Several months into my relationship with Blue, another panic attack swept over me at the worst of times, when winter was dark and David was traveling in Egypt for work.

"First of all," Blue said a couple of days after I called him in despair, "tell me how you're doing. It's been 48 hours."

Two days of palpitations and the trill of adrenaline still throbbed in my head. At high heart rates, muscle fibers in the left ventricle don't have adequate time to properly relax and allow the heart chamber to refill with blood. The body gets less oxygen. A TV nature special taught me that the smaller an animal, the shorter its life-span, and this correlates with how rapidly its heart pumps. Insects die within weeks, whales within decades. I surmised that a living thing is allotted only so many heartbeats in its lifetime; use them up too quickly and you're out of luck. The sense of doom during a panic attack isn't just subjective. If your heart is going at 120 beats per minute, you just are going to die sooner.

"I'm exhausted," I reported from the recesses of Blue's sofa. My eyelids were brittle from sleep deprivation.

"What started it this time?" he asked.

"I was thinking about Michael...."

I eyed Blue, from his black leather shoes to his face. His entire frame was watchful. Even though I was taking anti-anxiety drugs, my reflexes were still skittish. I had read that fear in psychotherapy is normal.

"I knew I'd meet him one day, in real life; maybe in a bookstore, or a concert. Maybe he would be my fantasy lover."

"So what upset you two nights ago?"

"I finally got the kids in bed. I'm sitting at the computer. And I started thinking about how much I miss Michael. I started reciting his history. That he was born overseas, that he had something vaguely Asian about his eyes and cheekbones, that he was half–American, that he immigrated and had to learn English and a whole new world, that he was smart but not showy, that the parents he knew as a baby died and he needed someone to rescue him.... And then I realized, Oh God.... He's not my lover.... He's.... *me!*"

Blue finished scribbling with a flourish and an exclamation point in his notepad. We had already doubled my sessions to twice a week. David wouldn't return from Cairo for another six days. Blue confirmed I wasn't suicidal, then gave me follow-up appointments for each of the next two days.

Carpenter

"See this rabbit?" Our teacher drew it crouched in profile on the far left-hand border of the blackboard, looking determined with its ears perked at an angle.

"It badly wants to eat the carrot." That he drew life-sized at the right-hand end. "But the rabbit has rules. It can only jump half the distance to the carrot each step. So it never actually reaches the carrot, but the distance there is approximated and the rabbit can get so close that it's practically *as good* as being at the carrot, right?" He beamed with a flourish of chalk.

My eyes widened in alarm. Rabbit could just crane his neck and eat the whole thing. I was sitting in a pre-calculus class. The teacher was the Carpenter, introducing the class by talking about limits.

Michael disappeared that hour. My head filled instead with the roar of Carpenter's voice, a rattle and a booming that made me want to stretch my arms out to the walls to still the vibrations. I understood every word he said, felt them stenographed one at a time, and followed his trail to the next, logical thought. I could feel his index finger as it glided along, mapping my brain.

I spoke little and just did math. Except one day, I failed a test. I knew I failed it as soon as I turned the test book in. But the day he gave us back our grades, I didn't get one. When I walked with trepidation up to his desk after class to ask for it, he waved my question away and said it didn't matter. Everyone has a bad day once in a while. He had destroyed my test.

"That grade had nothing to do with you." He looked a little embarrassed but also final in his decision, and I didn't argue.

I drew a portrait of him in charcoal and carried it around for a week. On the last day of classes I showed it to Sarah Highland. She took me in one hand and the drawing in the other, up to his desk. Through the crowd of girls, the voice boomed when he saw the picture.

"Who did that drawing!" Kids scattered and then we were alone. Did I paint, too? he wanted to know. Did he ask about my parents, how we came here, or did I bring that up? At the end of an hour, he wished me a good summer.

Carpenter taught me in another class the next year, and we fell into an easy rhythm. Several of us began eating lunch in his room—girls who were geeks, the gloomy, the rebels. "He's the only teacher I don't hate on sight," was the compliment bestowed by one. I sometimes lingered after school, helping to rearrange things on his shelves. We gave each other books. My *Gödel, Escher, Bach* for his Frank O'Connor anthology.

"I thought a lot over the summer about that drawing you made," he told me.

Carpenter introduced me to British Isles music and made me tapes of his favorite bands. I found an Archie Fisher record in the library and memorized a song, *Witch of the West Mer Lands*.

"I *love* Archie Fisher," he sparkled. We found the Kirksten Pass of the song on a map of the Lake District. He had gone on long walks there during his sabbatical in England.

Carpenter thought I had supernatural powers. He thought I spent every waking minute reading, drawing, or spinning complex thoughts. I in fact spent hours daydreaming, listening to pop radio, and talking on the phone. I didn't read the entire Bible as he believed I had, only Exodus, which just happened to contain the pro-choice reference that came up in conversation one day with him. I'd gotten bored at the begats. Another day, he asked for help on a New York Times crossword puzzle—13 across: the Three Unities....

"Oh, try Time, Place and Action" I said ... he stared at me, stunned, as the letters correctly dropped into place. It was no big deal; I had learned that in English class the day before. He watched me nibbling carrots at lunch and accused me of never eating. Rabbit. But I carried baby fat until well into college and ate junk food at home. He said I could pass AP computer programming blindfolded. I winced and avoided the class. I never lied but was anxious to the end that he might find me out. I believed he was blind to my mediocrity.

He gave me a small box of tiny French Conte crayon pastels one day in an off-handed way, in shades of brown, black and white, so I couldn't use my color-blindness as an excuse to not practice drawing. He never asked what I did with them.

"Tell me stories about you," I begged.

Carpenter hinted at a lonely childhood. When he was in grade school, his grandmother fell ill. She hadn't been kind to him. He remembered sitting on the staircase when his mother came down to say grandma had died. He remembered smiling a giant smile but afterwards had nightmares and felt guilty for months. There was another early crisis of conscience—he had spent many happy hours hunting frogs in a nearby pond and then killing them with a small gun. One day he startled himself by realizing the enormity of the destruction he had wreaked. The hunt stopped abruptly and forever.

He had that tendency to make complete and lasting judgments about things or people. He was convinced I was one in a million and nothing could knock that out of him. I insisted there were hundreds of girls before me and would be hundreds more. Already, I was jealous of passing on sixth-period lunch with him to the next class. He shook his head.

"No. There won't be another one like you. I won't let it happen. I've decided I can't do this again." He said it more sadly than I expected. I didn't understand or know what to say. I often didn't.

Carpenter carried knee-jerk politics from the sixties. We argued briefly one day when he referred to my parents' upper-class status in Việt Nam and made me feel defensive. This was years before my grandmother told me about her husband and I didn't know anything about my grandparents or how my parents came to Sài Gòn. He had a way of opening up terrible wounds with the best of intentions.

He stared wide-eyed into space and fiddled with the Albert Einstein-esque silver hair so it stood on end. He did this leaning back in his seat, feet on the desk, or pacing while absent-mindedly navigating islands of chairs and tables. He was left-handed, which made sense and which I deeply envied. He had warm chalk-stained fingers, thick carpenter's arms from hours of wood working on weekends, and a visage of deep lines in constant motion. He laughed loudly, then could withdraw into a deep, silent smile that I chased for yards and yards. He stooped over when walking, always slightly trotting. He wore jeans, sneakers, and flannel shirts sometimes misbuttoned. No one could think he was handsome. More like a hobbit, a romantic hobbit.

Unease about our relationship spread. Other teachers let me know there was a line, and they thought we were slipping over it. I was taken aback and defiant, seeing no need to categorize us and not seeing anything wrong.

At graduation, I descended the grand staircase at the Academy of Music downtown and landed in his arms, our long hug obscured at last by girls in white dresses and beaming parents. Otherwise, his closest touch was to occasionally ruffle my hair or graze my knuckles to bring me out of some reverie. I drew down the door blinds during lunch so people wouldn't look in while we talked. He quietly let it back up. He was more aware of boundaries than a sixteen-year-old was and respected them with a quiet discipline I didn't appreciate at the time.

My parents disapproved, especially my mother.

"It's not fair to his wife," she said.

"Leave her alone," Chương snarled at my mother, "It's all she's got."

I understood neither end of that argument. Key to Carpenter's charm were that I envied his kids having such a father, and the way he sparkled when talking about falling in love with his wife. Why would I want to disturb that?

I had no fantasies about Carpenter and never talked to Michael about him. I cried myself to sleep one night (I often did in high school) and dreamt I came through the door just in time to catch him on the stair landing. He turned and smiled, and kissed me on the forehead just once. It was the slightest touch, and then he had some other place to go.

I tried to tell him about Michael, but he didn't fully grasp that relationship. He smiled and said he felt relieved.

"I was worried something was missing from your life, Mai." He thought Michael was like any teenage girl's fantasy about a handsome prince.

He loved the immigrant story. A Cambodian student shared with him a story about her refugee journey in a rowboat across the South China Sea. He suggested we print it in the newspaper. We decided to devote an entire issue to stories of recent immigrant students, Boat People, the ones less lucky than me. We had them write in their broken English about their long journey to American high school-dom and contrasted the paltry support they got in our school with what students at my father's school got, where non-native students were a plurality. I wore an áo giài dress for the assembly to celebrate the issue. Carpenter told my friends I looked beautiful that day. My most treasured graduation prize was a history book of American Labor, for "excellence in the development of democratic human relations," for that feature.

I never saw the recommendation letter he wrote for my college application, and when all the school acceptances came, I just got a pat on the back while he effusively congratulated other girls. Was he surprised? Did I belong at Harvard?

I kept three yearbooks after graduation. He was in profile in the first, smiling politely in the second, looking at me obliquely through the page in the third. In my senior yearbook, he scratched a pen drawing of me sitting under a tree looking out beyond and wrote that he wanted to be there ten years from then when I picked it up again.

So it was baffling when he deliberately ignored me at a class pool party swarming with other girls and teachers that July. Our last meeting before college passed without a minute together. I sat poolside, knees under my chin and resentful, when I heard him behind my shoulder.

"Over here, Mai," he called. I turned obediently as the shutter on his camera clicked. What kind of a lesson was this?

"Why him, Mai?" Blue asked.

Had he not heard a thing I'd been saying?

"Because I could *hear* him, because he could map my brain, because he broke through the bubble." The bubble that isolated me from the rest of the world, that guaranteed my safety, that kept my secrets hidden.

"Why not let other people break through the bubble?"

I could barely make out the blurred outlines of Blue's face, warped by the thick glass wall between us.

"Because inside the bubble, you don't want many hands reaching in. That would be overwhelming, scary." My voice broke and Blue's figure became a mere blotch through the tears. "You want just *one* hand, a firm grasp…." I demonstrated with my own two hands tugging on each other in front of my chest.

"Yes…. It was him, Mai, because you had never felt a hand come that close before."

Altar

Vietnamese of my generation commonly had two wedding ceremonies—a smaller one at home with the couple in traditional dress, usually with just family and close friends, and a larger public one that in America was often Western, in a church, complete with tuxedos and white gowns, tiered cakes and banquet reception.

David and I had been together for six years when we announced our engagement, after a year on different continents—him on fellowship in England and me working in Boston, and three more apart while I finished medical school in Philly and he worked in Washington. My parents saw our steadiness over that time and rationalized away misgivings about his bookishness, ratty clothes, and not being Asian, let alone Vietnamese. It helped that Chương blazed the trail a few years before by marrying my Irish sister-in-law, Laurie.

The groom's relatives stayed at a Sheraton, then arrived at my "village" in mid-morning. Most hid out of view around the street corner while our cousins discretely brought out to my Jewish and partially vegetarian soon-to-be in-laws prepared gifts to bring back to us as symbolic dowry—platters of fruit and cookies, and one with a roast suckling pig in its oil-slick crisp skin wrapped with red cellophane.

The Malin Roodmans then formally processed to our front door, where my uncle Hải greeted and beckoned them in. Our four dozen relatives huddled in a horseshoe in our living room with junior members spilling into the adjacent sun porch. Everyone sweated profusely and smiled in the glare of giant spotlights that photographers had set up. After David's father formally asked Bố's permission for the marriage and it was granted, they called me down.

My parents had accrued significant social debt attending weddings of their friends' many children. Ân and Chương's weddings did not afford them enough decision-making authority to make it all up and adequately show off. Mine would be payback.

I staked claim to elements most important to me—that both parents would walk down the aisle with each of us—important to my feminist mother-in-law and as a Jewish inflection; that each parent would speak at both ceremonies; that my cousin Quỳnh Giao would work her magic fingers on the flower arrangements and my chef sister-in-law Như Mai would decorate the cake; and our western ceremony and reception would happen at the Mutter Museum of the College of Physicians downtown, so guests could wander with cocktails through exhibits of preserved distended colons and other medical oddities.

Otherwise, the day belonged to Bố and Mẹ. My mother gathered áo giài dresses for me to choose from. (Trying them on, I was the only one who realized that I was standing naked in front of both David and Mẹ!) Mẹ planned menus. Bố ordered bilingual invitations and insisted on choosing the Vietnamese photographer. Hence the unique video of the day, which interspersed scenes of our ceremonies and brunch picnic with inexplicable shots of Epcot Center and its water fountains, all streaming to an incongruous soundtrack of classical music they asked David to select beforehand.

For this occasion, my father wanted a much grander altar than the one they usually had on top of their credenza. He constructed a plywood base nearly four feet tall against the living room fireplace, draped in red velvet set off by enlarged framed photos of my grandfathers, stands of incense and flowers guarding each end, ribbons and lace hanging above from door frames and mantel. That morning, all material offerings on this temporary altar were for ancestors. In exchange, my father asked for their blessing as David and I bowed to them, and then elders in both families took turns coming forward to drop words of wishes and wisdom for us.

My parents spent weeks planning their speeches. Bố nervously penned multiple drafts and asked David for advice, not certain if his English idioms worked. He beamed, reading from his index card as

Dressing for our wedding home ceremony with my mother, Philadelphia, 1995.

my mother, aunts and uncles sniffled, "You bring us joy and pride, and are truly the apple of our eye. While we wish to keep you forever, we know you have to be on your way, to start your own family...."

"Is 'apple of our eye' right?" he had asked.

"Yes, Bố," David reassured him, "that sounds right."

At the museum, my mother stood small in a blue and yellow áo giài, yanking tears to say if she had chosen my life mate for me, she could not have done better than the one I chose for myself.

After a short night of little sleep, David and I left for Manhattan where my medical internship would start that week. I tried to shake off a nagging sense that my cousins and sisters-in-law saw the day's many imperfections, the awkward mash-up of not quite East and not quite West. It was two weeks before we made it back to Philadelphia to gather the rest of our

My father's speech at our wedding home ceremony. From left: Aunt Nhung, my mother, Uncle Tan (behind her), my father, sister-in-law Mai, Aunt Chinh, Aunt Khue, Ba Ngoai, cousin.

At our western wedding reception. My grandmother and her daughters (from left) Bình, Khuê, Anh, Chinh.

things before the honeymoon. My fastidious parents had cleared nearly all the wedding chaos, except in the living room where the altar and its finery stood untouched, quiet in the late June heat.

Memorial

The crash of TWA Flight 800 registered through my sleep-deprived fog only because the plane had taken off from JFK airport before exploding off the coast of Long Island. Living in Manhattan, we couldn't escape the news.

Two days later, a call came from a high school mate I hadn't heard from in years.

Carpenter and his wife were on that plane.

It was ten years after he signed my graduation yearbook; he wouldn't be there to see me re-reading it.

I met his daughters at the school memorial where he last taught. There was a second service three days later with six hundred people at a Quaker meeting house. Their friend, a writer of short stories, read a poem. One by one people rose to share memories while I sat mute. Sarah Highland gripped my left shoulder. They played a Jessie Norman aria. A man in a three-piece suit read a stiff condolence letter from the Governor. A pilot sent by the airline spoke while his wife sat thinking, "It could have been him." Back on hospital call in Manhattan the next night, my colleagues told me the memorial was covered even on local New York TV because the crowd seemed surprisingly large for a middle-aged public schoolteacher.

> Newsweek 7/20/96: Victims Were Unaware of Crash, Coroner Says ... instantly killed or rendered unconscious when the 747 broke apart with a force as sudden as a car smashing into a brick wall at 400 miles an hour....

I saw him only twice the year before he died, first at my wedding, then accompanied by my mother when we picked up the futon frame he made for us as a wedding gift.

"Is it sturdy?" I asked.

"Yes, I'm pretty sure. We tested it," he answered to my mother's giggle.

I didn't invite them to our home ceremony, just the western one. I knew he was hurt and disappointed. On our wedding video, he and his wife sat near the front, pointing out to one another carved wood moldings on the banquet hall ceiling.

Conversations with him were awkward that last year. Don't all relationships have those moments of veering back and forth around a baseline? Eventually, as sure as sine, I would have found a way to break through his banter, say it didn't feel right, ask if he had given up on me, and make us fit again. But I wasn't confident we would survive it.

He was exactly thirty years older. Three times my life when I was fifteen, but only twice at thirty. Poor, hopeful Rabbit. I had pouted in frustration one day in school, whined that I'd never catch up with him, never have as many stories, misadventures or friends, never be able to surprise him the way he did me. He smiled patiently.

Freshman year of college, I sent him long letters. I wrote to recreate the sensory overload of Harvard Square. I wrote of the subway vibrations, of squinting against the snow at night to turn people on sidewalks into so many noisy stars, of a busker breaking out the Beatles and Neil Young on guitar. I wrote out of loneliness and depression and because I had no one else to write to. He showed parts of my letters to his wife.

"What does she think of me?" I asked him on a call.

"She thinks you're a good person," he'd say. So, what's the problem? I wanted to ask.

My spiral downward accelerated late that autumn. One weekend, a roommate talked me into going to see Oliver Stone's movie *Platoon*. It was my first full dose of a story about the Việt Nam war and I was unprepared for the violence such an American perspective did to me. The camera drilled into expressions of American cynicism, American suffering, American anger. Every combat scene cast shadows over anonymous Việt Cộng soldiers, and civilian voices were relegated to background chatter or simplistic captions. Even in my most fluent language, the world conspired to hide the most basic facts of Vietnamese experience from me.

Too upset to want company, I huddled alone by the phone. I worried about waking Carpenter up at midnight but dialed anyway.

"It's ok, I'm awake now. What's the matter?"

I tried to explain—you never saw a Vietnamese face the whole time—but couldn't make sense of my own reaction. He let me sob for fifteen minutes.

"I'm trying to understand. Is it just the movie?" Of course it wasn't. He gently coaxed me to bed. The next week he said, "I don't know, Mai. If you had been my daughter, if I weren't married, I would've been on that next train to Boston, and then I don't know what."

When I met David, Carpenter did not equivocate. I told him over the phone that summer, "David's the first Mt. Airy person I've met here."

"This guy is going to be for a long time, and I can't believe you're so young and this relationship is already happening…."

Even in my adulthood, he refused to call me at my parents' house.

He asked if it was ok if his wife came along when we met. She was lovely and always interesting but I never understood why he needed to ask or she needed to come. Did he need a witness? I didn't think the idea was hers. It made me slightly paranoid.

At the services, his daughters made a kind effort to tell me how much he had talked about me, how happy he was when I married. I didn't ask what he did with my letters, my sketches, that photo he took of me at eighteen by the pool. Where was this other half of my memory?

* * *

A couple of weeks after the memorial, I sat in a pub with his best friend. Bill was the tall sarcastic Irishman to Carpenter's stocky romantic Jew; the perfect odd couple. Bill was also a teacher, used to anticipating what young people needed to make sense of things.

"He loved you. In some sense, he wanted to spend the rest of his life with you."

I thought I knew that already. "There was a lot that got said, and a lot that didn't," I began. "I didn't want to do anything that might scare him away."

"He couldn't say them, Mai. You weren't ready, you were just a baby. You don't tell people you have fantasies about that you have fantasies about them." He meant, what would have come of it? Carpenter would never cross those lines.

"Sure you do. People do it all the time."

Bill looked skeptical. "If five years from now, if you weren't both married, and he asked you to come away with him for the weekend...."

"I would have said yes, what do you think I would have said? I would have said yes..." I would have been on that next train, I thought, and then I don't know what....

"...I don't think he knew that, Mai."

From their seats one row behind where investigators believe the explosion began, it must have been flash and deafening noise and done—the shattered, shimmering vapor to hover for just a moment, for me to ache. Then sky so thin it hurts to breathe. An instant transformation I thought—he would like that—into whatever it is that surges between neurons, into memory.

Michael and David both blanketed me in their arms at night, but a few hours of respite in the dark didn't heal anything underneath, or help me understand what should come next.

In my last dream of him, Carpenter stood in an empty parking lot, coaching me. I sat astride a motorcycle, not a Vespa but a real hog, its threatening purr vibrating up my spine. I rode toward him slowly, then veered away in a careful figure eight, each turn perfectly symmetric as I expertly placed an inside foot down to pivot. After six laps, I heard his urging over the engine.

"That's good, Mai! … Now, when you're ready, just stop and get off…."

I cut the engine and left my helmet on the seat, keys tossed inside. I walked to the street and beyond, not bothering to check if he was following.

Then he was gone, snatching away the illusion that I could rely on surrogates to rescue me, on something borrowed to substitute for gaps in my own history, on anyone to hand me what was mine. Even as my year-long, grief-fueled depression set in, I knew how my pattern of passivity would break. It was the end of waiting for heroes, of childhood.

Clock

"I want to go back to Việt Nam for a year after residency," I told David barely three months after Carpenter died. How he felt about that or whether he wanted to come along were lesser things to negotiate.

Without understanding that reflex completely, I acted on it with clumsy efficiency. I cold called every American nonprofit in Việt Nam with a listed number, pitching that I was willing to do anything for a year. An American organization focused on reproductive health took the bait and said all I needed was to come up with a research idea and get a grant. No problem at all, for someone without any research training or fundraising experience. Their office was based in Hà Nội, where it was easier for the Vietnamese government to keep tabs on foreigners. Their director wanted to plant me in Sài Gòn to help establish a foothold there.

From the library on campus, I pulled every article tagged with the search terms "health care" and "Việt Nam." Even though my host NGO focused on reproductive health, my eyes kept drifting to sociology articles on the emerging private sector in health care. Infrastructure in the public health care system began breaking down after the Soviet Union collapsed and Việt Nam lost much of its foreign aid, forcing the "đổi mới" (renewal) policy of economic liberalization. Because public wages were under such pressure, the government began allowing doctors to see private patients while keeping public sector jobs, and I could see the kernel of a natural experiment. This project marked the beginning of my years-long obsession with how health care providers respond to financial incentives—the ethical and economic underpinnings of those behaviors, and how they shape the good and dark realities of a health care system. That intellectual journey would eventually lead me to high profile publications, my psychic break in middle age, and Blue's sofa.

I begged my hospital division chief for a crash course on how to design a research study and got him to summarize the essentials of a two-semester course in ninety minutes. To win a grant, I spent another six months drafting a proposal on rare days I didn't have clinical duty.

"That's a terrible idea!" My parents were frantic. "They could arrest you." My mother's worry surged through telephone lines to all her siblings. They enlisted Ân and my uncle Hải to talk me out of it.

"I'm a U.S. citizen. I'm not going to do anything illegal." Their paranoia was unconvincing. Few in our tribe had gone back, but my grandmother had visited relatives in the north just a couple of years before and returned without incident.

We planned an initial scouting trip for me to meet my new boss, negotiate a working relationship with my local sponsor in Sài Gòn, and help find David an in-country sponsor. Once they realized my mind was set, Bố and Mẹ turned to listing relatives they wanted me to contact, splinters of family flung along the country's north-south axis. I remembered that my father was the only son of my grandfather's first wife. He explained his father had been the oldest son and for a time, the village chief. That made Bố the village chief in absentia, and my parents' expectation was for me to represent him. How well would this go with my awkward, grade school Vietnamese?

Each escalation of expectations made the project seem more preposterous. *David and Michael both did their best to calm me, stroking my hair and shushing me at night, but the relief never lasted into day.*

By the spring after Carpenter died, stress and doubt had worn my sleep to almost nothing. I called my favorite medical school professor for a reality check. He was a child of the '60s and would understand the pull of Việt Nam. He had hit it off with Carpenter at my wedding.

"I can go and no matter what happens it will have been the right thing to do?" I asked.

"Yes, absolutely."

"I can go and completely fail on my project and it will be okay?"

"You should go and finish the project as you've promised…. And it will be okay."

My grandmother wasn't worried. She was pleased I was going.

"I will give you all our relatives' addresses and phone numbers," she promised. So one weekend David and I took a bus from Manhattan to my uncle Hải's house in New Jersey where Bà Ngoại was staying. My aunt Liên and uncle Hải set out lunch while squealing with delight at David's fledgling Vietnamese.

Bà Ngoại showed us pictures of relatives in Hà Nội. The family resemblance was startling; apparently not all Asians look the same. We explained to her that David would study economic development and the environment with his Fulbright scholarship, but he needed a Vietnamese sponsor. She opened a plump wallet and walked her small fingers through an inch-thick stack of business cards.

"Could Chú (uncle) Dzũng help?" she asked. She explained that this was the son of her beloved younger brother. His business card read Deputy Minister for Science, Technology, and the Environment, and Director for External Relations. His father, she said, had been the Minister until he died. David and I passed the bit of card stock between us, dumbfounded.

"Yes, Bà, I think Chú Dzũng could be very helpful," I said lamely.

Why did she have to flee the north with such an influential brother in the Party? How would his family feel about an American relative returning? My head splintered with other half-formed questions at this sliver of light on my family's secrets, but I didn't have enough Vietnamese to ask most of them and she had already stood up and moved on to wondering what fruit to cut for dessert. We would learn through subsequent attempts over the years that she couldn't talk about her brother for very long before quieting into a deep sadness.

We returned to the city and didn't pack luggage so much as battlefield gear—demure clothes, anti-malarial pills, letters of introduction, a dictionary, several forms of identification, phone numbers and addresses, a crude diagram of relatives in the canopy of my family tree, chocolates and other small gifts, a camera. David's visa came on schedule, but our anxiety built until mine finally arrived a few days before departure, only after my boss in Hà Nội had her Vietnamese handler ask discretely about its status. It was June 1997, a year after Carpenter died.

At the check-in counter at JFK airport, we realized my visa was missing. Overseas Vietnamese needed different visas than other foreigners, and David had kept it in a different folder than our other paperwork so it still sat in a dark file cabinet back in our apartment on the Upper West Side. Even if a friend could get to it, there was no time to bring it to us with the flight boarding in less than an hour. The airline agent looked at our distraught expressions and suggested we board anyway. She gave us contact numbers for the Vietnamese consulate in Singapore, where we were scheduled to catch a connecting flight to Hanoi.

"Have someone fax the visa there and they should be able to attach it to your passport."

I whispered with uncharacteristic calm to David, who was tense, "It's okay. Whatever happens, happens. This is the adventure."

After the roar of take-off as our jet peaked on its eastward climb over early summer life on the beaches of Fire Island, David reclined in his seat and opened a book. I sat straight, fighting nausea, eyes straying from the window down to my watch and back again. Eight minutes. Cloud carpets unfurled in fanned patterns all around and the unfiltered light was piercing. Ten minutes … time reared up and swayed. Eleven … twelve. Here. It was here…. He died here. In the seconds it took for David to notice and touch my back, the engines catapulted us through a wormhole to the other side of the world and decades ago.

Part Two—Native

Homegoing

My mouth flooded with saliva as soon as the hatch opened and petroleum laden heat on the tarmac of Nội Bài International Airport hit my nostrils. I slammed my lips shut and swallowed giant gulps to keep from vomiting. Through dust wafting on warm air, I tried to decipher Vietnamese directions on signs and orders that unsmiling brown men in uniform barked at us, but I ended up just following their gestures and flows of other people disembarking from our flight. David depended on me to navigate all conversations now. My temples seized with the start of a headache. The Hanoian accents were lilting and contrived, like Boston Brahmins come to Indochina. My accent marked me instantly as a child of former northerners, triggering just a flash of recognition and mild hostility from the customs officer before his face slipped back into its rigid mask. He didn't find anything offensive in our luggage or my paperwork; the fax to Singapore had worked.

Our taxi cruised twenty miles, then turned off the highway, winding down a warren of slim dirt paths by Hồ Tây (West Lake), just outside the city. Tin and concrete shacks gradually gave way to attractive sandstone and stucco two-story houses. Along the airport road, small men and women had crouched in front of wooden store signs and small towers of cheap canned food, cigarettes, and hand-wrapped foodstuffs, their feet bare or in thong sandals above swirling dust. They sometimes rushed out into traffic waving wares to tempt drivers. But in this neighborhood, stores skirting mansions sold neatly shelved European brands of fruit juice, milk, and boxed goods. Some abutted paved yards strung with lanterns and coarse speaker systems swaying gently above plastic tables and chairs. Our taxi stopped where the path narrowed to the width of a rickshaw, and our driver led us on foot past men hauling cinder blocks and rusted metal equipment in wheelbarrows. Fragrances of jasmine and bougainvillea floated past, tropical plant fronds peeked from behind wrought iron fences and gates. It took several days before our eyes adjusted enough to make sense of the visual cacophony and recognize the restaurant, convenience store, and construction crew for what they were.

At the end of the path, we came to the newly built mansion my boss was renting. Talking with her in English gave me a small island of ease. We dined family style, the meal discretely laid out then cleared away by her Vietnamese cook. Everyone who worked for expats, we would learn, was expected to spy and report on their employers' movements and conversations.

I made one last burst of effort that evening to phone and arrange meetings with relatives. We only had a few days in Hà Nội to apportion between work, time with each side of my family and a former school friend of my father's, without offending anyone. My aunts and uncles were happy and relieved I landed without incident, and forgiving of my halting Vietnamese. They patiently repeated instructions for where and when we should meet until I understood.

On the ride to the office the next morning, my boss asked me about my grandparents. After I told her the little I knew, she explained that I would meet her second in command, a Vietnamese obstetrician hand-picked by the government to be her handler. By then in his sixties, he had a storied history of delivering babies on the Hồ Chí Minh trail as a young man and making a daring escape into the ocean during an American air raid. She had gone to him when my visa was delayed, and after some discreet probing, he told her not to worry about me. They had checked on my family history.

"Maybe there's some Party guilt over how your maternal grandfather died?" she guessed. Not so about my paternal grandfather.

The charming American anthropologist, with her breezy confidence, and the sober, patrician Vietnamese operative had formed a trusting relationship, in an environment where trust was dangerous. She had gotten his intellectual and personal investment in common goals—improving reproductive health in a country where HIV was starting to spread and denial was deep. In exchange for his guidance through the many cultural, legal, and political landmines, she submitted to his watchful minding, and avoided doing anything to embarrass him. This was the standard for the relationship I had to build with my sponsor in Sài Gòn.

The next afternoon, a taxi dropped us off on a busy avenue in downtown Hà Nội. The row house there belonged to Chú (uncle) Dzũng, Bà Ngoại's nephew. He was handsome, slim and spry, with a confident reserve—a dapper, Russian-educated deputy minister who helped arrange David's paperwork and smiled at us with genuine warmth and protectiveness. He switched effortlessly between English with David and Vietnamese with me as we sat shoeless on the floor of his dining room. Over bowls of rice and tea, he matter-of-factly explained his father's position as a scientist, his own inheritance of it, and local, district, and national authorities he had maneuvered around to find David a sponsor in the south. I understood his charge; it was my duty to make sure David did nothing to embarrass or endanger him.

"One brother was a scientist, and he lived," my father had once explained about Bà Ngoại's family, referring to her chemist brother. "One brother was a politician, and he died." That was my grandfather. It began to dawn on me the wreckage of guilt, grief, fear, and confused loyalties that a family reunion in post-war Việt Nam would trigger for every relative we touched, and that they would try to mask. I wondered how much of it my parents had anticipated.

Back outside, the rush of traffic, bicycles and xe ôm (motorbikes) flowed in a slow rumbling river around cobblestoned medieval streets and wide French boulevards. Commuters' faces were relaxed but unsmiling. There was no music or chatter, just whistle shrieks from stern policemen.

We took a long cab ride east to new, treeless exurbs with arc after arc of two-story row houses still under construction. My father's nephew-in-law greeted us and proudly pointed out the pastel-colored house he and his wife, my cousin Hảo, had recently bought with "cooperative" money pooled from a large group of relatives and friends. As each member repaid their withdrawal, the next family would have their turn to invest. Their new house was simple and elegant with high ceilings and a courtyard. He ended the tour with a satisfied smile.

View from the home of my boss in Hà Nội, overlooking West Lake, 1997.

At the home of my father's niece, Chị Hảo, Hà Nội, 1997.

When we arrived at the house he was still living in, my cousin greeted us in a dark courtyard, the walkway cramped from stacks of crates and scrap metal. We had dinner while small poodles yelped inside cages in one corner of the room; Cousin Hảo raised dogs to sell for meat. When we asked what other work they did, they chose their words carefully. Relatives on this side of the family were political second-class citizens. Some relatives used to run a small business, but taxes (or extortion from officials to avoid taxes) on their truck became so exorbitant that a few years ago they dumped the vehicle in a pond at night. We left them chocolates and photographs my parents had sent, promising to visit longer when we came back the next year.

Nhà (House)

At the end of the week, we reversed our taxi ride to the airport and landed in Hồ Chí Minh City. A cousin on my father's side, Anh Sử, was waiting outside with his brother-in-law. He found me easily in the crowd.

"Anh nhận Mai ở đâu cũng được (I'd recognize you anywhere)," he said.

I wasn't sure if I remembered him or if he just seemed familiar because his delicate cheek bones and mouth were the same as Chương's and my father's. He was slim and walked with a steady, fluid, almost regal gait, unperturbed by the chaos of whistle-blowing policemen and small hordes dragging luggage carts. They escorted our taxi to drop off luggage at our hotel. I shed my backpack and climbed behind Sử on his xe ôm while David got on behind his brother-in-law, and we wove through the thigh-shaking drone of rush hour traffic for dinner with his family.

After a mile or so, Sử wordlessly leaned left and turned off the main road down a street with one-story bodegas and houses. I heard children calling and clattering dinnerware, motorbike engines turning on and off, the shuffle-slap-shuffle-slap of feet sauntering in flip-flops. This was the street where my friend Chau lived.

"Quẹo trái (Turn left)," I said as a T-intersection came into view.

"Nó nhớ (she remembers)," Anh Sử said confidently. Roof tops passed by us on the other side of the street, tall, short, short, alley, tall, short, alley…….

"Ngừng ở đây (stop here)."

He touched his left foot to the ground and eased the motor to off.

"Cái nào (which one)?" He quizzed me.

"Cái đó (that one)," I answered firmly, pointing across the street to a house not smaller or bigger than any other, with a tiled foyer fronted by an iron gate painted blue. There was a small balcony on the second floor, just high enough to see into the yard of the house across the street. An alley bordered its right side.

"Ai ở đó bây giờ (who lives there now)?"

"Người lạ (no one we know)," he said. He waited but I didn't dismount. I could see everything from my seat behind him—that I could now cross the foyer in six steps, that the walls were scuffed to a dull gray with patches of plaster missing, that clothes fluttered haphazardly from a cord slung over the balcony as a grandmother and two children stared out suspiciously at us. This was the house of my princess childhood.

"Đi chưa (ready to go)?" Anh Sử asked, and the xe ôm made a wide turn back to the highway.

* * *

Downtown Hồ Chí Minh City, 1997.

During the rest of our week in the south, I met with my sponsor and translated for David when we met with his sponsor. We ate with relatives almost every day. At our last dinner, my aunt, Anh Sử's mother, handed me a plastic bag filled with old, yellowed

Riding with my cousin, Sử, Hồ Chí Minh City, 1997.

Nhà (House)

In front of our old family house, Hồ Chí Minh City, 1997.

Kodak projection slides to bring home—family pictures my parents had left behind in the rush of fleeing in 1975. We held them up to the light, squinting at traces of memories Bố and Mẹ had not told me.

My Vietnamese didn't improve much over this trip, but I got better at skimming what I heard for context and otherwise faking it. I kept my responses simple while nodding and smiling. Each meeting began with an offer of hot tea, and I was so grateful to be able to hide behind the cup and slow conversation down however temporarily, I made the rookie mistake of drinking from every cup instead of politely faking sips. After we landed back in New York, the caffeine withdrawal headaches were so severe my ER attending was tempted to order a spinal tap, before settling for slamming me with painkillers and a sedative.

Hear, Say

Our real plunge into Việt Nam began the following year. David immersed himself in reading classics about the war like *Fire in the Lake* and *A Bright Shining Lie*. I couldn't bring myself to crack them open. My *Platoon* experience still lingered and made me resist getting soiled with American-centric perspectives before groping the realities for myself.

Instead, I gravitated to Neil Jamieson's *Understanding Việt Nam* because it wasn't just about the war. Neil had lived and worked as a sociologist in Việt Nam for years before American military involvement, and viewed the war as merely a brief modern arc in Việt Nam's ancient narrative. He interpreted events through the lens of Vietnamese cultural, historical, and literary legacies, with the advantage of actually speaking the language. Reading that book was a gift. I wrote a letter to thank him, and became friends with Neil and his wife, Ginny. I learned that he was among black ops volunteers on the tarmac in Sài Gòn at the end of April 1975 when our cargo flight took off.

By September of 1998, David and I were back in Hồ Chí Minh City. We rented a house in the oldest quarter of what was historic Sài Gòn, far enough from the city core to give it some buffer from the thrum of tourists. Among spindly, winding walkways, we found a newly painted three-story row house furnished with a pleather settee, carved wooden beds and a clothes washer, an amenity only found in houses on our side of the alley where expats rented.

Eight feet away across the alley were older, squat two-story structures with dark rooms and no air-conditioning, where some of the landlords and northern naval officers and their families lived. Echoes of clanging pots, scraping chairs, and conversation ricocheted down the air corridor between the alley walls, hitchhiking one on top of another with such clarity, it was impossible to tell if a spousal argument we heard was happening next door or eight houses away.

An implicit set of expectations ruled decorum between Vietnamese and expats in the neighborhood. Europeans, Australian-New Zealanders,

Chinese, Japanese, Indians, and Americans would behave as became the moneyed and privileged, divulge the minimum amount of information necessary about their professional activities, and serve as an important revenue source by hiring locals to buy and cook their food, chauffeur and nanny their children, clean their houses and clothes, or serve as interpreters. In exchange, Vietnamese would honor a respectful distance, exercise discretion, and offer useful tips to navigate the bureaucracy for amenities like Internet access or buying a car.

We violated all these expectations. We swept our own floors and walked laundry up to the washing machine on the roof, where we hung clothes to dry. We snuck out discretely for street food and a few cheap restaurant meals a week but otherwise bought and cooked our own food. I didn't want to forfeit my thrice weekly trips to the local markets, to trigger childhood smell memories and to explore. I fingered vegetables with unfamiliar skin textures, ogled baskets of giant prawns and squirming eels, and indulged in different permutations of "chè"—a snack-in-a-glass, layered with preserved fruit, sweet beans and flavored tapiocas, stirred into a primordial sludge with ice chips and coconut milk.

To our neighbors, these lapses in etiquette served as invitation. Hương, the plump naval housewife across the alley, first sent over her four-year-old to investigate. Quỳnh was a similarly large-cheeked, audacious package, just one-fifth her mother's size. The hair was cut pixie-style, the clothes usually plain shorts and a box cut shirt dusty from play dirt, the short body stocky with muscles, and because the name was androgynous and the voice somewhat husky, it took us several weeks to determine with confidence that it was a girl and not a boy. She fell in love with David, grabbing the broom and dustpan out of my hands to sweep the floor to impress him, pushing her way to his side at the laptop to ask about what was on the screen. He practiced his new Vietnamese with her, to her delight.

"This language is harder than I thought," he said at the end of an afternoon visit from Quỳnh.

"That's because she's sometimes speaking gibberish to you," I retorted, "She's four!"

Hương herself then padded over in flip flops to survey my kitchen. She took in the books and important looking reports on our coffee table, laptops with their black rats' tail adapters. She hid nothing in her punchy smile and Northern accent, loudly peppering conversation with questions about my quê hương (ancestral village), our salaries, what our parents did for a living, whether my brothers married Vietnamese women, and making cheerful observations about our odd cardboard cereal boxes. Then, having politely excused herself as I put out dishes for dinner, she efficiently transmitted the new intelligence to all her girlfriends. "She's not here or there (north or south)," I imagined her saying, "the accent is all muddy."

The exchange wasn't symmetric. Hương revealed that her husband was a naval officer, but nothing about family they left in the north. She volunteered his salary, but nothing about rental income their neighbors collected from expats. Privacy or embarrassment kept her from ever inviting us into her house.

To help penetrate the unsaid and feel more competent at work, David and I registered for private language classes at a university.

I was assigned to a stern marm from Hà Nội about my age. She sat across a desk from me, impeccably dressed in silk blouses and a bomber jacket, her face framed darkly by a severe bob Anna Wintour could envy, and led me through brisk oral exercises that always seemed to circle back to comparisons between America and Việt Nam.

Americans love pop music and movies but they have to borrow real culture from elsewhere; Vietnamese have thousands of years of literature and history. Americans expect everything to be fast; Vietnamese are much more willing to work hard and wait to see the fruits of their labors. I tried to focus on new vocabulary but couldn't stop my irritation from spilling over.

"I see so much in Việt Nam that's unique and beautiful. Why do Vietnamese not believe it? Why do Vietnamese keep comparing themselves to Americans?" I asked her.

She wasn't startled by my challenge. "Isn't your husband named David? Don't you remember the story of David and Goliath? Why should David have believed he could defeat a monster so much larger and mightier than him?" She redirected me to the short essay I had written for homework and began redlining my awkward grammar.

"Chị (miss)," she said, "when you speak Vietnamese it sounds natural, but not when you write it."

Vietnamese try to avoid direct confrontation. Centuries of reliance on communal water sources flowing serially through neighboring properties to feed rice fields ingrained in them the wisdom of finding every which way to maintain stable relationships in one's community. Make enemies, and you will starve. I let her change the subject. Even if my language lessons did little to directly enrich my vocabulary on emotions, they allowed me to begin hearing and speaking stories that illustrated them, and that was enough.

Mirror, Door, Whore

Vietnamese who live in-country refer to those in the diaspora as Việt kiều—sojourners, those that wander. The label conjures ghosts, free floating and aimless, robbed of destination and forever yearning. The living hold them guardedly at a distance, viewing them with a mix of pity at something disowned and envy of the freedom wanderers enjoy.

I was one of those ghosts, living in the soft middle land of a certain cohort of first-generation immigrant, too young to have rooted loyalties in the homeland, too old to forget it, comfortable enough in both places but uncertain where to settle.

As with my language teacher, I sensed accusations from other locals, foreigners, sometimes my own relatives, about aspects of my half-status, a fascination and skepticism about how much of my otherness was involuntary versus subterfuge.

A Canadian expat friend often reminded me, "Please move around wherever we're going to meet so I can find you. When you stand perfectly still, I can't tell you apart from the locals. When you move, you look like a member of the People's Committee and it's easier to spot you."

I carried my shoulders broadly, walked with long un-ladylike strides, and seemed taller than I actually was. When I was in a hurry and flagged down a xe ôm, Manhattan taxi style on my tiptoes with legs spread and a commanding wave of my hand, only more daring drivers with new, larger motorbikes came. When I stood still and instead demurely signaled with just a tilt of my head, I could fool anybody. Drivers would be oblivious to my provenance until I couldn't understand their thick southern accents when asking about the fare and asked them to repeat it.

When I wandered into a linen store to look for embroidered tablecloths my mother had asked for, the clerk patiently laid out samples and explained the classic Chinese scenery and symbols on each. Then she sized me up. She checked that no one else was in the store and asked me where I was from.

"I live in America," I said, and that was enough for her to begin confiding secrets.

She had tried to flee the country, paying smugglers hundreds of dollars for a boat ride to the Philippines only to see police boarding the vessel in the harbor as she approached it. She was ready to try again. She would bring food and papers, one change of clothes, and money in her shoes, to avoid drawing attention with more than one bag. This time the boat would leave down river, outside town. The trip might take a week, and once in Manila, she would contact relatives in Australia to sponsor her immigration. She wanted my opinion, wasn't it a good plan?

I froze in the moment, taken aback by her belief that a chance connection with me would confer luck and safe passage to a better life, and my own unwillingness to scuttle the fantasy that I was her live talisman, because hope was so precious.

I tried not to draw attention to my "muddy" accent. I adopted a mild southern drawl that surfaced when speaking to shopkeepers and hotel clerks. When I spoke to doctors at the medical school or clinic, my clipped northern accent kicked in instead. If anyone detected the fraud, they were too polite to say.

My vocabulary expanded exponentially as language lessons stretched on. Newly familiar words leapt off store signs and newspaper headlines but it was still easier to read signs than try to catch all the guttural syllables hawkers squawked at market. I made purchases by pointing to what I wanted and signaling numbers with my hands. If the seller gave me more of a vegetable than I needed, I just took it.

Sometimes locals decided the exoticism and status of associating with me wasn't worth the risk. I wanted to see a hospital not affiliated with the medical school. Someone introduced me to a young surgeon who met me at his hospital. He was just older than me, smartly dressed, sunglasses dangling from his shirt pocket. He led me through operating rooms pointing out anesthesiology equipment, and explaining how patients were selected and scheduled, the allure of training slots in Singapore or China. I asked him about his pay, his caseload, how patients got rehab the hospital couldn't provide, and he answered all my questions with an unhurried directness. He told me not to use the term "nhà thương" for "hospital"; it was a holdover from pre-revolutionary days that in modern Việt Nam meant an insane asylum.

After our tour, we walked to a café and it was my turn to answer his questions about America. Before we parted, I told him I was working for a U.S. organization, and thought the government was tracking me because we noticed suspicious responses in Hà Nội after I sent a less than flattering email about Vietnamese health care to someone abroad. He stiffened slightly. We said good-bye and he didn't answer my calls thereafter.

Others were willing to take extreme risks to make and keep connections with me. I couldn't be anonymous at the foreign-funded clinic where I saw patients part-time. I built a panel of regular patients after just a few weeks because they insisted on seeing Bác Sĩ Mai (Doctor Mai) and not a substitute, despite having to wait longer for appointments. Our nurses told me patients were intrigued by the free-thinking young woman doctor who bothered to explain their illnesses to them and charmed by my gestures, like bending down to tie an elderly patient's shoelaces at the end of an exam.

Because it was an American-Vietnamese joint venture, the fees were hefty, though not exorbitant, for the targeted demographic of independent-minded Sài Gòn-ese and villagers from surrounding areas drawn by the promise of modern care. Some traveled over a hundred miles. They didn't seem to mind my awkward Vietnamese, and nurses translated my more technical instructions. I tried to cram basics of self-care into the first visit for any patient with diabetes, worried they wouldn't be able to afford another visit. I saw advanced stages of conditions we only read about in America. One man with severe arthritis and an elevated iron level had true hemochromatosis (iron overload), something I had never seen in New York, and dutifully returned thrice weekly for us to bleed him.

The gynecology residents conscripted to collect data for my research study were all southerners and of an adventurous sort, also unafraid of associating with me. They knew what they were recording for me of their professors' clinical practices wouldn't be flattering, and I was barely qualified to be teaching them research methods I had learned myself just six months before. Yet they assessed our discussions about how to critically read medical literature as a fair exchange for risks they took on my behalf. Any kind of critical thinking implied irreverence, and southern, post-war twenty-somethings seized the opportunity to ride in the slipstream of an American-funded study, to question authority and push on boundaries.

I wandered into other forbidden places. My boss brought me down to the Mekong Delta one weekend for fieldwork. We camped overnight with a gypsy community of gay, lesbian and transgender outcasts and runaways, an exercise that was part trust-building, part data collection to better understand the cultural fault lines allowing HIV transmission to rip through the country. I wasn't officially contributing to that particular project, but my boss could sneak me and not white staff members into her entourage because I blended in and could be discreet.

In February, when I recognized signs of my early pregnancy, the Australian radiologist at my clinic insisted on performing a free ultrasound. She showed me the tiny sac and its throbbing blob of life. Inspired by the print-outs she gave me, I went to an upscale custom clothing shop and had them embroider the front of a mommy-sized and a baby-sized T-shirt each with "Sản xuất tại Việt Nam," and the backs with the translation, "Made in Việt Nam."

In early spring, out of clothes that fit, I passed over tourist shops and instead opted for cheap locally-made tent dresses that were easier than skirts and pants. Now when I walked with David, there was more staring than usual from people we passed, some cold, some warm depending on whether they thought I was cheap or smart to be carrying his child.

My condition didn't seem to deter any of the women, from teenagers to middle-aged, who wanted to flirt with him. In the late 1990s many Vietnamese women assumed most white men were gateways to a better life, but David was particularly easy on the eyes, and something about his slow smile, open expression, and earnest attempts at speaking Vietnamese made him seem approachable and desirable. The Vietnamese for "Jewish" (do thái) literally means "intelligent and clever," and they had no trouble typing him as such. What was not to like? They discounted the ring on my finger or didn't notice it at all. Why wouldn't they compete with my near-whore status?

Newsman

Michael hovered and watched me but otherwise let me navigate Việt Nam on my own. With every discovery I made or insight gained, every new nugget of family history reclaimed and every professional milestone, he raised an eyebrow and his body smiled with pride.

"But he wasn't actually present with you in Việt Nam?" Blue asked.

"No." I thought back to the muggy roads in Sài Gòn, trying to imagine him on a xe ôm, or weaving through crowds in flip flops. "He didn't belong there. As a mongrel back then, he would've stuck out even more than me in Việt Nam." And standing out would make it harder for me to gather the stories I was searching for.

* * *

We naively believed we could hunt down "truth" in Việt Nam like investigative journalists. David and I developed gendered approaches to family history. Ever the deep analyst, he has always been much better than me at tracking third-party evidence and searching for official documents. I focused on collecting stories from relatives and the occasional history book for context. We greedily interviewed historians and researchers that friends introduced us to, including one who said lots of Việt kiều like me were similarly sleuthing their histories.

We imagined all these pieces would fall into a neat jigsaw but learned, after running headlong into blind alleys and contradictions, that truth is many tentacled and incorporeal, alternately seductive and deceptive, particularly when reported through lenses of trauma, jealousy, and yearning. No one, even eye-witnesses, sees it all or monopolizes it. The same informant might share different versions from telling to telling. Try holding onto something too tightly as fact and it will disintegrate into puffs of contradictions and mirage.

No piece of family history was as vaporous as the mysteries surrounding my maternal grandfather (Ông Ngoại). I learned to let my understanding of him hover in a cloud a little above the ground, not settled in any one place.

He was born in 1908, one of five children of a low-ranking bureaucrat in the colonial government. Because they lived in the city of Khương Hạ rather than the countryside, he had the rare experience of finishing ten years of primary schooling.

In the social and political turmoil of the 1920s, many of his teachers effused a withering distaste for both French colonial practices and Confucian traditions. They exposed him to new ideologies, questioning Việt Nam's passivity toward French oppression. This generation of "petit-bourgeoise" student activists dared call for aggressive opposition and dream of independence. They would not wait for history to come to them.

My grandfather's path began with joining local nationalist groups alongside his older brother, Chính. He earned revolutionary bona fides when the French imprisoned them both in 1931 in a widespread campaign of repression.

My maternal grandfather, Nguyễn Đức Kính, Hà Nội, early 1940s.

Those prisons, especially Sơn La where Ông Ngoại did hard labor and Côn Lôn where his brother was jailed, were prime recruiting grounds for the fledgling socialist movement. International Communist bodies helped funnel material and moral support to prisoners while indoctrinating them in Marxism through whispers and shards of literature.

Among the new recruits was a young man named Trần Huy Liệu, who would become one of Hồ Chí Minh's most trusted political advisors and the Vietnamese Communist Party's master propagandist, and later devote segments of his autobiography to how my grandfather sheltered him and helped him find work after they were released from prison.

My grandfather, his brother, and Trần Huy Liệu were among writers and newspaper publishers that were prodigiously active in the 1930s. The worldwide Depression and prejudice they faced from colonial authorities left them few other options for work. Ông Ngoại started a paper called Đổi Mới (Renewal) in 1935 that lasted just a few months. More followed,

> Em Kính,
>
> Mới hôm nào anh em còn bíu cửa sổ nói truyện từ trại « Chín gian » sang trại « Cô-vê » ở nhà pha Hỏa-lò, thế mà nay đã người Sơn-la kẻ Côn-đảo.
>
> Chả biết ngục Sơn-la của em thế nào, chớ ngục Côn-lôn của anh thì khá lắm: tường xây cao như những tảng đá dựng xửng; cửa hai lần, một lần là song sắt, một lần là tấm tôn giấy và nặng, khi mở ra đóng vào nó nghiến răng ken két nghe rùng mình. Ở đây chỗ chứa tù không gọi là nhà giam mà gọi là banh (*bagne*); chỗ nhốt phạt không gọi là buồng kín mà gọi là hầm (*cachot*). Ở đây người ta không ăn cơm... à, phải cơm, nhưng một thứ cơm đỏ, trông ngỡ sôi đậu đen, lại rắn, hôi, lộn sôi, lộn châu. Cá thì thối, mục... để nuốt chớ đừng nên ngửi. Anh đã được thấy những củ-ngoéo⁽¹⁾ to tướng, những giây xiềng loảng-xoảng, những bộ mặt dữ-tợn. Cái cảnh âm-ti mình vẫn hãi-hùng tưởng-tượng hồi còn nhỏ nay thực-hiện ra trước mắt!
>
> Ấy hoàn-cảnh ác-nghiệt nhường ấy. Song anh cứ muốn phấn-đấu xem ai được ai thua.
>
> (1) Tiếng Nam-kỳ, chỉ cái ba-toong quắp.
>   *Lời chua của người xuất-bản.*

First page of a letter to my grandfather from his brother, Nguyễn Đức Chính, from prison, November 1930.

including *Le Travail*, involving Ông Ngoại, Trần Huy Liệu, and other future Party luminaries including Võ Nguyên Giáp, the military titan of the revolution. The band of brothers convened at a small concession stand my grandfather's sister ran at the Metropol Hotel, and became close knit.

Although the three men were all listed in French records of the time as "troublemakers," the numerous broadsheets they produced flourished because of a paradox of relatively permissive French oversight that lasted just a few years. The leftist Front Populaire briefly ruled France during this time and were sympathetic to anti-colonialists. Colonial authorities in Việt Nam were also eager to promote use of western script by the natives.

In this heady political context, and without birth control, my grandfather's family expanded to seven children (one died in toddlerhood). It was clear from the beginning how different my grandparents were. Both were devoted to their children, but while my grandfather splurged on gifts, made up games to play, and rarely raised his voice, my grandmother meted out discipline and ran a tight household, sometimes favoring some children like my mother too much over others. He wafted between jobs while she squirreled money away for emergencies.

Their friends and relatives thought him too much the idealist, his feet not quite on the ground, but that was what she loved about him. She let him soar and clung on for the ride, providing the ballast. To compensate for his meager earnings, she made parcels of food to sell at roadside, mended clothes for wealthier families, and opened a one-room schoolhouse named Khuê Anh Học Hiệu—after her daughters, my mother Anh and aunt Khuê. Trần

Huy Liệu sent his son to study there. She learned to keenly watch Ông Ngoại's habits. She guessed money was going to drugs, a prison habit the French encouraged. He even took his younger son Hải to an opium den once, curling up with the boy until his spell was over. He tried to quit the habit many times, but became so violently ill in withdrawal, my grandmother resigned herself to it.

Over time, Ông Ngoại's relationship to the Party grew complicated. He was in and out of trouble with colonial authorities but was also able to intervene with the French on behalf of friends and got official approval to publish his brother's prison letters. Theories abound of him being a spy or courier whom the local Party eventually suspected of being a double agent.

A page from the annual report of the French Service de la Surete au Tonkin (Security Service of Tonkin), about my grandfather's publication activities. Translation: The *Đổi Mới*, from March to April 1935, had undertaken this task: the searches carried out on April 26 in its offices and at the homes of its principal editors were to ruin its efforts in a few days, and the *Đổi Mới* ceased to appear. The same group of publicists, comprising notably Trần Huy Liệu, Nguyễn Đức Kính, etc.... who published *Đổi Mới* then got their hands on other susceptible newspapers, under their direction, to play the same role. They succeeded in introducing themselves, successively, into the writing of *Kiên-van tuần báo* in Hà Nội, *Hải Phòng tuần báo* in Hải Phòng, *Hà Nội báo* in Hà Nội, *Tiến Bộ* in Bắc Ninh, *Tiếng Van Lang Báo* in Hà Nội, but failed in their attempt to seize *Trang An* in Huế.

We encountered a dead zone in our research from 1939 until 1947 when Ông Ngoại died, a period when Hồ Chí Minh reasserted leadership over the Communist movement, and Ông Ngoại's friends rose to more prominent positions on the front lines of battle while he remained in Hà Nội in murky activity. He and Trần Huy Liệu stayed in touch. According to my uncle Sơn, Trần Huy Liệu invited my grandfather to join him in 1945 on a delegation to witness the abdication of Việt Nam's last emperor, Bảo Đại.

Maybe Ông Ngoại played both sides to make more money to feed his rapidly growing brood. Maybe he was vulnerable to French manipulation because of his opium habit and growing distance from Party leadership. The truth is likely buried with all the other secrets of that generation of comrades, because Ông Ngoại purposefully told my grandmother little about his political work, in an effort to keep his family safe. That wasn't enough to avoid the summons and his disappearance.

Another revolutionary and friend with complicated ties to French authorities, Mai Ngọc Thiêu, tried to warn Ông Ngoại that suspicions were swirling. "You should leave immediately with your family," he urged, just before fleeing that night for Sài Gòn with his own son. But my grandfather didn't sense danger until it was too late. Agents knocked on their door the next day.

My mother maintains it was Trần Huy Liệu who turned her father in to local authorities, but most of my relatives disagree. It's hard to reconcile such an accusation with the seemingly genuine warmth with which Trần Huy Liệu writes about my grandfather in his autobiography.

The 1940s were chaotic and dangerous even, or perhaps especially, for the ascendant Communists. Different factions competed through mutual assassinations. Because French authorities also routinely captured and pressured known Party members to inform on one another, killing one's own comrades became a potential matter of survival. Purges ripped through the countryside, some orchestrated by Võ Nguyễn Giáp.

Ông Ngoại's assassination by his comrades left my grandmother bereft, radicalized his children into staunch anti–Communists, and seared into my relatives' collective psyche the folly and dangers of loving a dreamer.

I long puzzled over why I became the only one of Bà Ngoại's grandchildren pulled early to public interest work with a political tint, and whether the summation of "1970's television morality + urban public education + community-minded father + liberal mixed-race neighborhoods" produced my lean to mending the world. I rejected rigid ideology but wanted to find pragmatic solutions to large problems. My family was bemused or indifferent when I volunteered at a heroin treatment center, and my parents couldn't hide eye rolling (though accompanied by some pride) when I took a large pay cut to go into federal government.

> Tòa báo *Đời mới* ở số nhà 17 phố Hàng Khoai. Người xin được phép xuất bản tờ báo là một người không làm báo, ông Lê Viết Hồ. Ông Hồ cũng như bao nhiêu sáng lập viên của các báo khác, dưới con mắt của bọn thống trị Pháp, nếu không bảo đảm về sự trung thành đối với chúng thì ít ra cũng phải là người không có vấn đề gì về chính trị. Tòa báo là một căn gác chật hẹp. Cách trang trí không có gì khác hơn là một gia đình. Trong "gia đình" ấy có các anh Lê Văn Hòe, Thành Thế Vỹ, Nguyễn Đức Kính, Nguyễn Mạnh Chất và tôi. Theo lời Phờ-lơ-tô thì đây là một ổ cộng sản, nói thế thì cũng hơi quá. Tôi vừa đến, nói chuyện với nhau một lát thì biết nhau ngay, biết ai là cộng sản, biết ai không phải là cộng sản. Tuy vậy mọi người đều chung sống thân mật, chẳng có gì xung đột hay phân biệt về chính kiến. Tôi đến thì tờ *Đời mới* đã xuất bản số 1. Tòa soạn chúng tôi không có lệ duyệt bài, nghĩa là ai muốn viết gì

A page from Trần Huy Liệu's memoir in which he describes his involvement in my grandfather's newspaper. Translation: The Đời mới newspaper house located at No. 17, Hàng Khoai street. The person who got publishing license for the newspaper, Mr. Lê Viết Hồ, was not journalist. Mr. Ho, like founders of many other newspapers, in the eyes of the French rulers, must be, if not loyal to them, then at least, free of political problems. The newspaper house was a cramped attic. The decor is nothing than family-like style. In that "family," there were Mr. Lê Văn Hòe, Mr. Thành Thế Vỹ, Mr. Nguyễn Đức Kính, Mr. Nguyễn Mạnh Chất and me. According to Fleutôt, this was a communist sink, that saying was a bit too much. Only after a while since I came and we started talking, we knew each other already, we knew who were Communists and who were not. However, everyone lived intimately together, and there was no conflict or discrimination in term of political opinion. When I arrived, Đời mới had already published its first issue. Our editorial board did not have any review schedule, which meant that anyone could write about anything. I got the opportunity to restart what had been left unfinished at the prison and continued to write Côn Lôn chronicle to publish from issue 2 onwards.

Bà Ngoại didn't seem distracted by muddy facts; she had a different equation in mind. She never considered my endeavors out of place in her world, even if she only half-understood them. Perhaps to her, it was inevitable that Kính's passions and faults would re-emerge in at least one grandchild, transposed into a safer place and time; a mixed inheritance with the pragmatic survival instincts from her and my father's side of my family.

"I often wonder at how much more connected you feel to your ancestors than to some of your living relatives," Blue observed.

Having chosen my role, I was searching for my model among the ghosts.

Trail

Her husband ripped from her and alone with six children in the increasingly dangerous countryside, Bà Ngoại decided to first move back to Hà Nội to stay with her brother, then to the port city of Hải Phòng. They were part of swarms of refugees flowing in different directions across northern Việt Nam to escape the insurgent war with the French or flee the Communists' scorched-earth campaign.

They lived off money she earned from tailoring clothes with her older daughters, and savings she wore in a belt. Having no electricity where they rented, my grandmother sewed by the light of an oil lamp. When the wick burned short, she gently nudged it upward with the tip of her needle to eke out a few extra minutes. Without money to send the children to school, Bà Ngoại taught them herself. She had argued with Ông Ngoại a lot over money their last few weeks together. Through connections, she eventually found a job in the colonial Ministry of Social Services, but it would not last long.

In the 1954 Geneva Accord, western powers pressured Hồ Chí Minh to accept a treaty that ended French rule but divided the country in half. The U.S. offered to evacuate northerners who wanted to migrate south before demarcation closed the border. Bà Ngoại discounted reasons for leaving. She tried to stay hopeful that her scientist brother could offer them protection as a high-ranking Party member. My teenage mother and aunts had made themselves inconspicuous black and brown clothes, preparing to work as laborers. But a friend and leader in Nationalist circles (competing with Communists for influence) who managed to escape Communist retribution warned Bà Ngoại that if she stayed, her children would never escape the stigma of Ông Ngoại's record as a potential traitor. They would be *thộng xuống đất đen*—hidden in the black ground—suppressed and without a future.

Bà Ngoại reluctantly prepared to migrate, promising to bring along a nephew and my orphaned great-aunt for a total of eight children and leaving behind her beloved brother Khác, who would die before she returned to Hà Nội. My aunts and uncles remember the migration differently—whether it was just uncle Sơn, the oldest, who went south first, or if Bạ Ngoại took both sons to scout out their new city before sending word for the girls to follow.

They stayed with another family from the north. One day a Việt Cộng rocket hit the house, killing the mother of the other family. Bà Ngoại found a different house to rent with several families. She and her children ranging from seven to twenty-one years old settled into one windowless room.

Bà Ngoại could now take stock. She tracked down the same friend who warned Ông Ngoại about his imminent arrest. After she aced civil service entrance exams and with her colonial government experience in the north, it was not hard for him to help her get a job at the South Vietnamese Social Welfare Ministry, where she eventually became its director.

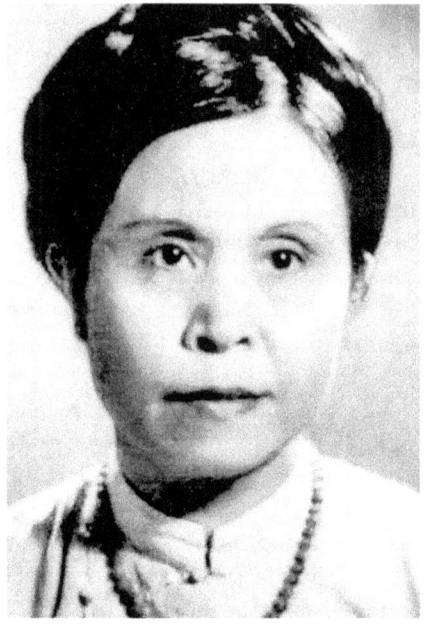

My grandmother, Lê Thị Cạnh, Hà Nội, early 1940s.

She focused on building as much stability for her children as possible, except when an acquaintance in Sài Gòn whispered a rumor that Ông Ngoại might still be alive, sending her into a weeks-long frenzy of fruitless investigation only to feel his ghost float away and out of reach.

Seed

My parents began to plan their visit to Việt Nam as soon as we landed there. Our Sài Gòn relatives impatiently and repeatedly asked us when they would arrive.

"Later this year," I answered a little tensely.

In September, my father made flight reservations. In October, he cancelled them without explanation. My mother emailed us the news. I emailed back.

"It'll be good," I promised. "Everyone wants to see you and you can do so much in a few weeks."

He made new reservations and cancelled them again two weeks later. He never explained his ambivalence and all the shrouded secrets meant I had little confidence I could reassure him about the things he wanted to avoid. By then it was late November. I had to keep the pressure on. Come the new year, tickets would be twice as expensive with the diaspora coming back for Tết, too convenient an excuse for him.

The next evening, I sat up at dawn to catch him coming home after work in Philadelphia with the twelve-hour time difference.

"I need you to come now," I begged. "I need you to show me all the places you know."

He let my mother book one last flight to arrive just after Christmas. I let myself relax just a bit. With only a month before the flight, it was too late for him to cancel and get a refund.

We had been living with such intensity since we arrived in Sài Gòn that spending the holiday in the city with throngs of revelers seemed a chore I had to gird for. On Christmas Eve, a friend suggested we hire a driver for a getaway. We rode up the coast to a new beach resort we couldn't really afford, where we paid for the cheapest private cabana, perched luxuriously on its own sandy knoll. The vast property was idle except for six expat guests and an army of Vietnamese staff overeager to please. We strolled on the pebbly beach in moonlight and gorged on canapés at the poolside buffet, then guiltily dipped into our hot tub. These were indulgences grossly out of step with the rest of our Sài Gòn life.

Frozen then thawed, lying in dark with the city behind me and knowing my most important work of the year—bringing my parents back to Việt Nam—was done, I told David, "I'm ready for the baby now."

We conceived Benjamin that night.

Missive

Growing up, the top drawer of our dining room credenza always held two short stacks of paper; one white for typewriters and random notetaking, and one of translucent air mail paper. The air mail stack was replenished more often. My parents wrote and received long letters from friends and relatives in Việt Nam, and from the diaspora around the world. Accent slashes and swerves in their cursive were as mysterious to me as Japanese kanji. When my mother pushed an air mail letter toward me to read so she could keep her hands occupied with sewing or cooking, I failed miserably and she snatched it back in exasperation.

Gossip lines came to life, and over time, my parents' contact book filled with far flung addresses of re-found acquaintances in France, California, Australia, Maryland, Arizona, Texas—high school classmates, neighbors and friends, colleagues from the embassy and Teachers' College. Many were twice hardened survivors who first escaped the North then the South.

One friend had taught with my father in Sài Gòn and fled to Canada. Delighted to have found where each other landed, they began an elegant correspondence. Bố composed his news as a multi-stanza poem in classical Chinese form and sent it north. His friend took a few weeks to consider and sent back his response in an equally complex poem, and they carried on this one-upmanship for years as their children grew up, without telling us what they wrote about. My parents steadily stitched back together their virtual community, a safer one to write to than people left in Việt Nam living through the purgatory of Communist rule, and where happy news did not trigger jealousy, guilt, or despair.

As an empty nester, Bố finally acquired the time and desktop computer to write for pleasure. He pecked out short stories, snapshots of American immigrant life, parables about parental and filial love. He stacked them in two piles. In English, they seemed a bit trite and I wasn't sure they taught me anything new about the human condition, but then, I was living them. In Vietnamese, they were unusual, relatives in Sài Gòn told me, his voice crisp and direct with none of the affected flourishes of traditional Vietnamese literature. He pointed to an oil landscape hanging on my living room wall, and I recreated it in watercolors for the cover of his first anthology. He found a printer in Philly's Little Sàigòn to produce the yellow-colored paperbacks.

My father sent the book to everyone he knew in the States and packed fifty copies to bring to Việt Nam when David and I lived there. But when he reached Customs at Hồ Chí Minh City Airport, nervous security officers scanned the first few pages and with their reflexive risk aversion confiscated the whole lot, allowing him to import only one.

Bố tried to hide his upset when we picked them up; he had been in the country for less than an hour and already so much loss. But we smiled with relief and reassured him. This, we could fix. The next morning, David walked him and the sole remaining book to a photocopy shop, where the crew efficiently cranked out a hundred contraband black and white copies on cheap paper and bound them with a plastic cover and cloth tape at the spine. The whole operation took a day and cost pennies.

"Your father writes like no one else," an auntie whispered to me. "Quite unique."

Over the following weeks, Bố slipped a copy to everyone he sat down with, pressing his open-faced stories and Việt kiều voice into his friends' hands, his relatives' bags. They floated across Việt Nam's length and breadth, strewing his American experience over his native land.

Legend

At the end of each day roaming around Sài Gòn or on day trips to nearby sights or beaches, my parents came back to dine with us. My mother delighted in serving up whatever exotic foodstuffs she had scored at market, as if they had waited for her all these years and were joyously sacrificing themselves to celebrate the reunion. Or we meandered on foot to one restaurant or another.

Thus the rooster crowing and bread hawkers at dawn, the backfire of early commuters on motorbikes, swarms of tourists and schoolchildren, men laughing in beer halls, thin young hipsters in jeans congregating at pop-up restaurants past midnight until suddenly the city fell silent before refreshing itself again for the next day—all gradually bore their rhythms into my father's bones, until he allowed something to crack open, a connection between this modern Việt Nam and the one he had left behind.

Through that portal, I managed to jostle loose a few stories. I would revisit Bố's stories with him over later years, after our kids were born, and again during my time with Blue. Each interview yielded a few more morsels, a nuanced shift in his perspective, progressively less tidy and more crowded with dangling regrets and contradictions.

Back in medieval Việt Nam, my nội (paternal) ancestor, Nguyễn Trãi, served the first King Lê, Việt Nam's hero king. Nguyễn Trãi was a trusted advisor, poet and scholar, so astute and elevated in his Majesty's esteem that the jealousies of other royal advisors swirled incessantly.

King Lê Lợi died and his son ascended the throne. Nguyễn Trãi had his own household and many wives and concubines, whom he treated well. One in particular was a noteworthy beauty, and one day the new King asked to have her.

"For just one night," my ancestor reassured her, though he couldn't have been sure it would stop there. But during the tryst, his Majesty suddenly died, and the beauty ran back to Nguyễn Trãi, terrified.

He made a quick calculation that his rivals would accuse him of a plot and regicide. He packed his family as the court prepared warrants for their arrest. They stole north in the dark, leaving the Perfume River and citadel of Huế at the slender waist of the country's spine, traveling until they reached boggy countryside west of Hà Nội, in the Red River Delta of Hải Dương Province. He changed his name to Phạm.

This was what my father remembered being told about his origin, an ancient story of political catastrophe driving a rooted family to flee, seeking renewal in a strange land with half their identity erased. These snippets of trauma and resilience lurked in my genes for generations, natural selection preparing Nguyễn Trãi's descendants to survive migration.

The legend defies written history but cannot be dismissed. Through the centuries, Việt Nam succumbed many times to Chinese invasion. To better control the populace and historical narrative, Chinese commonly destroyed Vietnamese books and replaced them with their own. Each time Việt Nam finally repelled the invaders, scholars carefully tried to reconstruct their native truths in writing, from memory, with all the inevitable biases and imperfections. It's reasonable to wonder if oral traditions might be as, or more, valid.

The books say Nguyễn Trãi was born in Hải Dương and trained in the mandarin system. After Chinese invaded in the early 15th century, nationalism stirred him to leave the comfort of his position to join rebel forces led by the upstart Lê Lợi, landowner turned champion of the common people. Nguyễn Trãi grew close to the future king, and through military poetry, came to define core philosophies and stratagems that made the Lê insurgency successful. Central to these was his dictum "it is better to win hearts than conquer citadels."

After the second King Lê died during the night, the court arrested Nguyễn Trãi and executed him and all his family, though rumors suggest that one wife or concubine escaped with a son in utero. Many in Hải Dương trace their ancestry back to him, perhaps from children born before he met Lê Lợi, perhaps from the in utero child who survived the family's execution.

My father was well schooled and would have known all this, although perhaps not, in his childhood, that Nguyễn Trãi's military writings had become foundational reading for Hồ Chí Minh and his advisors. My ancestor was so influential, his descendants would be killed or left bereft and chased from their homeland by revolutionaries inspired by his own philosophies, his legendary success fueling my family's epic losses.

Generation

Among favorite places David and I wandered in Hà Nội's Old City was the ancient academy of Văn Miếu. There, generations of scholars who passed grueling entrance exams trained for years before rising to fill coveted seats in the Confucian hierarchy that governed hamlets, villages and cities, from the first millennium to the end of the Lê Dynasty in the late 18th century.

Once dominating in the city scape, Văn Miếu had been subdued by surrounding flows of motorbikes, taxis, and ever-multiplying modern buildings, though its stone outer walls and walkways were respectfully kept clean of vines or litter. Through the majestic temple entrance, we could walk past a sequence of gardens, statues, and low buildings carved of wood and stone housing prayer halls, rooms of study, and a phalanx of giant turtle statues to honor the most accomplished scholars. City sounds evaporated along its perimeter, the courtyards unexpectedly hushed except for squeals and chirping from an occasional school group on tour.

Long ago, similar if lesser temples of study dotted the countryside, serving as oases of calm and reason as colonial incursions roiled the old order and sowed seeds of chaos. My father's father trained in one of them.

My grandfather was one of ten children of a plantation owner who farmed enough neem trees to build homes for them all, cotton to clothe them, and rice, vegetables, chickens and pigs to feed them. His prosperity allowed his children to marry into families of station. My grandfather chose the daughter of a mandarin.

Ông Nội watched five daughters born. He believed that lacking a son was among the most devastating deficiencies in Confucian filial duty, even keeping a concubine to produce my half-uncle Tùy to serve as a back-up son until my father arrived.

His oldest daughter, my aunt Chịnh, was a full twenty years older than Bố, and had her first baby the same year my father was born. My father thus entered the world with nephews and nieces as playmates and siblings old enough to toss him over their heads. He was of two generations, foretelling how the arc of his life would span other gulfs, between continents, between democracy and not, between a life of washing clothes with wooden clubs or threshing rice with rocks, and one in the Internet Age of instant everything.

Book

The basement of our final house in Philadelphia somehow became a neutral zone, a rotating refuge for different family members where we rarely interrupted one another if we knew it was already occupied.

Halfway down the stairs was where my mother or I stooped to fetch canned food from the makeshift pantry. Sometimes I paused to daydream or grit my teeth, depositing in the dark all the rage I couldn't direct anywhere. Sometimes my mother would be the one to linger down there, meticulously tending to laundry in one dark corner under a fluorescent light. My father helped my brothers set up their weightlifting bench on one side of the room where Ân and Chương disappeared for hour-long sessions. My father used the other side of the room to store tools and materials for his classes, where he tinkered on weekends.

My space was between the tall metal shelves rigged as bookcases. They housed a hodge-podge of used textbooks on finance and taxes from my mother, on algebra and calculus from my brothers; Vietnamese-English, French, and Spanish dictionaries, and world history books from my father; tattered paperbacks on Greek mythology and great American novels. Whatever required reading my father had to teach or my brothers had to learn, ended their lives in the basement. They had no place in the public spaces of my mother's house, and were not worthy of daily attention, but it was not imaginable to anyone to throw them away.

They had a different authority than my library finds because I worried vaguely about missing something in chasing pretty binders or finishing a favorite author's series. The basement books mapped out what lay ahead, what one needed to know to graduate from high school, to finish an accounting degree, to be culturally literate. If I felt my parents and brothers didn't fully appreciate their power in banishing them to the dark, I thought I could get more out of them, a foothold on the future. I leafed through nearly all of them, and read most. No one disturbed me.

* * *

In 1999, the Internet was available in Việt Nam, but only accessible through government desktops or large businesses, monitored Internet cafes, or the laptops of expats and Vietnamese working for foreign companies. For the most part, information was still analog.

As David and I strolled, we saw men and women, schoolchildren and retirees, completely engrossed in reading. Reading anything. Comic books, newspapers, magazines, used books. Used bookstores far outnumbered ones selling new books, crammed with hundreds of uncatalogued volumes in a multitude of languages and varying stages of decay. Many were brought in country by foreign transients, like a throwaway English-language novel we found with a hand-written love letter inside the cover in 1971 from an American soldier to his girlfriend. We wondered whether it was still in Việt Nam because he died in battle or was evacuated, or if the relationship withered. You could have books for pennies, make endless photocopies with copyright impunity, yet bookstores wouldn't have done such brisk business unless their tomes had been recycled through dozens of hands and resells.

Even then, struggling to develop a middle class and in the wake of the Asian financial crisis, Việt Nam boasted a literacy rate of nearly ninety percent (now almost 100 percent). Vietnamese ingest books continuously, like finishing one breath and starting the next, a deeply ingrained reflex as old as the country itself. Some people we saw reading during the day had no jobs, and little else to their name. I couldn't tell whether they hoped books would help map out for them the future or the past.

My father's childhood was punctuated by the different schools he attended. Bố was born in 1937 the youngest child of Phạm Hữu Sán and his first wife, Nguyễn Thị Đoan. Ông Nội was Bố's first teacher. He was the village administrator—tien chi, the First Person, and before that the chánh tổng, principal administrator of a group of villages, widely respected and trusted, and known for his generosity and refined, genteel ways. The 1930s were a transition period between when Vietnamese was written in Chinese characters and the Romanized alphabet brought by French missionaries, and Ông Nội was unusual in being versed in both.

He built his own school and became a revered teacher of a generation of boys alongside my father, many of whom later entered the upper ranks of the local Communist Party.

Vietnamese form life-long bonds with their teachers, a deep-seeded extension of Confucian filial piety, repayment of the debt they owe those who nurture them. In modern Việt Nam, Teachers' Day is a national holiday with the emotion, excess, and public fanfare of Mother's Day, Thanksgiving, and Veterans Day combined. Children carry gifts and large bouquets to their favorite Thầy's houses until those foyers are buried under a floral carpet and muggy with the scent of lilies and mums. Grown men and women drive for scores or hundreds of miles to visit a former Thầy like salmon returning to spawning beds. They plan parties at dusk in beer gardens to fete Thầy. Each year, hundreds of people die from traffic accidents on their way to honor teachers.

My grandmother doted on her only son and was so overly protective that Ông Nội felt compelled to send Bố away to live with relatives to toughen him up, only to relent when both his wife and son became despondent. Bà Nối died when Bố was barely a teen. My father plunged into a dark whirlwind of loss—she was his sun and confidante, and anxiety over having to assume her household responsibilities. Ông Nội insisted Bố's education continue, including rarified French and guitar lessons that marked him as belonging to the elite.

This just as all of Indochina heaved with rapidly shifting military dynamics and simmering revolution. Japanese invaded in July 1941 and held an uneasy alliance with the Vichy authority. Seeing its southern border threatened, China nurtured a disparate mix of Vietnamese nationalist and Communist factions, ultimately putting its weight behind the young Hồ Chí Minh and his insurgency. Soviets made the same bet. Fire fights and bombings pocked the northern countryside. My father was shot in the leg one day while running to another village to warn friends about approaching Japanese. Japan turned on its French collaborators in spring of 1945 and took control of northern Việt Nam until the Allies defeated them in August.

My grandfather's reality twisted and somersaulted. Rooted in the old world, he was ill equipped to prepare his son for what was coming. At first, Communists were cautious and left the mandarin system of bureaucrats undisturbed, but Bố could feel their antipathy. His fifth grade teacher was a Communist sympathizer who disliked children of the old order. He recruited students as messengers for the Party but turned Bố down scornfully when he volunteered.

Despite escalating chaos around him, or maybe because of it, Bố anchored himself in any schooling he could find. One family fleeing Hà Nội stayed briefly at his uncle's house and left behind boxes of books. Bố found them and taught himself algebra, geography, and science, eager to grow beyond the Chinese history and philosophy Ông Nội knew. When a middle school moved from Hà Nội to their village, Bố walked several miles to attend classes, but warfare seemed to track the children down, and even that school closed.

Only thirteen, my father sensed his world teetering on extinction—Communists would take away the remaining family land and his life, already limited, would narrow to even fewer opportunities. Ông Nội's resources dwindled from Communist confiscations and disruptions in his teaching from warfare.

Bố flitted between a public school in the city of Hưng Yên, and an expensive private school run by a relative, then back to Hải Dương. He won a coveted job as a substitute teacher, to ease guilt about the financial strain on Ông Nội and other relatives supporting his tuition and living expenses.

When demarcation came in 1954, no one wanted my father to flee. Filial piety kept my grandfather rooted in Hải Dương to care for his ancestors' tombs and out of loyalty to the king. Bố's school principal also tried to convince him to stay in the north.

"Communists are going to take over the whole country anyway," the principal told him, "What is the point of going south?" But my father didn't want to be paralyzed by what might happen in two decades; he just wanted enough time and hope for the immediate future.

Communists began a propaganda campaign to convince northerners to stay. A man encouraged Bố to enroll in college in Hà Nội, claiming the war would quickly end. Bố was intrigued enough to take a train to Hà Nội but found nothing where the school should have been. He worried the man was Communist and had baited him. That train ride also exposed Bố to dispirited faces of Hanoians, and Communist youth bullying passengers.

He had already witnessed what he considered Party hypocrisy, when leaders dined in private on meats they took from Ông Nội's farm, then publicly slummed with soldiers over spartan meals of rice gruel and vegetables. Skeptics in the village whispered that Communists cared more about Party than country, and predicted they would sacrifice a generation of bodies to unify Việt Nam. A future in the north looked bleak.

"I also wanted to read books," he explained to me. "I wanted to read the best books, and they were written in English and French, not Russian or Chinese." He meant, he didn't want anyone denying him those books.

Bố couldn't bring himself to tell Ông Nội he was leaving, but neither could he imagine asking my grandfather to come with him. Life in Sài Gòn was a mass of uncertainties, and Bố didn't know how he would support even himself. He asked a relative to give his watch and gold ring to Ông Nội, who was both personally devastated by his son's abandonment and mourned it as a betrayal of our ancestors.

My father fled to the coast and boarded the largest piece of machinery he had ever seen, an American aircraft carrier, with thousands of other northerners. He floated down to Sài Gòn with little save addresses for a few relatives, and the promise of the best books in his future. He was seventeen.

Allegiance

A technocrat by temperament, Ông Nội was politically non-committal. He had willingly given rice and money to Communists when they asked for supplies to replenish forces between battles, but he was skeptical that any Vietnamese force could defeat Western powers.

In the binary world of insurgency, he became a target of suspicion and increasingly after the country's demarcation into North and South, of disfavor. Communists spied on him, eavesdropping through a hole in the house's mud wall. They knew he was not an active counter-revolutionary; they would have immediately executed anyone suspected of such. In the village, people pointed out those corpses with indictment letters hanging on their necks.

Neither did Communists do anything to directly harm Ông Nội. His former students had become important members of village governance in the Party; to kill a beloved teacher was public sacrilege they were not prepared to commit. Rather, they treated him with as much respect as one could muster while confiscating a man's home and putting him under arrest. Instead of trying him in court, they sent him to re-education camp where he eventually fell ill and passed away, a slower and more anonymous way to kill. Back in the village, Ông Nội's brother-in-law was tried and stoned to death. His son-in-law was also executed, despite having given his house, guns, gold, and rice to the revolution.

My paternal grandfather, Phạm Hữu Sán, Hải Dương province, 1930s.

Bố learned the news months later.

In America, my father considered himself a committed Republican and voted reliably, but for many years felt any civic engagement beyond that outside of his Vietnamese community was at best a waste of time, and at worst naive. For him, even being a Vietnamese outreach coordinator for the 2000 Census was about getting his community representation, not serving the body politic. Even if he could get over the low pay, he was mystified by my pull to public service, to solving sprawling social problems on behalf of strangers. Regimes come and go. Tribes endure.

Hustle

Sài Gòn is the unruly teenager city in millennia old Việt Nam. It has always been a raucous negotiation. Long a busy port in the Cambodian empire, it absorbed Vietnamese settlers throughout the 17th century, who eventually made the remaining Khmer a minority population but imbibed their foodstuffs and other cultural tics passed down from Indian and Thai influencers. After a brief century of centralized rule under the Nguyễn dynasty, Sài Gòn was again siphoned off in the mid-19th century, this time by French missionaries. They overlaid chaotic medieval streets with formal boulevards and imposing colonial buildings, and offered Catholicism, an alphabet, opium, and baguettes in exchange for plantations and subjugation. Việt Nam's last emperor, Bảo Đại, lasted all of a year there leading the Republic of Việt Nam until he was deposed in 1955.

Throughout its passing from hand to hand, the city persistently throbbed with commerce, irreverence, and flagrant passions. Conquerors intent on subduing it all eventually surrendered to its freewheeling spirit. I saw it in the impishness of my medical residents. It is where pirates and marauders gravitated, where migrants, artists, intellectuals, hucksters and unapologetic entrepreneurs were willing to try anything once; where the farmed and fished bounty of the Mekong Delta streamed in by cart, boat, truck, and on foot to feed the most complex culinary melting pot in the country; where money and ideas flew fast and laws were sketchy. Inevitably, it would one day become the country's financial capital. It is Việt Nam's Texas, New York City and western frontier rolled into one.

When David and I lived there and sometimes forgot to call it Hồ Chí Minh City, when most expats still had government minders, the national Party had struck an informal and uneasy truce with local realities. Hence some blinks of an official eye but tolerance of a widely publicized drag queen parade and the city's first condom sculpture contest in support of HIV awareness, at the underground modern art scene, the brisk market in bootleg recordings of perversions like the Beatles or cold war spy thrillers, or the outright adulation of Western idols like Bill Gates or Bill Clinton.

Sàigònese might not miss American military invasion, but they knew who had game when they saw it.

My father did not know when he arrived in 1954 that he was made for this place, that if the tradition-bound, studious, and dutiful ethos of his northern childhood had given him a solid ego and moral compass, Sài Gòn would launch him. It would offer him new dreams, push him to outrageous risks, and show him how far he was capable of going to not just survive, but win.

His first imperative was to find work. He had contact information only for a poor uncle and knew he had to make his own way. He tried selling vitamins for a pharmacy by walking streets with a box of pill bottles but was unable to overcome his anxiety at approaching strangers. Near a bus station one day, a stranger suggested he try delivering newspapers for American soldiers. Bố didn't own a bicycle, so he borrowed one without permission from his landlord, and stole out early each morning to make his rounds. But he grabbed the wrong bunch of newspapers one day, and they fired him.

Walking despondent afterwards, he came to an office for Operation Brotherhood, a non-profit run by the American Junior Chamber of Commerce. Operation Brotherhood hired doctors and Foreign Service professionals to treat civilians in formerly Communist areas. A sign in the window advertised for English-Vietnamese interpreters.

Bố had learned a smattering of phrases and how to sound out written English in Hải Dương from a teacher who only had books of poetry to teach with. It was a stretch to say he could speak English but in desperation, he amplified things on his application and got hired without an interview. The staff complained almost immediately, but his understanding written English bought him just enough time to become verbally fluent on the job.

One of his sisters (my cousin Sử's mother) also fled to Sài Gòn. Her family had lost land and an infant daughter whom her mother-in-law snatched and ran away with on the tarmac in Hà Nội as my aunt screamed. My father bought math and science books whenever he went downtown to see her. After a year, he wanted a better interpreter job at the American Embassy. He was astonished to find his old English teacher from the north already working there. His old Thầy hired him on the spot.

After long workdays, Bố had just enough money to enroll in night school. He prepared for entrance exams to upper high school. His class was full of other northern teenage migrants, slightly over age because of interruptions in their schooling. One of them was my willowy mother, with a waist so thin he could circle it with his hands. He had seen her before in an English class for Embassy employees where she had been the teacher's favorite.

The chaos of my parents' childhoods, the deaths of their fathers—all the losses that scarred them and fed their common ambition to make the most of a second chance in Sài Gòn led them to meeting in these classrooms, to falling in love and eventually to my birth.

At the time, a South Vietnamese law heightened pressure on young men to perform in school. Those who didn't enroll in college or get a threshold score on national qualifying exams at age eighteen were drafted. Education could literally be life-saving. My uncle Sơn didn't pass the exam and served in the infantry. Bố resented this law even thirty years later. When I told him the father of my college classmate was a judge in Sài Gòn and had, in a futile act of civil disobedience, refused to authorize the drafting of young boys who failed the exam, Bố's face lifted with a lock of the jaw and a look of admiration.

My father passed exams to earn two years of deferment. He was then eligible to apply to public university or a more selective college requiring additional exams. His dream was to go to medical school, but, knowing he couldn't support himself for that much more schooling, he applied instead for a scholarship to enter Teacher's College.

Bố aced the exams, only to hear the director of instruction announce that another favorite student would get the scholarship instead. My father spun in panic and anger. Every tactic, investment and minute of toil led to the promise of a college education. There was no back-up plan he was willing to contemplate. He formally protested to the office of the Minister of Education and a swift investigation got him back on the scholarship list. The other student was drafted and Bố earned the lasting enmity of the director of instruction. Hundreds of people took the entrance exam in hopes of avoiding military service, but my father's score ranked him third. He won one of only thirty slots.

Bố began his college career while still working for the American embassy. He cheated by going into work early, then sneaking out to campus for lectures before returning to the office. There was never a blip in his productivity for his bosses to notice, but the high-pressure multi-tasking wore him down within the year. He quit his job to focus on college full time.

In his third year, when Ân was just a toddler and Chương a baby, the embassy announced scholarships for young Vietnamese to study in the U.S. My father had only a passing notion of what he would do with such an opportunity. He casually wrote in his application that he would study sociology and psychology, so heavily discounting his chances that he didn't bother researching what it would mean to leave his young family or live in America and was already eyeing teaching slots around Sài Gòn. He had his pick of positions upon graduation and chose one in the Gia Định district.

He had not become anything close to a village chief in this metropolis but was poised to join the long line of teachers in his family after outcompeting a much larger and hungrier pool of rivals than his father ever had to. Just as Bố launched his career, he received news he had won the embassy scholarship, and the service order to go for his studies in America.

My father, Bính, Sài Gòn, early 1970s.

My father, Bính, Sài Gòn, early 1970s.

Each near-death experience and successive rung on his climb to middle class status seeded in my father the fits of anger we braced against in Philadelphia. His transmission of these stories, doled out to me in measured servings, gradually unknotted something rigid in my chest and belly.

"What were you so relieved about?" Blue asked.

"That my ancestors' suffering eased, knowing someone had started hearing their stories." Just as Michael heard and kept my stories.

Flow

My father was drawn to America in a tropism for the open-ended opportunity—novelty, money, prestige, and a vague promise that it might bestow some future advantage. He didn't fall in love with the place at first meeting.

He was, in fact, deeply reluctant to embrace this immense gift. He had guiltily left behind his wife and small sons—too close an echo of abandoning his father—watched his beloved pulsing Sài Gòn shrink away below his first airplane flight, and landed in Athens, Georgia, alone and bewildered by the cold of a winter so severe his nose bled every time he ran from his dorm to the cafeteria. Letters to and from Việt Nam took weeks to travel, the food was heavy and strange, and his social life confined to Vietnamese classmates at Peabody (later the University of Georgia College of Education). Even their company wasn't adequate defense against his homesickness; he needed more engagement than a small southern town could offer. After a year, he transferred to the University of Pennsylvania in a bustling Philadelphia with a metabolic rate that reminded him more of Sài Gòn.

His first summer in Philly, Bố saw signs posted by someone looking for a roommate. City rents were expensive, nearly a quarter of his monthly scholarship stipend. The ad led him to a lanky American named Dan Ross studying for his law degree. Dan's wholesome work ethic was familiar to my father and Bố admired his frugality, knowing his family was wealthy and influential. Dan had investments in something called the stock market. His father ran a diamond drill company and had connections to Governor Scranton.

Bố sent what he saved of his stipend in dollars back to the P.O. box of my mother's American supervisor in Sài Gòn, escaping government oversight and bribes. It was a precious remittance that allowed my mother to help support some of her siblings and buy gold for safe keeping, a defense against the inflationary pressures of war.

Dan found in my father a well-matched chess opponent and easy company. He didn't push too hard on the opaque parts of Bố's story, not even realizing until years later that my father was married with children because Bố insisted at the time that he was single. Had the scholarship favored unmarried students?

My father also hid from Dan the shocks of his American experience. One night, Bố stood to leave a restaurant after dining alone to find that the black umbrella he left in a stand by the front door had disappeared. Another diner likely accidentally snatched it, but my father could neither allow the innocent explanation nor recover from the loss. A thunderstorm lashed outside but soaked clothes and the wasted few dollars an unremarkable umbrella had cost couldn't explain the despair my father felt returning to his room. He had lost parents, land, a village, had barely clawed back a life-saving scholarship from someone else's cheat; an umbrella gone missing just when he needed it cemented forever his reflexive suspicion that he could never trade vigilance for trust in other people's good intent, or that the hustle could ever end.

Bố returned to Sàigòn with master's degrees and earned an appointment to train elementary school teachers. Inspired by teaching methods he experienced in the States, and frustrated that he couldn't find instructional material reflecting his new perspectives, he decided to write his own. When his textbook was published, covering everything from child psychology to sociology and education, students found it revelatory. The book demystified material in Vietnamese college entrance exams. All three editions sold out, and our housekeeper grew accustomed to strangers at the door asking for copies.

To supplement his teacher's salary, Bố's applied to the Staff Development Center at the American Embassy where he oversaw testing for people like him—Vietnamese employees and those hoping for scholarships for U.S. travel and education. It didn't take long for him to seize the next opportunity; as the Minister of Education changed national examinations from essay form to multiple choice tests to measure a broader range of skills, Bố drafted another textbook, this time with some friends, on English language testing and how to take multiple choice tests. It was just as popular.

With each conquered threat and milestone to build his new life, my father inched closer to his ancestors' expectations. Like Michael, he knew what his station in life was meant to be.

Her and Him

I met the shadow of a man at a wedding reception in Sài Gòn for a relative so distant the cousin who brought me there had trouble explaining the groom's relation to me. Shadow Man was of my parents' generation, grayed, with a gentle, carefully blank face. He wore a faded suit, slightly too large for him. We both finished eating quickly and neither of us wanted to dance. Instead, he quietly said he knew my parents.

Because his voice never rose above a whisper, I had to lean into his bent frame, hollowed cheeks, soft eyes to catch what he said. I liked him instantly. He had been a classmate of my parents and taught alongside my father. He, too, had passing associations with Americans, but he wasn't able, or didn't want to, escape in 1975. Communists sentenced him to re-education camp where he wasted away for ten years. My father's half-brother had met a similar fate and arrived in Philadelphia in the mid-1980s after my parents sponsored his relocation. But Shadow Man didn't have family in America.

After his release, Shadow could find no work and had to rely on relatives. All he had was time, so that was what he spent. He traveled to Hà Nội and surrounding villages and began hunting for records of his family's history. He traced his genealogy north to south, from government archives to village rosters, and wrote his ancestors' stories.

"Will you publish them?" I asked.

"No one would be interested in them," he said. "I do this for myself, not anyone else." I wondered whether he had children to bequeath the stories to but was afraid to ask.

Later in the week, David and I had lunch at my second cousin's house. Bác Vượng was orphaned in the north and brought south by Bà Ngoại but chose to stay in Sài Gòn in 1975. He reminded me of my uncle Hải in America—avuncular and generous despite hardship, nearly always smiling except when trying to fool you in some prank. He and his plump wife gave their children each a different, felicitous name starting with the letter "h,"—meaning "peace," "kind," "respectful," and approached every day with a boisterous laugh, convinced that enough bia (beer) and cà ri (curry) in company of people you love would set everything right.

He wouldn't deny me answers to any questions. Over bowls of rice, I asked him about Shadow Man. He and his kids traded side glances.

"Who is he?" I wanted to know. "Is he related to me?"

Bác Vượng smiled and said Shadow couldn't possibly be related to me. "He was very important to your mother once. She had two suitors—him and your father. This one was her romance, her poetry, and he loved her very much. But your grandmother preferred your father."

My face clouded ever so slightly and Bác Vượng's children were quick to jump in, "But of course your mother married the right man! There is no question."

"She married the one with the stronger life force, which is why you are here today," Bác Vượng finished firmly, ladling a fist-sized chunk of stewed pork into my bowl for emphasis.

After my parents arrived in Sài Gòn, I asked my mother about Shadow Man.

She frantically shushed me, "Don't ever mention him in front of your father! Bố will get very angry!" She didn't ask me where Shadow was, or whether he was well.

* * *

From an early age, my mother instinctively projected an inviting vulnerability and other qualities that made people care for her. She was smart with a bright, welcoming disposition; beautiful, but delicate. She survived childhood scarlet fever with a weakened constitution, leaving her panting with exertion such that Bà Ngoại let her ride to school on the family's one bicycle. In Sài Gòn, she suffered from repeated bouts of other feverish infections requiring stays in the hospital where my father would visit. It wasn't until she fainted from a minor stroke in her fifties that we discovered she had a hole in her heart from birth, stressing her lungs and limiting her oxygen capacity.

And she was competent and generous. Soon after arriving in Sài Gòn, she left day school in search of work to help Bà Ngoại support the family. Her English teacher introduced his star student to what later became the U.S. Agency for International Development (USAID), where she became the highest paid Vietnamese employee and tripled what her mother and siblings could earn. She took in my great-aunt as our nanny, was a favorite confidant among her sisters, gifted clothes and desirables from the U.S. Commissary to friends and siblings.

After turning over most of her earnings to Bà Ngoại, there was enough left over to buy a motorcycle, and return to night school to finish her degree. She was moving up in the world, and my grandmother eyed

My mother, Anh, Sài Gòn, early 1970s.

her protectively to guide the selection of a worthy suitor, through a nod or quiet word.

Even as an orphan, my father distinguished himself in Bà Ngoại's eyes with his talent and moxie. She tracked his academic accomplishments with approval. He courted my mother ahead of his entrance exams for Teachers College. My youngest aunt walked behind them one day and noticing a new intensity in their conversation, hung back to let them stroll off together. My parents thought themselves clever for sneaking secret dates around night school hours. Bà Ngoại didn't resist when their Catholic friends proselytized them, and they wed in Đức Bà (Notre Dame) Cathedral.

My mother, Sài Gòn, early 1970s.

They shared a house with Bà Ngoại for a time, which gave my mother some relief during my father's year in America, and through a subsequent miscarriage. When Chương was barely two, she wishfully thought going on a two-month rotation to the U.S. would help break her depression, but the unfamiliar food left her nauseous and feeling more helpless than ever. It was a relief to come home.

Shortly thereafter, Dan Ross was posted to Sài Gòn as a procurement officer in 1968 and rekindled his friendship with Bố—visiting our house before returning stateside. The quiet didn't last long.

President Nixon's decision to begin drawing down American military involvement rippled through my parents' lives. Their increasingly desperate search for a way out lasted three years. They were even willing to split the family, most concerned about what would happen to Ân and Chương in a Communist Việt Nam. They chased leads about smugglers and random Westerners willing to take teenagers. They were furious when my great-aunt's American husband turned down their request and instead helped another family. They packed emergency luggage, stowed away in a secret crawl space in the house. They wrote careful instructions for Bố's sister on how to divide among relatives any belongings they might leave behind. They converted as much Vietnamese currency as they could to twenty-two ounces of gold leaf, carefully wrapped and taped shut, which later generated anxiety in Philadelphia when Dan took Bố to sell the gold and the pawn shop owner insisted they first remove every shred of tape so he wouldn't be paying for its weight. They had those tin dog tags made for their children.

In mid–April 1975, Bố wrote Dan asking for help and waited for a response. My mother's USAID supervisor, James Groves, tried to reassure her—he promised to not leave without her or us. But by April 23, he still didn't have concrete plans.

That morning, American leadership at the Army's Vietnamese American Association School of English told their assembled Vietnamese staff—nearly all married men—that the Army could evacuate them but not their families. Bố left despondent and without protest. He rode his scooter to Mac Vi headquarters (Military Advisory Command of Việt Nam) where he saw empty yellow buses clearly waiting to transport people out. That American commander had just told his Vietnamese staff that Mac Vi would evacuate them *and* their families.

My uncle Tân worked there, and happened to look out the window as my father looked in. They huddled briefly then left in different directions to gather the rest of my mother's family. The next day, James Groves came to our house with news of a way to transport us out, to find it abandoned and the gate locked. Curious neighbors told him we had fled.

In Philadelphia, Faye was tending to three-year-old Kevin, baby Eric, and her elderly parents. She had never met my father, but when Dan raised the question, she agreed without hesitation to sponsor us, doubling the size of the household to an even dozen. By the time Dan tried to telegram back to my parents, it was April 30 and the Telex office was in chaos with news of Sài Gòn's fall.

When my father wrote him again from Fort Chaffee, Dan repeated his offer of sponsorship, by then one of several my parents had received. They considered heading to Washington, D.C., with some of my aunts and uncles, but it was such a popular relocation site that Bố and Mẹ decided instead to take a chance on Philadelphia where they might have less competition in finding work.

Brood

Leaving Fort Chaffee and landing in Philadelphia severed for the first time in her thirty-nine years the connections that bonded my mother, grandmother, and her siblings and cousins through poverty, murder, migration, and years of toil in Sài Gòn. They were now scattered across four states and thousands of miles.

Without their chatter and tempering presence, she was left to tend her anxieties alone. She had no sisters with whom to compare their respective sponsors or housing prospects, no brothers to consult about job searches, no nephews and nieces to play with her kids. She realized Bà Ngoại could never live independently again. She was terrified for cousins left behind in Sài Gòn. She worried about how my younger aunts' journeys would end with babies in tow. Two of her sisters were still shaken by separation from their husbands (one was still with his military unit in the Mekong Delta when our cargo flight left, and another had official duties that kept him in Sài Gòn; they both escaped later).

So many of the competencies and advantages my mother had accrued in Sài Gòn vanished. She traded a high-ranking position at USAID working under devoted supervisors, for entry-level secretarial work with strangers who didn't think her English anything special. The months we spent in the Rosses' house were temporary respite. She would no longer have a motorcycle to move about independently without crowded, hourlong bus rides, nor a housekeeper to nanny her bewildered children or to shop for and prepare meals by the time she arrived home from work, spent after a day of living her own alien status. She worried about whether gold they brought from Việt Nam amounted to anything in America; about how her teenage sons were adapting—she thought Chương was especially sensitive; about how to pay to fix Tuấn's teeth—so rotted and misshapen that Faye spent many days with him at the periodontist; and about my increasingly dense muteness.

Despite generous support from the Rosses and Faye's parents, anxieties piled on. She looked forward each night to when she and my father could retreat to the Rosses' sun porch for privacy, and she could let her guard down to speak Vietnamese.

My mother knew we were likely the first Vietnamese refugees arriving in Philadelphia. Yet over our first summer, as she did errands around Mt. Airy with Faye, she occasionally spotted other Asian women and couldn't help rushing down the sidewalk or crossing streets to ask in Vietnamese if they were also from Sài Gòn. The Korean women all shook their heads in puzzlement and backed away.

It only took a few weeks to re-establish contact with her siblings, but her village was gone and would take years to rebuild. In the meantime, there was little in her new world she could exert control over as she was able to in Sài Gòn, except me.

Hạnh Phúc
(Blessed Happiness)

My parents were celebrities everywhere they went in Việt Nam. In the month between booking flights and arriving, they spread word of their trip to all their family and friends. My adolescent narcissism finally gave way to the realization that they had full lives separate from their children's. They too had once been young and rebellious with outsized ambitions and gauzy daydreams despite or because of the dark of war, navigating complicated factions of relatives, intimates, and frenemies.

They had left as many if not more people in Việt Nam as had migrated west, and they vibrated with excitement anticipating all the reunions. Before they stepped off the plane, their calendar was already crammed with plans for meals and meetups.

Relatives, including some I hadn't yet met, arrived in a steady stream to our house to visit, or took us to restaurants tourists would never find so my parents could indulge in the delicacies they missed. Distant cousins tried to best one another in giving Bố and Mẹ the most nostalgic memories to take back to America. Some drove for hours from smaller towns. Anh Sử did his best to manage my parents' exposure, occasionally curtly cutting off a conversation to give them time to catch breath before the next social commitment.

Even when they took strolls or went on casual errands, my parents generated buzz. They beamed and widened their eyes with childlike delight at things they recognized and novelties alike, and shopkeepers found it infectious. They rushed over to talk with Bố and Me, showing my parents how to count the unfamiliar currency and engaging them in faux haggling over prices, just for the fun.

One priority, especially my father, was seeing old classmates and teaching colleagues, the adoptive tribe that sustained him when he migrated south. These were young Turks mostly from the north, the best and brightest, many of whom won scholarships to study abroad before 1975 in Japan, France, or America, and who collectively had tried to modernize Vietnamese education.

Hạnh Phúc (Blessed Happiness)

One day, we went with Bố Mẹ to an open-air restaurant at lunchtime, where a group of eight or so beaming men met us and greeted my father with shouts and vigorous, back-pounding hugs. Most spoke some English. Their laughter, reminiscing, jokes and ribbing were so loud that I subconsciously ducked my head to get out of the way.

When waiters cleared main dishes away and the table was only littered with beer and tea glasses, someone patted his full belly and talk turned to heavier topics—friends who had died since 1975, how their family and work situations deteriorated under Communist rule, things they weren't allowed to teach. The group grew quiet. My mother didn't seem bothered, but Bố's face was no longer beaming.

In the pause, one teacher turned to me and said, "Your mother brought your father a lot of hạnh phúc (blessed happiness). Not all of us had that." He was referring to how my uncle Tân had found our family's escape route in 1975.

I realized then that relatives showering my parents with attention might have also been hoping to win favor in how much money Bố and Mẹ would continue sending back to Việt Nam. Anh Sử was protecting my parents from more than just too exhausting a schedule. No matter how much they gave, it would never be enough. But blessed happiness—that was even harder to bestow, and impossible to allocate fairly.

Monkey

My horoscope was destiny. I was born in 1968, the year of the Monkey. Long before I met Sarah Highland and wanted to out-tomboy her, I loved to climb. I didn't climb to lord over what I left beneath but because I craved what loomed above.

At age three, I climbed my mother's motorcycle just after she dismounted it after work, oblivious to glints of the scorching hot engine. I kept stubbornly climbing even while crying after the metal burned a neat three-inch oval on my leg, until I could straddle the seat and reached the prize of holding both handlebars as if to rev the engine as my mother did. At six, I climbed the tree limb stretching over our neighbor's wall to reach its forbidden apple-y fruit. I climbed to the top of our dining table and roamed it on all fours, to take in a view of the entire house, while Bố laughed and my mother scolded.

"Con khỉ! Con khỉ! (Monkey! Monkey!)" my father had called.

Now that my parents were back in Việt Nam, they did their own excited scampering. This was a welcome

On my mother's motorbike, Sài Gòn, 1971.

break from emotionally fraught reunions with family and friends. They took off by themselves to boat down the Mekong River, attend Mass at the cathedral, shop in the tourist district, and gorge on favorite fruits at market.

They also hailed taxis to take me to the Catholic hospital where my mother birthed all her children, pointing out the corner room where I was born, and to my elementary school where remarkably, a statuesque woman with gray hair in a bun opened the gates and recognized them with surprise. This was the very headmistress when my brothers and I were students. She gave us a tour, pointing out knee-high drinking fountains and holding her hand flat against the wall to show me my height when I first came to school.

One morning, my parents strolled through the French Quarter. I followed a few paces behind as they rediscovered favorite haunts—the lobby of the Continental Hotel, the Cathedral courtyard where they stole away from Bà Ngoại's strict eye for a forbidden date. After lunch, we walked a mile east toward the river until traffic ebbed and houses thinned and a grove of once grand palms marked the entrance to the zoo. They loved coming here when it was a destination, after night classes or for lunch.

That day the zoo had mostly emptied. Việt Nam's economic revival had begun but there wasn't yet a robust enough middle class to fill recreational venues like this one. On the best days, a few dozen visitors might stroll on the cracked cement walk. Exhibits were nearly bare, their neglected artificial habitats tinged red and gray from rust and lichen colonies. The few half-starved animals remaining lay or stood listlessly, as uncertain about their situation as their keepers, their ribs and facial bones jutting sharply through fur and skin.

After passing once around the zoo's perimeter walk, we came to a ten-foot-tall rusting cage in the middle of the promenade. Inside, squatting halfway up on a bare branch, were a pair of thin, raccoon-eyed golden monkeys.

My father paid a man at a cart for a bag of his warm peanuts and began passing them through the bars, slowly at first as one monkey then the other cautiously leapt down to retrieve them. The smoky aroma of nuts mixed with that of monkey urine and sweat. When the bag was empty, he went back to the cart for more.

His tossing tempo quickened with the second bag, and more with the third. He didn't feel my mother tugging at his arm. He was now trafficking peanuts between the cart and the cage as rapidly as he could, his eyes glassy and his arms clenched around multiple peanut bags at a time. He forcefully heaved peanuts in handfuls, littering the cage floor with unopened shells, then handing half-full bags over to one monkey then the other.

"He's going crazy," my mother hissed at me. "We have to get him out of here."

But I did not want, or have to, intervene. Two, three bags more, then he was spent and out of small bills, and we trailed him out the gate.

Quê Hương
(Ancestral Land)

After my parents spent two weeks in Hồ Chí Minh City, David and I flew with them to Hà Nội. From our room in a kitschy walk-up hotel in the Old City, we taxied to visit cousins, to watch water puppet shows on the big lake and gather for family dinners at late-night seafood restaurants. We strolled through cobblestone streets of art galleries, some crammed with unceremonious bins of ink or oil pastel drawings covered in plastic sheets, others with air-conditioning, credit card machines, chic lacquered wood floors and luxuriously spare white walls dotted by an occasional gilt frame. In just such a fancier gallery, my father chose a watercolor of layered jungle foliage with a village in the distance and paid to have it shipped back to Philadelphia.

At midweek, we dressed in restrained finery in keeping with the Puritan aesthetic of the north—dresses and pumps rather than jeans and sneakers, my father and David in dark suits and overcoats—and set off in a motorcade westward, away from the city. We rode in my cousin's sedan while a small band of city relatives from the nội side of the family followed in a second car and on motorbikes. Outside, the air gradually lost its petrol-infused afternotes and grew quiet, crisp, and sweet with crushed hay and wet winter soil.

More than an hour later near the far end of a two-road village, we stopped in front of a stone house. When the engines cut off, we entered to find two dozen men and women forming an arc inside the front room, and my mother and I followed Bố into their embrace.

In the center stood the smallest figure there in a dark áo giài, her still-dark hair rounded into a bun, betel-blackened teeth curved in a familiar smile, wide moon cheekbones moist with tears. My father stooped into his beloved eldest sister's arms. Bác Chịnh was the one who mothered him after my grandmother died; they were each other's favorites. They clung like that for many minutes, until someone at her elbow reassured her that we were staying. He gently pulled her arms away from Bố and turned her to lead us all into the back room.

We lunched sitting in a circle on the floor, on expensive grilled dog meat and red sticky rice, sautéed greens and shitake mushrooms, jasmine tea and sweet dried fruits, the kind of feast reserved for holidays. My cousins peppered Bố and Me with questions about everything and nothing. But my father and aunt had written many letters to each other over the years; she had few questions for him, and mostly sat beaming, basking in his face and voice. When she spoke he leaned in to listen, and the words were cloistered between them. I lost track of conversation, my eyes slipping from one parent to the other holding court.

Hours later, they led us back to the cars, but rather than turning around, the motorcade, now lengthened with more cars carrying my aunt and her children, pushed further down the road as it branched at repeated right angles and devolved into rough grooves lining long earth berms between rice field lakes. The fluid quilt of squares and quadrilaterals of water multiplied on each other's margins, until there was nothing on the horizon but the glistening green hair of rice plants.

When we finally stopped, we were on a rare plot of solid earth, barely wide enough to fit the cars and all the family, with remnant walls of a stone building and several neat rows of slim, waist-high vertical stone and wooden markers jutting out of the ground with names of the dead marked in Chinese characters chiseled or burned on their slim faces.

Visiting my father's oldest sister, Bác Chịnh (middle) with Chị Hảo, Hải Dương province, 1999.

I eased out of the back seat and moved away from the car. My city shoes sank into the mud. I breathed in water droplets and let January cold seep through my coat. In the thin air, I hallucinated wafts of incense and echoes of wailing.

This was the loamy ground that made me, nutritive matte black and fed by deep strata of decayed bones and sinews; the sky that watched my father born and his mother pass away; the crop that fed my ancestors; the half-destroyed barn where revolutionaries stoned my father's uncle to death and one of Bố's cousins now stood weeping; the marker where my grandfather lay.

My father stood there alone with his head bowed,

My paternal grandfather's grave, Hải Dương province, 1999.

the village chief come home after fifty years. He and I both wondered whether, confronted now with the safe, prosperous life and granddaughter Bố had made, Ông Nội forgave him for leaving.

My pride in helping this moment happen was marred by the way gray clouds rained memories and accusations down on Bố's shoulders. I flinched at the pain I was again triggering for him but tried to reassure myself that this was the last thing I'd ask him to endure, for now. When he finally pivoted and retraced his muddy footprints, we followed him silently and reconstituted the motorcade as the wind of centuries whistled around us.

Shield and Sword

Pregnancies are selfish by necessity. The expanding, parasitic placenta worms into your tissues. It leeches nutrients and recodes reflexes to get the new life what it needs. My body swelled after Bố and Mẹ flew home. I took my time swimming and eating, reconfiguring my walking and sleeping posture as the baby demanded.

The incubation in my belly also forced a new conservation of energy. It chipped away at the forbearance to let others project their fears and desires onto me, the openness and vulnerability required to gather morsels of history, the disciplined self-editing that kept my blunt American voice from smashing fragile, fraught relationships branching out in every direction of our lives in Việt Nam.

I had taken and given plenty since coming back to Việt Nam, and lost track of the effort it took to sustain a fair exchange, or even to do the accounting. Who owes how much of what to whom? At the end of June, six months pregnant and yearning to settle, we made farewell visits with Sài Gòn relatives. We gave Hương our remaining household items and boarded a flight eastward over the Pacific.

My parents met their grandson *in utero* at Newark International. We slept together on the car ride home to Philadelphia, three generations of Việt kiều ghosts with our layered migrations still in flight.

Back in America, we could let our guard down and be anonymous again. We began new jobs (a think tank for David, a research fellowship for me) and feathered our rented nest in downtown Baltimore. But for months, we couldn't stop talking about Việt Nam to anyone who would listen and thinking wistfully of street foods and cultural mysteries we left behind. Sometimes when the baby moved, I wondered if family stories we recovered there had seeped into his bloodstream.

My mother and Bà Ngoại stayed with us the week after Benjamin's birth, taking turns expertly swaddling and tending to him. David snapped a photo of us three mothers asleep on the same futon, with the baby between us. Sensing a new urgency, he videotaped me re-interviewing Bà Ngoại about my grandfather and their love story.

Shortly afterwards back in Philadelphia, Bà Ngoại began to deteriorate, as if the digital maw of David's camera had excised and snatched away the last thing she had to bequeath. At first we just noticed that she spoke less and forgot little things. Then over the next few months her pacing around the house slowed, and she stopped gardening.

She smiled but rarely laughed except when we put a baby in her arms. There are twenty-one cousins on my mother's side, and we birthed her great-grandbabies in a steady rhythm. She laid them on the carpet and laughingly cooed over them—"Sấu quá! Ngu quá! Hư quá!"—"How ugly! How stupid! How naughty!"—to ward off jealous evil spirits. I watched with a mix of gratitude and wistfulness, wondering if each transmission of love to the next generation sapped her and left her with less to live on.

Within two years, the most rote acts became frightening puzzles to her, the tiny sweater she crocheted for the newest baby showing tell-tale gaps where she dropped a stitch or changed direction prematurely.

I've written in a medical journal about how it all unraveled the year after Alexander's birth. How her medical care fragmented across doctors in multiple cities as she migrated among her children's houses, how we lost track of her thyroid medication while she got treatment for breast cancer, how insidious her onset of heart failure was, confounded by a quiet depression and vacantness that made it hard to take measure of her symptoms.

On her last weekend, my mother and her siblings took Bà Ngoại to the emergency room as she labored to breathe and, when confronted with the specter of intubation, decided to bring her home. They called Ân, the oldest grandchild and the type of talented clinician who could take her physical over the phone. He told them to increase her diuretic dose, and call everyone to come say goodbye.

By late the next day, lungs temporarily drained of fluid, she was awake and alert enough to sit. My uncle's house teemed with subdued relatives. I squatted in front of her and saw one last spark.

"Mai!" she said, a quiet last claim of something familiar in the sea of dark overcoming her. And then she was gone.

Hers was my first family funeral. It introduced me to the droning Buddhist service and yellow and white mourning headbands at temple, devastation on the faces of my mother and her siblings, the blinking hazard lights of our lazy motorcade along the route to and from the cemetery, muffled conversations over lunch afterwards.

I came to understand these to be all we could manage in our depleted state, after depositing her, alone, deep in a hilltop in suburban Maryland, half a world and a century from her ancestors, brother, and Ông Ngoại, in a foreign wind without polyphonic Sanskrit chants and prayer drums, without any of the muggy sweetness of overripe mango or jackfruit, of incense or dried mushrooms and radishes in open baskets at market.

My mother recovered a diamond necklace she had given Bà Ngoại and had the stones reset into a ring she passed on to me. In bed at night, before curling up in my usual dream posture, I turned the tiny stones to the palm side of my hand and folded my fingers over it. I will keep you, I promised her. You will ride to all the places I go and where you belong. You will see what I can do. You will be the shield on my back, the sword at my side.

Part Three—Remains

Un-Altered

Dissociation takes myriad forms. At one end of the spectrum, it's a natural human state. You are behind the steering wheel and realize you've driven twenty miles without remembering any of them. In that gap, you rehearsed a joke or planned tomorrow's chores, leaving the waking Self with its trained hands and feet to handle the car. It's normal and induced by boredom or random neurons firing in free association. The mind wanders but remains anchored and recognizes its host as one whole, homing back to a single consciousness.

At the far other end of the spectrum, the Self splinters into parts that may not be aware of or recognize each other, share memories, or even want to coexist. Some people refer to these parts as Alters. The mind erects barriers to contain each in its place with its own particular wounds and talents. This is the pluralism of multiple consciousnesses traveling in the same body and not normal. It is induced by trauma.

"You aren't quite there, Mai." Blue explained. "But you are much closer to that end of the spectrum than to normal."

I pushed him, "Nothing that terrible happened. My family wasn't murdered. I wasn't tortured or kidnapped. I don't live on a flood plain in Bangladesh."

I had seen unfathomable ghetto poverty in America, Việt Nam, and India, watched homeless patients die alone and anonymous in hospitals; my privilege was undeniable. Blue's advocacy on my behalf ran headlong into what my upbringing had drilled into me—my needs could never surmount others' needs; it was my job to endure through them.

He pushed right back. "You lost everything literally in one day. You wandered streets in Philadelphia alone. You felt like an alien. You were seven. And you weren't safe at home because someone was always watching you critically and with hypervigilance. The measure of what happened to you," he spoke slowly for emphasis, "is that you dissociated. It's a wildly creative and intelligent response, but not a trivial one."

"But my brothers went through similar things, and my parents went through worse…."

"They aren't my concern."

Even accepting that my dissociation was justified wasn't enough for me to own that it happened to *me*, rather than to Michael.

Between the poles of normal and splintered, the land is murkier. Descriptions in textbooks and comments from other dissociatives in online forums never quite mirrored my psychic experience. The best documented cases involved people who "flip" in and out of the material world and their inner world, or between one character and another.

That wasn't how I lived it. My awareness of and relating to my inner world was fluid and interwoven with material reality. While it was sometimes easier to focus internally in quiet times like while waiting to fall asleep in bed, that inner world often evolved or injected itself into my consciousness throughout the day. Usually, new awareness washed over me in cumulative layers as days passed, in flashes of understanding and subconscious "editing" to get at the psychically truest version of a story or character. I can't pretend to know what was happening concurrently in material reality in every instance.

Hence for you, Dear Reader, this part of the book might be particularly challenging. I mark events in my inner world with italics and try noting whenever possible where I was externally at the time. But in truth, boundaries and markers were rarely that clean. If you feel challenged to map the two realities into a unified whole, you're feeling echoes of my psychological experience.

Throughout my time with Blue, I functioned with what one of my bosses called "frightening effectiveness." I earned promotions at a regular clip while inspiring deep loyalty among my staff, made family dinners most nights, and was thoroughly immersed in my kids' joys and needs. I felt brittle and often on the precipice of shattering, but as far as anyone else could tell, I was fully present in every arena of the material world. Dissociatives make excellent compartmentalizers.

"Every dissociative configuration is different," Blue tried to reassure me, but I found the lack of benchmarks frightening and disorienting.

One Self, holding many versions but separate from them all, and feeling far away from other people. If this begins early in childhood, the adult feels hollowed out, disabled and missing memories and awarenesses, having not noticed the fragments coming off and misplacing some over the years.

If your leg were amputated and went off on its own adventures, what would you say to one another if it returned? Would you undo everything your other muscles had learned to compensate for its absence, and take it back?

"I'm crazy?" I asked Blue hopefully. I'd feel relieved and on more solid ground if he confirmed this.

"No, you're definitely not. Dissociating is what kept you from going crazy."

He grew quiet at the disappointment on my face.

Seven

Photographs do more than preserve memories. They project them from dusty recesses into consciousness, and even into flesh.

Several months after we labeled me, I brought in a manila folder to Blue, carefully packed with old pictures sampled from each life phase that I culled from my own sloppy stash and gummy albums in my parents' storage room. Nearly every face in them was smiling, snapped immediately after my father harangued us into posing.

"I thought you'd like to see the cast of characters," I explained, looking at him expectantly. He nodded eagerly. Blue confessed that therapists starve for these extra bits of data patients rarely share. He buckled his long legs together at the knees to hold the pictures on his lap as I handed them over one by one.

"These are from Sài Gòn." A family portrait with me looking sideways at baby Tuấn in his blue satin áo giài; four-year-old me under a tree at the zoo, in a yellow dress and white leather Mary Janes, toddler tummy jutting out.

"You look exactly the same," Blue said wonderingly.

"First week in Philadelphia," I announced for the next one. And there she was, the Seven-year-old. She stood in front of the Rosses' arbor gate in late spring, leaning back with Chương's hands on her shoulders, brown legs peeking out under the hem of a white shift dress, bobbed hair pulled neatly to one side under a barrette. I could barely look at her; I could feel how soft she was, even across the faded film surface.

We met the first time a few weeks before this session with Blue. I figured if Michael might leave and never be known to her, she'd need someone else to watch over her as she grew up. So, I looked for her on the path to school. I said "Hello" and crouched down to speak at her eye level. She saw I looked familiar and reached out to feel my face. I felt grateful she was so—flexible—she didn't seem to mind being the only one to see or hear me.

I took her hand and we walked to school. I told her little things in class. "See Ms. Schwartz? She's going to be Mrs. McNeil someday. That's why she's acting that way in front of Mister McNeil!" *She smiled to be in on the joke.*

Seven

Seven haunted me after that. Suddenly unmoored from her proper time and place, she hovered on the edges of my current, waking life. She appeared in the corner of my office, once on an empty subway seat. She never complained or asked for anything. She wasn't hungry or tired.

My chest filled with a suffocating burden. Neither she nor I knew what to do next. Now everywhere I looked, she was watching and waiting for help. My hesitation turned to dread. I saw a creeping puddle of inky purple spreading wherever she stood or sat. It was the color of oblivion.

"I can't take care of her," I wept to Blue. "I have enough things to worry about already. She's cold and I don't know where to put her." It was the middle of December.

"What do you need to feel more in control?" he asked.

"I just need to put her some place safe." Then my eyes widened with an idea, "How about here? Can she stay here? You could take care of her for me?" I pleaded. His office was warm with lots of soft surfaces and things to distract her.

"Of course, she's welcome to stay," he said cautiously, "but we both know that's just a temporary solution, right?"

I didn't care. I needed a break. So I left her in his office that weekend and the next. She scanned the place and explored his shelves. She spun in his chair with her feet spreading from the torque, watched while he typed, caressed the strap and buckles of his leather bag. After he turned out the lights and locked the door, she curled up in one corner of the sofa and slept.

After a couple of weeks, she felt stronger and restive. To ease her boredom, I suggested Michael take her out. It wasn't until he opened the door that I realized they had never met. O God. She startled at his height and overcoat, and the wintry air he swept in. He kept a safe distance and let her track his movements. She slowly resumed play with one eye spying his expressions. He answered questions as she asked them. Hours later, he held out a periwinkle wool coat from under his arm. They rode the elevator down and she let him take her mittened hand as they stepped out to find a snack.

"This is how a mother feels leaving her child at an orphanage," I said to Blue, my frame convulsing with guilt and fatigue, "What will happen to her?"

"You're leaving her with the person you trust most in the whole world, Mai."

I spied on them over the next few days. She tried everything Michael suggested—walking with him all the way to the river, visiting the zoo.

Then one night I came downstairs after putting the kids to bed and there she was on my sofa. Her coat was gone and Michael nowhere to be seen. Even on the dark gray upholstery I could see a creeping pool of indigo *purple spilling outward from her, viscous like an oil slick. I turned away and busied myself with dishes. At least she was warm by the radiator.*

"But she's a part of you, isn't she?" David asked. Something irritated me about his trying to shove the two of us together.

She was a living memory of me, but autonomous in her likes, dislikes and trajectory, visible to me only through a gauzy haze. She grew her own relationship with Michael in just a few weeks. And here she was clearly waiting for someone to give her something she needed.

I puzzled over her. I brought her paper and crayons, put out milk and soup, showed her where the kids' games were stashed. She glanced politely at my offerings but didn't budge. She began to shrink, as if someone were turning down her dial.

"I give up," I announced to Blue. I was failing.

"You're a mother; you'll figure it out. Why not just hold her?"

Because I'd get smeared with all that ink, I thought.

Then one night, it hit me. The damn dress and shoes. They were stiff and itchy and weighed her down. I rifled through closets and brought down clothes for her to pick through. She perked her eyebrows and chose a stretchy red, pink, and black Custo Barcelona shirt with embroidery and mesh down the sleeves, a pair of flared jeans, and white ankle socks. We threw away the barrette and roughed up her bob with pomade, for a little punk. I found an old pair of glasses that fit her; the prescription hadn't changed all that much.

She bounced off the sofa and cruised around the house inspecting toys and cookware. She peeked over Benjamin's shoulder at the marble chute he was building and tapped gently on a few piano keys.

Then she saw David. She climbed onto the kitchen stool next to his and watched his hands on the laptop. She looked my way and, sensing permission, reached out and touched his face, the five o'clock shadow pleasantly gritty beneath her fingers. She liked how his eyes were hazel enough to see the pupils' outlines. His eyelashes curled, which was novel. She compared his pink skin to her brown and traced one large vein up his arm. He swung her onto his lap and brought up a new web browser screen to show her how to use it. I saw her mouthing the order of the Q-W-E-R-T-Y keys.

Over the following days, her cheeks plumped out and she developed a voracious appetite. Something about the way she now moved atomized the ink and made it evaporate. I strung a hammock across the second-floor landing and made her a bed in it of blankets and cushions. She read books and Googled her way around the world. She listened to indie rock on the radio and made paper monsters with Alexander. My girlfriends took turns taking her out to museums. Every day there was something new.

Little Girls

Seven paved the way for others to appear. Soon after she settled into her routine, a Four-year-old and a Baby arrived together at our house. Four took off on bare feet around the first floor, while Baby cruised haltingly on furniture edges. Seven heard their ruckus and came to sit at the top of the stairs, scrunching her nose at the whirlwind below. Four opened up cabinet doors and spilled out board games and puzzles. She began to hum ditties in French and English, looking up occasionally to repeat them for Baby.

I strung up a second hammock for Four, realizing Baby would have to sleep in bed with me and David, and then I glimpsed a shadow by the kitchen counter. This one was taller and quiet, a Teen, with early curves around her breasts and hips, long hair spilling limply past her shoulders, and the saddest face of all. She watched the others' movements protectively. Whenever Four temporarily settled in one spot, Teen moved through the room restoring order. Tidying up seemed to cheer her. I strung up a third hammock.

Seven finally came downstairs when she saw Teen. She carried a sketch she had worked on all morning to show her older sister. Four begged loudly to see it too, ignoring Seven's scowls, until Teen refereed a compromise and they each went back to their own spaces. Brat! I heard Seven thinking. But Four was happy and oblivious, barely pausing to take a breath between her songs.

"The house is filled with little girls," I said cheerfully to David that night. I told him about the hammocks and that Baby was between us in bed, asleep in the shadow of his heat, her dimpled arms and legs wrapped around a hot dog pillow, a koala on a limb. I felt him stiffen.

"She doesn't take up much space," I reassured him, but he said nothing.

"Are you just tired, or freaked out?" I asked more quietly.

"Freaked out, I think."

I was afraid to move. I heard his breathing slow and waited for sleep to drug the whole house, then snuck downstairs and lay down on the rug in front of the stove, tucking knees to my chest. David found me there in the morning. My eyes were puffy and I averted them from everything.

"How are you feeling?" he asked.

"Crazy."

It took three weeks to negotiate with Blue to let David come into session with me, so Blue could explain to him that dissociation—the experience of it—often becomes more dramatic before it would seem, from the outside, to get better as one achieves "recovery."

"Tell David how you want to be listened to when you talk about it," Blue nudged.

I wanted him to recognize that I'm still me, to believe I'm doing my best and moving in the right direction. I wanted to feel ... safe.

Blue looked past me to lock eyes with David, "Safety is *very* important to a dissociative."

David nodded almost imperceptibly.

By then it was late winter. I craved any excuse to curl under bedcovers, sinking into warmth radiating from David. But my sense of safety was an illusion; remove external stimuli and all that's left is the dangerous quiet of within.

Hold me, I begged Michael. So he did. And then a new temptation came, one so brilliant I wondered I had never thought of it before during all the past bad times.

"What would you do," I gingerly asked Blue, "if Michael and I switched places?"

I sounded matter-of-fact. Not seeing any impishness in my face, he arched an eyebrow and straightened in alert. "I would work *very* hard to get you back, Mai."

"Maybe you could get farther with him than with me, you know? You two could work while I rested. No one would notice. He could do my job with his left hand. And he loves Benjamin and Alexander. He'd take good care of them. It would just help to have a break."

I could go back to Rich's house. There wasn't much of it left, but surely I could find one bedroom with thick walls, a bed with a deep mattress and lovely white sheets and pillows, someone to close the drapes and remove clocks to let me sleep as long as I wanted.

"Maybe that would be true," Blue said, unconvinced. "It sounds like a very compelling place; or at least, it was. It's a *memory* of a very compelling place ... but it's not real, Mai."

I brushed him aside. Real is what I felt.

A few nights later I tried willing it to happen. I slept so deeply in a bed in Rich's house I didn't feel the hands pulling on my wrists at first. It was Michael. I squirmed to loosen his grip, but he heaved me off the mattress. Icy air. Searing pain in my throat and ribcage. He shoved me out of the safe house, back into my body. Nooooo! I screamed, but he cupped his hands over his ears and disappeared.

I crouched in a heap on the floor, groggy. Before my eyelids fell, my friend Phoebe rushed in. Hey there! Up you go! She shoved an empty garbage bag into my hand and hustled me around the room. The place was a mess. I shoved trash into the bag. More girlfriends came with bags and brooms. I was exhausted but they stayed in my face with persistent cheer until we piled bags high.

I glimpsed Blue slipping out the door. Phoebe whispered, It was his idea for you to clean out this place, you know. They wrapped me in a coat, then shoved a ticket in my hand. Time to go! You'll miss your train if you don't hurry. Someone drove me in the dark to the station and pulled me up to the platform. I boarded, knowing I just left my house, and yet was headed home. I fell into a window seat, soaked with fatigue. Blue dropped into the aisle seat beside me to keep creeps away. He tipped my head onto his shoulder, and I slept all the way home.

I looked at him quizzically the next day in his office. "What a lot of trains you must have to ride...." I said.

Cells

Over the following weeks, the Little Girls wandered farther and farther from the house.

I tracked them while walking to the metro, alone in my office, or at night just after Benjamin and Alexander were in bed and David was deep in his own head with reading or computer coding. They tended to come out when other stimuli ebbed.

But Michael began to fade. At least, he hollowed out, not just receding from my consciousness as he often did whenever my waking life was consuming, but fading, losing random pixels and mass. It now took effort to see and feel him at night. I had betrayed him by speaking too much about him out loud. Harsh daylight and Blue's scrutiny vaporized him. I strained to recover him, retold myself his story again and again to reinforce his flesh, to little effect.

"This feels like speed therapy," I said in a strained voice.

"I think that's accurate," Blue agreed. "You work very fast in here, just like you do out there in the world. But you're the one setting the pace, Mai, not me. I advise slowing down."

My grief was overwhelming. Blue braced for it and seemed relieved each time the sobbing began. I was the only one who could mourn Michael and I wept because of that, too.

He had no house left, no family, no Rich.

My despair ballooned, loud enough to speak for them all. It was nothing like watching a friend die of illness with time to say goodbye. Michael thinned, his layers peeling off, until he was no more convincing than a sketch. I wept for the memory of him.

"I can't imagine what it's like to have something so integral ripped out of you," Blue whispered, "especially when it's you doing the ripping."

My wailing got louder. "*You* did this. *You* made this happen!" I hurled at him.

"Mai, it's really hard for me to accept responsibility for this. I'm the one who tries to point out that Michael protects you. You're going through a rough time, and you could use some protection. I'm the one who's been urging you to use Michael more, not less."

He was wrong. I could still conjure Michael but now saw him through a one-way glass. *His focus shifted to some inner work of his own; he couldn't take care of me anymore.*

"It doesn't matter what I want. Once there's a crack in the bubble, all my stories fly out."

"…Well, I do buy that imagery." But all Blue seemed capable of doing was to watch with pity.

Focus, I coached myself. What can I salvage? Michael was the keeper of all my stories as I was of his. He guarded the safe places we built, the ways we had grown up together. I had to recover everything he remembered before it was lost. That flash of understanding recalled my sense of relief with the recovery of each of my ancestors' stories over the years. Safeguarding our stories were table stakes, an existential defense against the void of forgottenness.

Over the next few weeks, I reached into what was left of his gray eyes and clawed it all out, one fistful at a time, blinking as his blood spewed and mixed with my tears.

And as I did this, my insides roiled and reorganized, each cell negotiating a new state of being. My metabolism went wild.

Now when I walked out the house for work each morning, breathing felt like drinking pure oxygen and made me giddy. I had to stop still and swivel my head, slowly scanning the horizon to find solid bearings. I could see farther than before. My joints creaked from expansion and my hands swelled, not with fluid but muscle, adding pounds to the strength of my grip. My fingertips felt more calloused than I remembered. My stride lengthened. And when I spoke, my voice rang with a new, deep timbre and pounced forward, leaving just a ghostly echo in my head.

I remembered feeling bulky walking around Sài Gòn as an adult, swinging my arms while staring passersby straight in the eye, taking up space and oxygen like an entitled Westerner. But now back in Washington, the American capital of power and ego, I warily waited for people to notice what was happening to me, and for signals that I was overstepping.

"And has anyone said anything remotely like that to you?" Blue challenged.

"No, but I can't tell what they're thinking because they're all three feet taller than me."

He eyed the length of me. "How tall *are* you, Mai?"

"Five foot one."

"Hmm. I have a very odd relationship with height, you know. Partly it's that I'm taller than most people and it's hard to judge the height of someone shorter. But most of the time, I'm also talking with people who are sitting down. I've found I grossly mis-estimate my patients' heights."

"Do you tend to overestimate or underestimate?"

"Both. I'm so grossly wrong all the time that I realized it must be purely psychological."

"How tall did you think I was?" I asked timidly.

His eyes widened, "Much taller than five-foot-one." He leaned in, "You are doing all kinds of things Michael used to do. *You* are taking care of the Little Girls. Everyone in your professional life *does* listen to you. They *do* turn to you. It has been obvious to everyone except you for a long time, Mai. You are six feet tall when you open your mouth. You just hadn't been willing to accept that before now. Could that be why you're sending Michael away?"

Art

I considered myself an art pretender. Chương was the talented one in the family. My parents and I competed silently over the years to squirrel away things he made that he was willing to part with—casual charcoal sketches, paintings, small classical plaster and clay sculptures. When his engineering firm transferred him to a new city as a recent college grad, he decided to ditch his old furniture, sketched out designs for a table and went in search of a fabricator to make it. The carpenter he found offered to pay him for the drawings instead. He was frustrated that my parents were not willing to pay for him to leave an Ivy League school to enter an art conservatory, though his engineering, law, and business degrees eventually gave him the financial freedom to return to art in midlife. His house was covered in murals painted in free hand, his basement populated by silent clay statues, the garage and porches taken over by boxes of resin, sculpting tools, and paints.

I had decent enough draftsmanship to win some school awards, but realism was effortful for me. Instead, I gravitated toward the fantastical, hugging a book about the

Warrior. **Watercolor and pencil on paper.**

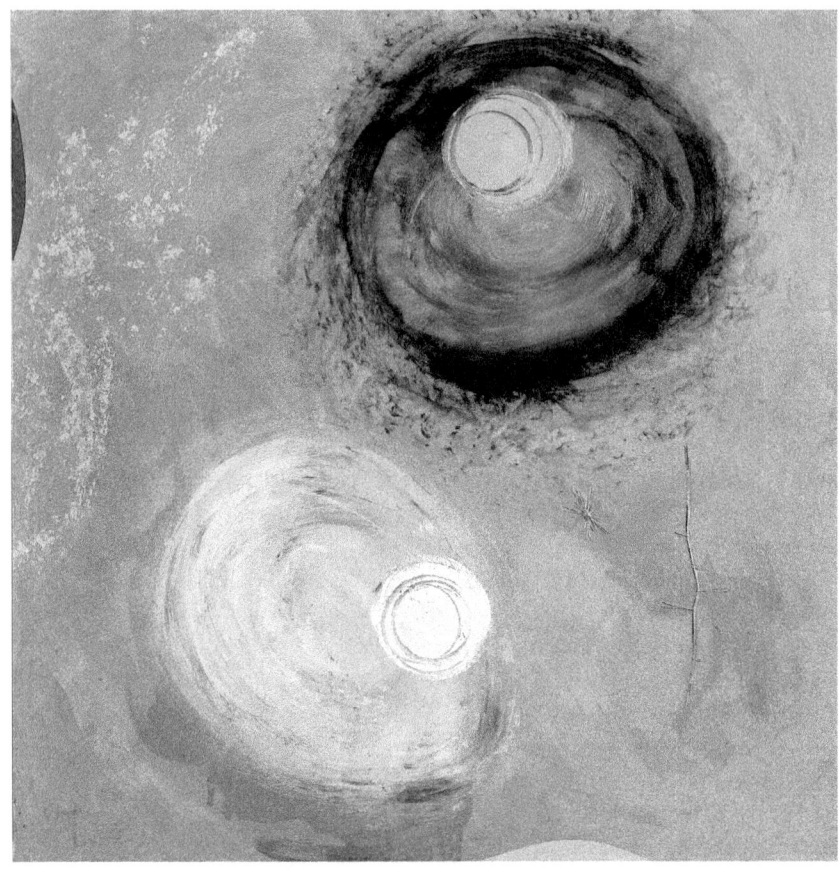

Ovale. Acrylic and silk thread on canvas.

painter Florine Stettheimer for years and gifting Bà Ngoại a portrait of her in that style before we returned to Việt Nam. It felt amateurish and flat, more valuable for the sentiment than anything else.

I finally found my art through my time with Blue, at first using large canvases to portray my psychological journey and eventually finding confidence to let go of self-editing and insecurity about my colorblindness, straying into a variety of media. [Maiphamart.com]

I claimed Reds of my childhood dreams and Oranges of my quest for Tibet.

I painted a portrait of Blue in swirls of indigo and purple.

I recorded my sense of fragmentation on a diptych of bisected trees and leaves swept by wind.

I honored our time in Việt Nam by painting abstract jewel-toned weavings from ethnic minority tribes.

Split. Acrylic and paper on canvas.

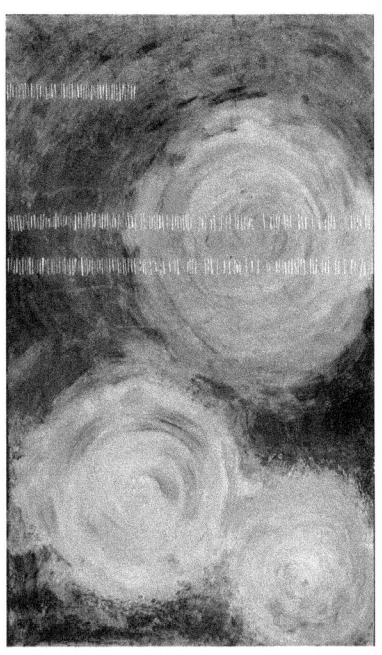

Matte Blue, No Purple. Acrylic and paper on canvas.

I experimented with themes of transformation in paper sculptures.

I collaborated with Benjamin and Alexander on a meditative piece of wood shavings that took years to complete.

Threads. Acrylic and paper on canvas.

Rotation 1. Paper.

Rotation 4. Paper.

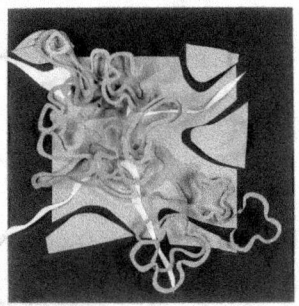

Rotation 2. Paper.

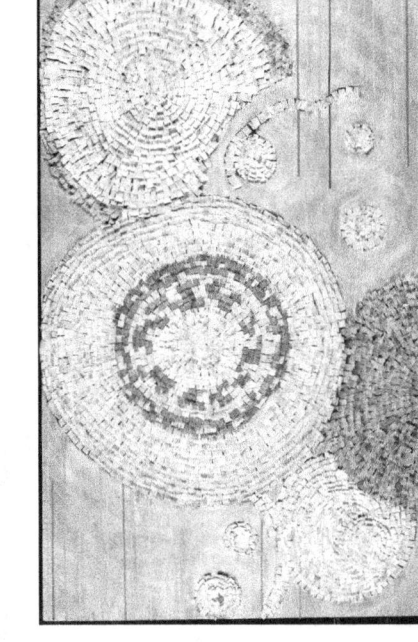

Salvage. Acrylic, paper, and wood shavings on canvas.

Rotation 3. Paper.

Tango. Steel washers.

Treasure. Steel washers, Japanese glass fishing buoy.

She Waited Until. Steel washers.

I used steel to explore the dualities of softness and strength, the safety and permeability of relationships, motherhood, and dreams.

I'm never confident in the value of my art to others, having only ever sold pieces for charity auctions. But I know creating it was sublimation of all the creative mental energy that had previously gone into building my inner world.

Tango

Summer dance camp was six days of fluttering REM sleep. Every August since our children were out of diapers, we went to the same family dance and music camp. We fled the city to exhale in the twenty-degree temperature dip, to indoctrinate the kids in folky ways, to let them see grownups unafraid of being silly, to waft lazily uphill when the dining hall bell clanged and downhill when the trombone and ukuleles called. We packed the car with board games, clogs and flip flops, ideas for a skit and fancy things for the parade. Just beyond the edge of Washington's megalopolis civilization, north of Winchester, Virginia, we'd bend west into West Virginia and up into the Alleghenies on a red dirt road winding through summer storms and thirsty trees, past the fossil quarry nearly spent from three decades of invasion by summer children, to Timber Ridge Camp on the bank of the Cacapon River.

The summer after the Little Girls arrived, I picked a tango class at camp. When class was over on the first day and people streamed to the large hall for family gathering, I hid away in our cabin while my sweat evaporated, lying down with what happened two days before in session. Blue believes patients tend to keep conversations benign just before vacations in kind of a wind-down mode, but rarely was that true of me. I wanted to talk about Michael.

"What happened to Michael between when his parents died and when Rich found him?" Blue asked.

"He lived in his uncle's house for a year before Rich rescued him."

"What was his uncle's house like?"

It was a predictable question, yet for some reason I hadn't been aware of the answer until Blue asked. His office began to feel cavernous, the corners darkening and receding. Or I was getting smaller.

"What are you feeling?" Blue asked gently, seeing my forehead furrow.

"...I don't know." It was puzzling, this sensation of a heavy, dark lens falling before my eyes.

"That's okay." He leaned back. "Why don't you just feel it for a while?"

The drowsiness of my self-induced trance was a long, silent suction. It wasn't interrupted by narcoleptic jerks into consciousness; it wasn't sleep. An anesthetic potion, a portal. Red, the color behind my eyelids except my eyes were open, if just barely. Red, the color of my dreams.

"I'm backing away," I struggled to slur out.

"Why?"

"To keep my peripheral vision as wide as possible." My breathing deepened. My eyes swung to the left, to the right and back to center again. "There's a light." Flicker.

"What happens with the light?" His voice traveled to me in slow motion.

"It's coming towards me." My tongue was so heavy I had to itemize instructions to the muscles to make it move.

"Am I in the room with you, Mai? Or am I behind the light?"

Flicker. He couldn't be behind the light; I wasn't afraid of him. "You're in the room with me. I'm backing up. They're coming closer." The words came with too much effort to explain that the zone of light was much wider than me, wind licked the back of my neck, and They were circling around me. I knew I would surrender in the end.

"Who? Who's coming closer?" When I couldn't answer, he raised his voice slightly. "You don't have to stay in that place, Mai."

No, no. Please let me see what happens. Flicker. Hand. Cool air. Flick. Fingertips landing, tented on something smooth, shadows underneath.

"My hand is on the wall." It's such a little hand.

"You don't have to stay in that place, Mai." His tone was sharper, loud, then stern. "Look at me a minute!" Fighting gravity on my eyelids, I finally obeyed. He sprang into action.

"It's Friday morning in August 2009. It's a beautiful sunny day in Washington, and you are wearing a fabulous blue dress. Come back to *this* place."

Unable to telegraph him or fight his increasingly urgent rhythm, I slurred out through lips disengaged from my jaw, "I can't move my legs!"

Was I going to die, frozen like this? Where were my thighs?

He nodded and softened his tone. "You have vacation coming up. Tomorrow you're leaving the city with David and the kids and you'll have a lovely week in the mountains. Then we'll both come back here and talk more about today, but not until then."

In a leap, my right hand flashed up to grab the pendant at my neck and my legs gradually thawed. Palpitations made my head jerk slightly from each volley of blood.

"I don't like surprises. I've never liked them. I don't like Beethoven. I don't like loud noises or people sneaking up on me. It took David years to learn that; he still pounds on the piano. It's not *funny*!"

Blue pulled his chair forward, nodding. "In this room, you don't have to say more than once that you don't like surprises…. What would help right now, Mai?"

"I don't know…." I hesitated for just a moment, "…fried chicken."

"Really?" He sounded disbelieving but impressed. "Well, did you know," he leaned in conspiratorially, "there's a Popeye's at 14th Street?"

"No way. How do you know that?" What I wanted was for him to be quiet and let me think, but he kept pricking me with his prattle.

"I know things," he crooned like a girlfriend. "I used to live around here. I'm constantly frustrated by how hard it is to find good soul food in this supposedly southern town. And the best thing is, Mai—it's a *drive-thru*."

"So I don't have to park the car?"

"Nope. You just roll right in and out!" He smirked in satisfaction.

I fingered my pendant furiously, craving for the drowsiness to return, searching for the wall. "This banter is fine," I told him, "but now I know this thing is out there."

Only three minutes left in the hour. He scooted to the edge of his chair and got in my face. "Listen to me. As your *shrink*, I'm telling you to not think about this for the next week. Stop thinking about it *right now*! You haven't thought about it for many, many years; one more week is not going to make a difference."

He pointed a finger at me then at his own chest. "You're going away, and I'm going away. This is a really bad time to start opening stuff up. Go dancing and be with your kids."

In the first day of tango class, our debonair teacher gave a tutorial about Argentine tango. His face pinched in bliss as he described his love affair with it, the high cheekbones tilted up and eyes softly closed as if to inhale the dance.

"Tango is an invitation."

He asked us to name the most essential elements. "Being connected to the floor," someone said. "Being connected to the music. Eye contact." He straightened at that last one.

"Is eye contact really important? Where are the answers in tango?" he asked rhetorically, looking at each of us in challenge. "The answer is not on the floor, so don't bother looking there. It's not where the musicians are. And the answer is not in your partner's eyes. The answer … is on your partner's *chest*."

He placed his hand on his sternum for punctuation and pulled a svelte teenager into place facing him. He demonstrated, pushing and pulling their collective weight forwards and backwards, pivoting slowly until her legs were scissored between his, then reversing the rotation.

"If my chest moves, your chest moves. If your chest moves, my chest moves.... If my chest moves and yours doesn't, we will fall apart."

He asked the men to stand in a circle, facing outwards, then the women in another circle around the men, facing inwards.

"Close your eyes!"

The music began and hands groped within each pair to find her waist, his shoulders. We swayed in place, motored by the piano baseline and something else. After a few minutes, he had women rotate one man over. And in the darkness behind my eyes, every sweaty, tall, short, lean, fat, strong, wispy, shy, confident man had his own palpable center of gravity. My chest blindly centered on his, and this centripetal force bound us to the circle and the dance.

After class the second day, I snuck into the arts and crafts cabin and tore off two yards of butcher paper, then picked out markers in three colors—for streets in Mt. Airy, for buildings, and for places I couldn't remember well. Back on our cabin floor, I began with Lincoln Drive intersecting Mt. Pleasant Avenue on one end and splintering into side streets. Next I drew squares for the Rosses' house, our house, school, the library, the Lutheran church where my Girl Scout troop met. With the last color, I drew splotches where the entrance to Wissahickon Creek might've been, the Egans' house, and the MacGregors.' I pulled a pen from my purse and etched a broken line along paths I walked over thirty years ago until the sheet was covered in ant tracks. I carefully violated Blue's instructions; so many of these places had walls.

The next week, I showed the map to Blue, unfolding it on the floor between our feet.

"It's so barren," he said. "Where were the trees and flowers? Where were the people? Did no one hear you walking all those places?"

"No, they did not." I drew horses, people, and pretty scenery throughout years of art classes. This map was about finding the wall. I left enraged, not caring what he did with the map. He carefully stored it in his closet, pulling it back out when I asked a couple weeks later.

For months, I seethed at our failure to find our way back to that place, that room, where surely all the answers lay. I couldn't forgive Blue for interrupting my trance. He was indifferent to my anger at first, but years later would say he regretted being so overprotective in the moment; he hadn't expected it would be so hard to reproduce that state of awareness in me.

I once asked if he or someone else would hypnotize me, but he discouraged the idea, worried I was so suggestible that neither of us would know whether insights under hypnosis were reliable.

Eventually, we pivoted this way and that, our chests in locked in synchrony, and found our way into other rooms, as he knew we would.

Eight

Two more seasons passed after the map, by then my third year with Blue. It was late spring, when I should have had no reason to think of an icy bridge. My triggers usually came in moments of mindfulness, shoved forward by a rebellious subconscious. I was merely lazing on our sofa after clearing away dinner one night, when the scene flitted in front of me.

Flash. My boots clapping on bent wooden steps of the foot bridge over train tracks, the one on my way to school, slipping when I stepped on bird crap. Wooden walls, holes in the roof, an arch in the center. Stairs bend into a blind corner at the other end of the bridge.

Commuters pass in opposite directions as floorboards shake with the putt-putt-putt of a rail car half a station away. Why don't they mind the smell? Mildew patches creep on the planks. Peeling paint the nauseating color of manila hangs and waves dementedly from the rafters.

Bird shit lacquers the mold and my eyes spin in shades of gray, yellow, brown. More feet pounding. Bird shit. DON'T TOUCH IT. WALK FASTER. CAN'T MOVE. KNEES WON'T FLEX. DON'T TOUCH! CAN'T FEEL MY FEET. FUCKING BRIDGE.

"What pisses me off about that bridge," I leveled at Blue the next morning, "is there are actually people in the neighborhood campaigning to have it restored." I had searched online to see if it had changed at all in thirty years.

He waited.

"You can't restore something that *rotten*. You can't save it. You have to blow it up. THEY SHOULD BLOW IT UP."

He eyed my fists and froze, averting his eyes. This was his playing-dead technique whenever I verged on violence. "How would you go about that?" he asked in monotonic deadpan.

"Dynamite. Not the kind that makes a pile of rubble, the kind that vaporizes everything."

"And then what?"

"I'd put up a new bridge. People still have to get to the train platforms somehow. A steel bridge maybe; something modern. *That* won't rot or rust.

It should have a real roof so fucking birds can't get in so easily, and plexi-glass for walls."

"Why?"

"So people can see in."

"See in. Who can see in?"

"*ANYBODY.*" The shout faded after four heaving breaths.

"There's a Little Girl curled up in a fetal position on the bridge," I said quietly. "She's naked. Her body is scorched. She looks like a piece of bacon, like how Napalm girl in that Việt Nam war photo would've looked if she stopped running from the bombs. You know the picture I'm talking about?"

"Yes, I do…. How did she get that way, Mai?"

"I don't know. She's in a coma. She can't say anything."

I couldn't tell if there was soft tissue left on her bones. There had to be; she still had hair.

"How old is she?"

"Eight. Maybe nine. No, Eight. Seven knows something's up. She got so agitated last night, I had to bring her into our bed so she wouldn't wake up the others. She kept blubbering, 'Where's my sister?' I didn't even know she knew she had a sister." *She must've caught me looking at the Eight-year-old. It's hard to sneak things past them.*

Blue raised an eyebrow. "What happens to the Eight-year-old if the bridge blows up? What would Seven think?"

He often played this maternal card on me. I stared back threateningly. "Sometimes you just do what you have to do." *You make sacrifices.*

"You could. But that won't really solve anything, will it?"

I left hissing. I hissed at Blue, at the Fucking Bridge, at her. This one was *not* going to fall on me. I would have *nothing* to do with her.

I left Blue's office and pounded down inert escalator steps above the metro station. The digital message board announced a train in four minutes then changed its mind to eight. Fucking Red Line. Change trains. Close the office door; don't slam it. My throat closed. Open Outlook on the desktop. Fucking Microsoft. Useless email. Delete, delete, delete.

Spent by night, in bed with my back turned to David and the soles of my feet planted on his thigh for warmth, something relented slightly. I was all she had. I let the scene play out before falling asleep.

I dialed 911 and told them what they needed to know. An ambulance pulled up alongside the bridge. Oblivious commuters passed as paramedics lifted a gurney up the slouching steps and wrapped her in white sheets while leaving the stretcher's nylon straps to dangle unbuckled, afraid the friction might rub off what muscle was left.

The hospital burn unit droned with monitoring equipment and redundant alarms. She lay in a glass-walled cubicle, melting into shadows after her nurse turned off the light. They didn't bother putting a catheter in her bladder; with organs shut down and tissues desiccated, it would be eons before she could make pee. She should have died, but wouldn't.

After watching her sleep a few moments, I fled from the hospital back to our house to put on rubber soled shoes, then grabbed David's work gloves and an axe; I don't know how to use explosives. I snuck out and in an instant flew to the bridge.

Angled light beams from lamps towering over the tracks clearly marked a wall panel. I swung the axe from right to left, then up to down. Each crack rent the cold quiet and left my arms and shins vibrating from the force of contact, my boots swiveling on bird shit. When the splintering had made a jagged hole the size of a suitcase I moved on to the next wall panel. At the top of the arch, I'd made my point. My shoulders burned as adrenaline ebbed. I let the axe drop on the landing in case someone else wanted to finish the job. The handle had no fingerprints.

Rain

My external life completely masked the turmoil in my inner world during these years of confrontations with Michael and my other characters. I got another promotion at work and had enough interesting projects to turn away new ones. We helped to start a charter school in our neighborhood. I was part of the team organizing the art gala fundraiser, which meant I also made art to put in the show. And David and I arranged our work schedules so we could pick the kids up after school almost every day. My afternoons were filled with playdates, scrambling to put dinner on the table, and teaching Benjamin and Alexander that nature is wondrous, by bundling them under blankets on the porch to watch storms.

We learned about Alexander's autism when he was eight, in a meandering string of evaluations from multiple psychologists that we would only realize years later took too much precious time. We smilingly reinforced for him that this was just one of the things that made him special. He still oozed an elfin charm and confidence then. His doctors gave little guidance. We didn't foresee or understand all the traps and worry that lurked in this new territory of parenting.

I casually mentioned to my parents that I was seeing a therapist and taking medication but told them and my brothers nothing about the roiling contents of my mind. They didn't probe.

May, and it was gray.

"I'm not depressed," I explained to Blue, "My legs aren't giving out under me. See?" I stomped on the floor to demonstrate. "I'm doing everything I need to. There's just a ... sadness."

He nodded.

"Have you ever been to the tropics?" I asked him.

"Yes."

"The kind of tropics with dry seasons and wet seasons?"

"Yes."

In Sài Gòn, it rains most days. Even in the dry season, at 4:30 every afternoon, skies open and weep. You can set your watch by it. Rain washes away all the dust, sewer smells and exhaust so everything can start over.

But in wet seasons, rain is constant. Wet seasons in Hanoi are cold and filthy. A towel left on the floor for three minutes will grow mushrooms. In Sài Gòn, sometimes the rain is "lai rai"—on and off, light, pretty. Hold your hand out flat with palm downward and spread the fingers, then wave it gently back and forth in a figure eight the way a light breeze helps an oak leaf float to the ground. Like that.

"Your seasons are changing?" he asked.

I ignored him. Sometimes the rain isn't lai rai. Then it's torrential, but everyone still has errands to do. Our moped drivers, two brothers-in-law who loyally perched at the end of our alley and always prioritized me over other fares, thought I was crazy to go out with them rather than in a taxi in such weather, but I'm a lady and they took me where I asked to go.

Streets were much emptier when it rained like that. Most people held back and waited. I wore a poncho and the electric blue bike helmet made a small ledge over my eyes, but it didn't matter. I was wet through in seconds. Sheets and sheets of water. When I got to wherever I was going, I dripped from my neck, my legs, the seat of my pants.

"You don't want to go where you're headed?" Blue tried again.

No. It's raining. My eyelashes were poor windshield wipers every time I blinked but I couldn't turn back because I was far from home by then and I'd have to go back out in the rain to get home.

Blue's eyes wandered to the clock, "I'm afraid we have to stop now."

Something crumpled inside and my hands flew to my face as the tears began. With a quick collapse, he sloped his long frame down into the well of his chair so his head was on level with mine. The chair had not moved, yet somehow I could now see every eyelash and detail on his face. He dropped his voice to its gentlest and most confiding.

"Tell me what you're feeling...."

It's hard to exaggerate Blue's empathic powers when they're fully unleashed. They are so reflexive I was sure they were mutant, superhuman and innate, not possibly a result of training. His face often reflected my emotions almost before I was aware of them. The feedback loop compelled honesty.

"I feel like I'm failing. I'm doing everything I'm supposed to, and I feel like I'm failing." My internal ripping was almost audible.

"You couldn't be more wrong, Mai. You feel like you're failing and you are so profoundly not. You've been walking in the rain this whole time."

Smash

Pluralitas non est ponenda sine necessitate
(Entities should not be multiplied unnecessarily)
—William of Ockham

I'm a physician and scientist. An honest living for me depends on knowing when and how to apply Ockham's razor. Ockham, a medieval Franciscan friar, was the unlikely anti-mythologist, the killjoy who derisively rejected all supernatural causes. He promoted the theorem that the simplest explanations are likely the truest ones.

In medical training, attending physicians drill a version of this principle into their trainees—Don't go looking for something that's not there. You don't need to give the patient three diseases if one will explain everything.

Except, sometimes there was more than one. That's why we perked up at grand rounds, not only to catch glimpses of the fascinomas—cases of rare diseases named for dead white men who first identified them—but also for the unsolved mysteries, cases where no one or two concomitant disease states explained everything going on in the single human being, when stray facts dangled outside the neatness of diagnoses.

These mysteries imposed humility. They forced us to let go of tidy explanations, of the need to know everything with certainty after a patient recovers and we still don't have all the answers. Reality often disrespects Ockham.

I asked Blue if being a refugee with a lonely childhood alone was enough to trigger dissociation.

"Yes, absolutely."

"So do you think I should stop searching for whether something else happened?"

"That's not for me to say, Mai. I will follow you to wherever you feel you need to go."

A few weeks later, Eight was still asleep in the ICU, but her condition had stabilized.

I walked to work past Victorian row houses and their tiny gardens spilling over with spring flowers. Around the corner, the stoops grew grander, porch lights marking eleven foot tall ceilings. These houses faced onto the park and had English basement apartments tucked under them with a smidgen of light passing in.

I didn't understand why my feet hesitated at the first house. Steps curving down to its basement were half the width of normal, its narrow door so shrouded in shadow I couldn't make out the color. As if the passageway was not tight enough, a locked bicycle on the railing blocked half of it.

I lurched forward, thinking of things that might hide in the dark tunnel. But the next house had a dark basement door too, and the next. I crossed the street and cut across the park. I couldn't remember anymore what was hopeful about the day or feel where the pressure from my feet should have transmitted through my femurs to my pelvic girdle.

The next morning before the kids woke up, David lightly ran his fingers across my shoulders, back, and thighs, his usual signal that he wanted sex. I kept my eyes closed against the early light.

"I'm tired, but you can use me if you want," I said softly. He went about it quietly.

Then I felt his arm under my chin. He was bracing himself. My eyes sprang open and my throat closed. When he finished, I exercised restraint to give him a gentle push to free myself.

"What did you really want to do?" Blue asked.

"Throw him against the wall and listen for the thud."

"Why? What did you feel?"

"Nothing. I felt nothing. I still feel nothing. The whole way to work and here I kept jabbing myself with a fork, just to feel something." I demonstrated with a fingertip in my left bicep, eyeing the divot it made with satisfaction. His left eyebrow rose in apprehension.

"Metaphorically," I reassured him.

"How often does this happen with David?"

"Rarely. He rarely puts his arm at my throat. I should tell him I don't like it. He couldn't have known."

"It's true. After all, you did invite him."

Another couple minutes of silence and he tried a different tack. "Dark basement entryways seem rather vaginal, don't you think?"

I scanned the office, desperate for a change in subject. The framed paper sculpture I had made for him for our one-year anniversary hung on the wall to my left.

"Did other people give you everything on your walls in here?" I asked.

"Why do you want to know?"

"Because I'm curious whether you chose any of these for yourself. Like those photographs." I gestured to a trio of black-and-white pictures of a fountain, a building, and a park hanging above his desk.

"What would you guess?" he asked.

I stood up then and turned my back on him to walk over to the wall. Leaning over his desk, I inspected the composition, the contrast, the quality of the matting.

"Probably some things you chose and some things people gave you. I think someone gave you these photographs because they seem trite and inanimate, kind of inoffensive. I think you're more likely to choose less neutral things for yourself."

I sat back down.

He tilted back onto his headrest. "That was kind of aggressive, and flirty."

"Isn't flirting always aggressive?" I retorted with a smile.

"I suppose…….Did you, by any chance…. Did you do that just to feel something?"

"Yeah, I'm pretty sure I did."

Numb

"Did you tell David you wanted to throw him against the wall?" Blue asked.

"No, why would I do that?" It was only one week later. Not enough time had passed for me to process.

He raised an eyebrow. "How do you talk with each other about sex?"

"The sex is wonderful," I reassured him, not answering his question. "It's wonderful now, better and better all the time, much better than in the beginning."

"How so?"

"In the beginning, it hurt. Penetration hurt. We used condoms back then; I think the spermicide was irritating on my tissues. I found ways to minimize it. I gave him a lot of hand jobs." I said it sheepishly.

"Did he complain?"

"No. He was always very sweet. That's why I wanted to make him happy. We did it that way a lot. It was almost meditative. I could think while doing it."

"What would you think about?"

"...mostly Michael."

My Vietnamese boyfriend in college talked me into the charade that sex without intercourse would maintain our virginity. One afternoon, I lay on my stomach on his bed, drowsily scanning a philosophy text. He undid my socks, my jeans, gently slid the book onto the floor. When I thought he was done, I drifted off to sleep. He whispered to me as I woke up,

"Don't ever do that again. Don't ever go to sleep without finishing me off."

I only told David the story in our fifth year together.

"Sometimes I'm just tired, I explained, and I don't want you to start sex because maybe I won't have the energy to finish it."

He was furious it had taken me so long to tell him, furious at the old boyfriend. "That was just mean," he hissed under his breath, holding me tight and soaking my tears into his shirt.

And yet by this point in our marriage and my time with Blue, I had become familiar with and quietly enraged about a duality within David—that he could project protectiveness and tenderness outwardly toward other women as easily as he would inwardly toward me.

They tended to feel some sort of void in their lives or had a taste for variety. Often it was just someone who felt safe and comforted talking to him, though sometimes chemistry during a folky social dance would be a sufficient trigger. They were also beautiful, like me (he would say).

When his interest in them was superficial and from a distance I could play it like a shared hobby between us. People watching. But occasionally a woman triggered an incorrigible drive in him to make contact, then sink deeply into intense connections. Wounded birds crave the safety of such gentle and persistent attention, and for a while he might send long letters or have hour long calls with her. But the intensity was usually unsustainable, and they would lapse into awkwardness and avoidance, or a cooler friendship.

He would sometimes describe it as a biological imperative—women are pickier because pregnancy and childbirth are huge, high-risk investments, whereas men just want to spread the genes as far and wide as possible. He didn't fully have vocabulary then to explain that the emotional elements were as important for him. I couldn't empathize with it, this level of craving for romance and the appetite for even more complexity in our lives, even when there wasn't sex between them. But sometimes there was. Then I would just play dead, dissociating from my anger and hurt. The most galling part of these episodes was when I could find little in common with this other person. How could he love me and people so different from me?

In one case, the tryst came just as my work with Blue spiked in intensity. She was aggressively friendly with me and bent over backwards to reassure me that she respected that I was primary in David's life (which I never doubted), so it took weeks for me to figure out why I had a panic attack when she brought me a bag of granola, which we don't eat, or why her late arrival to our holiday party where she began slicing her contribution of spelt bread next to my roasted duck and gorgeous hors d'oeuvres so rattled me that I ended up in a fetal position under covers in the dark of our bedroom.

"She comes to me with an offer. She doesn't really ask me what I want," I said to Blue.

"That is right on the mark, Mai. She bears an uncanny behavioral resemblance to your mother."

And my not stopping David's pull toward loving other women was just me playing possum under the sheets when my mother wandered through my teenage bedroom at night.

Tree

Eight couldn't stay in the ICU forever; they needed those beds for people they could help. Once she stabilized, what more could they offer? There was no extra skin to graft, no clue to her coma. They didn't even know what language to use when testing whether she heard them. They tried infusing Michael's blood. They managed to take her off oxygen and relax the rigor in her limbs, but that was all.

Unlike the Little Girls, Michael had faded beyond where I could speak with him directly. Even when we inhabited the same space, I didn't believe enough in his voice anymore to hear it. But I let him self-conjure when the Girls needed him, with the timing and reflex of a parent with one eye open, one eye closed. To them, he was wholly Real. I watched with gratitude.

Now Michael sat by Eight's side almost every day. He didn't want to be there but couldn't bear the thought of not. Seven, on the other hand, was desperate to visit and convinced the adventure could only turn out well. She bounced from foot to foot, pestering me with questions.

"Is Sister awake yet?"

"No."

"Does she need socks or a teddy bear?"

"The nurses will take care of that."

"Can we see her? Please?"

"They don't let children into that part of the hospital."

"What's wrong with Sister?"

I hesitated, then took Blue's advice and said something vague about her having been hurt and no one knows how. I tried to distract Seven, but she got the others into it. Four bounced in a circle holding Baby's hands and chanted "Sister, Sister" to the tune of Frere Jacques.

My head was foggy with the Little Girls so agitated. I hoarded my time alone; it was hard to sustain external conversation without real effort.

The ICU staff asked every day if we had plans for Eight's care after she was discharged, but I had nothing new to offer.

As I puzzled over this one morning, I headed toward the double doors of my office building. I saw my hand on the glass, felt its chill underneath. In the same moment,....

I was also lying in the ICU behind Eight's eyes and wondering with Seven when it would be safe for her to visit.

I sat on the floor in Blue's office the next day to get more circulation into my tired legs.

"I can't do very much for her. I'm farming it out to Michael and the nurses."

"And in that way, you're taking care of her, Mai."

"I wish the Little Girls would stop moving around so much."

"Moving around. What do you mean?"

"I see them moving out the corner of my eye. This one then that one, this way then that way. There's too much commotion. I wish they would sit still for a while. I can't keep up with all the activity." They pricked my consciousness the way a toddler tugs persistently on your pant leg. My voice was thin and my throat parched.

"They seem like they're anxious to get to know one another. There's tremendous progress in the way you've found and brought together all these different pieces of...."

"I DON'T KNOW WHO I AM!" I screamed. And then as suddenly as they began, the sobs stopped, like an August storm. I sat still, my brain washed glassy and blank, my eyelashes lapping against swollen tissues under my eyes.

Blue waited until my breathing was normal again. I felt his eyes tracking my clinical trajectory, where I'd been, where I was headed. To me this felt like backsliding into chaos.

"No, you're on the right path. It may be hard to believe, but you're getting closer to normal...."

I wasn't sure I'd survive the journey.

Suddenly, our house wasn't safe enough for Michael or the Little Girls. It was too easy for random people to wander in off the streets. It wasn't safe to have them spread out in various places either—at home and the hospital, sometimes tagging along with me to work.

We needed to consolidate. I found a tree house perched in a giant baobab tree tucked in a forest clearing several hundred yards from the nearest road. It had a wrap-around porch from where you could see everything around the clearing's perimeter. A rope ladder hung next to a pulley and both rose to a hatch door in the porch floor. A basket attached to the pulley was large enough to hold a small person.

The other Little Girls climbed up, then I called the hospital to bring Eight to the road. Michael and I carried her to the tree and raised her up in the basket. Then he pulled up the ladder and let the hatch slam shut with a thud and small puff of dust as I watched from below.

I went home and slept soundly for the first time in weeks. Blue called to check on me the next day, worried my depression might deepen.

When they slept in the tree house, I slept. When they moved around, my adrenaline surged and Michael took his look-out post. I moved the tree house to a tropical island. An uncharted one, like Blue suggested. Only I knew where it was, and there were hundreds of miles of ocean all around.

Pieces

Weeks after Michael and the Little Girls withdrew to the island, I still saw them occasionally. Their tempos never seemed to coincide; one character launched into motion just when he or she sensed my focus had landed on another. Once or twice a day, I managed to get them all down to sleep up in their aerie, and exhaled briefly.

"Do they talk with you or each other about the Eight-year-old?" Blue asked in my next session. "Do *they* know why she's the way she is?"

"You're making them move around again," I said tensely. I just needed everyone to leave them alone so they would settle down.

"Hush—shhhhh," he commanded. I cried softly from the exhaustion.

"Maybe there's a way for you to put some distance between you and them for a while…."

I tried leaving them to their own devices. They had plenty of food and water and mangos at this time of year, for God's sake. Nobody would find them. The island faded to a dot on the map, the cloying smell of tropical fruit fading into night air.

Unable to see them on the island, I wandered through work, kids, and groceries over the next few days. But now my fingers typed autonomously to finish editing my next journal manuscript. I watched distantly as my legs alternated on the sidewalk and my hands choreographed supper over the stove on their own.

At the end of the week, I sat down on the bathroom floor to consider my options. I could stay hollow and calm, or let them come back and risk chaos again.

Regardless of which option won out, I needed a system to track everything. So on a Sunday morning as the kids fought over bacon, I opened a laptop and built a spreadsheet, labeling row headers with their names in age order. Column headers listed characteristics to index. I started filling in easy ones, adjusting column widths and font sizes and hitting "Wrap Text" as the descriptions lengthened.

	Color	Flavor	How I met them	How they relate to each other	How they relate to people
Baby	Magenta	Soft, trusting, watchful, observant, needs a lot of sleep, can crawl but mostly sits or leans against people	Showed up with Four. Slept in our bed		Sleeps on David
4-year-old	Yellow	Bouncy, loud, bossy, laughing, likes to climb on anything, quiz people, bobbed hair and dresses with petticoats	Showed up after Seven, runs around trying to get attention, opening everything	Likes to teach Baby things. Likes to ask questions of everyone	Has her run of our house
7-year-old	Blue	Competent, efficient, self-directed, quiet explorer, methodical, wore a white Twiggy shift dress, short hair	Went to meet her on her way to school. She saw that I looked familiar, but was accepting. Didn't mind that she was the only one who could see and hear me. Went to classes with her. Sat in a puddle of untouchable purple ink for a few weeks	Finds Four annoying, trusts Teen, adores Michael	Curious. Likes to ask other people to teach her things. Likes to have a companion when she explores
8-year-old	Black	Burned, bruised, cringing, a giant startle reflex, tentative, afraid to move, numb from the waist down, naked	On the railroad bridge	Is the last to become aware of the others. The rest want to take care of her.	Doesn't want to have anything to do with anyone except Michael and me
Teenager	Purple	Moody, pensive, solitary. Caretaker.	Came with the Little Girls	Big sister	Quick to help. People trust her.
Michael	Gray	Strong and silent, always available, empathic, multi-lingual, modest, musical	In waking dreams when I was 9, flying, super-hero	Takes care of everybody, including me. Everybody's confidant	Respected, modest, leader

Thirty boxes. The edges of the array were no longer visible in one view, having crept onto another screen page. The laptop might crack and explode any minute. I closed it and watched the power indicator light blink its blue eye into hibernation, then went upstairs and sank beneath bed covers where it was dark.

Michaela

> One and one-half wandering Jews
> Free to wander wherever they choose
> Are traveling together in the Sangre de Cristo
> The Blood of Christ Mountains of New Mexico
> On the last leg of a journey
> They started a long time ago
> The arc of a love affair
> Rainbows in high desert air
> Mountain passes slipping into stone
> Hearts and bones, hearts and bones, hearts and bones....
> —*Hearts and Bones*
> Paul Simon

David was born to a tribe of St. Louis Jews, of great-great-grandparents who had migrated from the land straddling Ukraine, Russia, Lithuania, and Poland. They settled in suburbs stretching north and west. Some became merchants and salespeople, accountants and business leaders, and prospered. Their descendants built summer homes in the Ozarks and joined synagogues where parking lots crawl with sport utility vehicles. Others struggled to meet middle class aspirations; many just wanted to assimilate. David's grandparents sent his mother to Christian Sunday school.

By the time his parents married, it no longer seemed compelling to pass on the old traditions to their children. Into this void poured the liberal, secular values of New England, where David's father began his career as a college professor, and the agitating social consciousness of his feminist mother and school teachers.

David learned to celebrate Christmas as the pagan holiday it originally was, and to warily eye all organized religion. By the time we met, I had been to more Seders than he had. We listened to Paul Simon sing about his and Carrie Fisher's relationship and joked, "Who's the one, and who's the half?"

My parents became Catholic in Sài Gòn, in acts of conversion that completed their separation from the Communist north and the most passive elements of their parents' Buddhism. They proudly had their children baptized in Notre Dame Basilica, the city's spiritual core, where twenty-nine years later and pregnant, I gingerly navigated herds of bicycles and romancing Vietnamese teens huddled together on the plaza outside.

Unlike for Ân and Chương, my baptism didn't take. Once in America and without memories of churchgoing in Việt Nam, I was buffeted by my parents' split allegiances. Some Sundays, we went to the Irish Catholic church in Mt. Airy, where they still used Latin for services and we were the only dark faces in a sea of ruddy complexions. Other Sundays we drove to the Vietnamese church in South Philly. Some Sundays we went to no church at all. My brief choir career was in a Baptist congregation. And because it was unavoidable growing up in Philadelphia, I sat through Quaker meetings too, with one friend or another.

The lessons were opaque to me. I did not feel host to a Holy Ghost. I was not comfortable with the notion that someone had died for me and sins I hadn't yet committed. I was never confident that what I did with the communion wafer once laid in my mouth was proper. I went into a confession booth once and left befuddled after five minutes, having said nothing. A pillar of the Irish congregation sponsored a Vietnamese refugee boy my age, and once invited me over for a playdate, at the end of which I was horrified at her hypocrisy when she screamed at him and he begged me to help get him out.

Except for the comfort it gave my parents, and the music, none of it was healing. No one sat me down to explain where the story began and how it ended. No one, it seemed, was willing to convince me to care. No one worried that I did not. When I was done admiring hats in pews ahead during services, I wandered off to meet Michael.

My grandmother's Buddhism stood as counterpoint to the church, but I knew that was also an unlikely home for me. I was too discontented, addicted to imbalance and the drive it breeds to make change. I would be a failed Buddhist even before trying, for just worrying about failing.

I had but a handful of Jewish classmates and they weren't my closest friends; my parents had none. But even from a distance, I felt a twinge of envy. In those houses, everything seemed fair game for discussion. It seemed normal to argue, question, doubt. Those families wielded sarcasm and irreverence like whips, and somehow at the end of the day, knowing what it was to be outsiders and having to pass, they remembered to feel simultaneously burdened and fortunate.

Those houses seemed much more expansive than Catholic chapels. If I had a house like that, I imagined, I could ask what place I have in the world, and what I should do for it. I could explore where my story began and how it might end. Somehow, I believed, that story would curve on itself, and bring me back to my grandparents.

I never spoke of my curiosity about Judaism with my parents. My father's Catholicism seemed to deepen as he aged.

Neither did I take much action to explore Judaism and that suited David just fine. We floated through our early marriage not committing to any spiritual home except our folk dance community, chasing Maypoles and other seasonal rituals because they were honest but not overly serious. We accepted Passover invitations and fought over whether our Christmas tree should be live or artificial.

Still, I would occasionally probe and listened for cues from Jewish friends.

David and an older Jewish friend struggled with the politics of Israel and were astonished I would consider converting. I asked one Jewish classmate in medical school what she thought of choice.

"Converts don't really fit with the whole Chosen People thing," she said off-handedly, shrugging. Her quip set me back from thinking about it again for years.

Then three months after Alexander was born, I began to wonder again. As progesterone drained from my body, I craved something more. I missed the music. A neighborhood friend suggested a visit to her Episcopalian church.

"It's very ecumenical," she promised, "And half the members are agnostic."

I decided to try. The half-mile walk helped me settle into a calm, reflective frame of mind. I sat on the end of a rear pew by the center aisle, to better see the minister and follow the sermon. When the singing began, I opened the hymnal.

There the problem lay bare. I couldn't speak the words "Christ" or "Savior," not even mouth them. How did this happen? Every verse posed this hurdle. My brain pinched and my tongue lodged in the roof of my mouth. I quietly closed the hymnal and slipped out. I used the walk home to forget what had happened. Just outside the door, my milk let down and the baby wailed inside.

I thought nothing more of it until several years later when I was exhausted from my tug of war with Michael's ghost. I could see the arc of my affair with him coming to an end. I needed new internal scaffolding, something convincing to take his place. And then came the quiet realization that it had been waiting there all along for me to claim.

I shopped for a conversion class. After three friends separately told me the same story of how their rabbi, Danny Zemel, had called all non-Jewish spouses up to the bema during Rosh Hashanah to thank them for their support, that seemed a clear sign. He sounded like a good rabbi to learn from.

We had a long get-to-know conversation by phone, near the end of which I explained how I always felt alone among my siblings and cousins in my need to probe family history, especially against so much resistance from our elders. It made me paranoid about missing something they already knew, or feeling cursed in some way they were not.

"Well that's an easy puzzle," Danny said, "In every family, Mai, there is only ever one keeper of stories. Sorry kid, but that's you."

Then he got down to business. "I only have one requirement for enrolling…. Do you have a good sense of humor?"

"It's excellent … but I thought you were supposed to turn me away three times?"

"It depends on how good your sense of humor is, and you've got spunk. You're in! See you on Tuesday."

I fell in love with him on the first night in the basement of Temple Micah, and again when we spent a quiet hour talking. Each class wound around his ongoing, internal dialogue about his inspirations, doubts, and associations with a given tenet or tradition. Another rabbi joined the class for a refresher. Danny stuttered with a child's excitement over every scholarly detail and whenever we stumped him with a question. He cried when talking about Israel and rolled his eyes when someone asked repeatedly how God could forgive us on Yom Kippur if the people we wronged refused to forgive us first.

"Not everything in life gets resolved, you know." We argued more loudly after that, and the low-ceilinged basement classroom felt as large as I had hoped.

One Sunday night the following June, I bathed and removed my nail polish and printed out my conversion statement. The next morning, David drove me and the kids to a conservative synagogue because Danny's temple didn't have a mikvah for the ritual bath. I passed before the beth din, the panel of wise people reviewing my desire to convert. Then naked, I walked into the dark mikvah waters.

When I emerged, flushed and lightheaded from the steam, Danny inscribed my chosen Hebrew name on the conversion certificate, and Michaela was born, again. I didn't advertise it with my family, but all my friends were thrilled for me.

"I already considered you a Jew," a girlfriend reassured me. "This was a mere formality."

It had been only eight months since I told Blue I wanted to convert. He's a rock guitarist and had solemnly warned me to think twice about adopting a tradition where nearly all the music was in a minor key, but he was astonished and proud at the efficiency with which I went about it.

"Michael was Jewish…," he began wonderingly.

"Half Jewish," I corrected him.

"His mother was Jewish, so he was Jewish," Blue pressed, "and you somehow knew that many years ago."

"Yes," I answered. Wasn't that always clear?

I am the one, and the half.

Well

"Ow! *OUCH.*" The screech out of me was like a cat being dismembered.

"What's happening? What's happening *right now*, Mai?" Blue hated it when things like this whipsawed him near the end of the hour.

Waking had terrified Eight. It catapulted her from sub-sleep into acute pain, a raw awareness of her blackness, of the smoky whiff of burnt flesh left to cool into coal, the threat of fresh air rushing past exposed nerve endings. Her eyelids fluttered.

In a throbbing panic, I swept her out of the tree house, down, down, to the bottom of a well.

When the scare of our flight subsided, she crouched and sat vigilant for days. She scanned the well's six-foot diameter stone wall, checking there were no openings where bad surprises might come through. The clay soil floor was solid. A trickle of fresh water skid down a crooked track on the wall. When it made a small pool the size of her foot, she was overcome with fatigue and lay down. This was sleep, finally, not coma.

On the fifth day, her eyes cautiously wandered up the wall. She heard soft scuttling noises up there and saw a teaspoon of dust sparkle on its way down. Around the circle of light above, small things moved—fingertips, a hand, dark hair. Seven, Four, and Teen lifting Baby up to peer over the rim, their faces silhouetted against the morning sky.

"She's a mess," I croaked. "I shouldn't have let her wake up."

"What's hurting her?" Blue asked gently.

"I don't know. She can't talk. Everything hurts," The despair might have been mine, or hers. I couldn't tell.

Blue insisted this was progress. She had woken up and was aware of the other Little Girls. She was safe in the well. And she knew who she was.

Wherever I was headed clinically, my psychological journey seemed to accelerate. Where it had taken months to watch Eight go from the bridge to the treehouse, now some fresh understanding pelted me every few days.

Eight had had enough sleep. She gingerly straightened out her limbs. She lightened from black to the color of an early summer tan, and muscle began regenerating in her limbs, buttocks and face. She lay waiting. I heard her call voicelessly; a craving, not a sound.

I jolted out of sleep in my bed, head lifting off the pillow.

But ... it wasn't me she was calling.

Michael stood waiting against the well's wall when something clawed and snagged him, and wound him backwards on a thin spindle of time. He grew younger—thirty-something, then nineteen, fifteen—regressing so rapidly that his clothes disintegrated and none of his younger revisions had time to blink before he passed back to earlier in childhood.

At ten years old, the clock slowed and baby fat filled in his jowls. The glasses were gone, his hair brightened to a golden red. At nine years old, he lay down, naked, next to Eight. He had no memory of Rich, of meeting me, or of the man he had been.

She stretched her fingers to reach for him. Where her fingertips touched his, their fleshy pads fused. They turned to each other, ten fingers on ten, while their fibers comingled and his plasma coursed through her.

"What do they say to each other?" Blue asked.

"He's just so relieved to be reunited with her. I don't understand anything else they're saying."

"You mean they're describing something that doesn't make sense to you?"

"No. They're using a language I don't understand, just snippets of thoughts and phrases. He doesn't talk to me. He doesn't even *know* me anymore."

Flash. Her hand, fingers tented on the wall, a long time ago, as it happened in my trance. When her back pressed into the wall's plaster, Michael budded off from her, taking the vital yang with him, leaving her desiccated, black and alone in that dark room.

He stood watching a moment, frozen and helpless, before flying up-up-and-away. I drew a sharp breath at this reenactment of their moment of fragmentation.

"He didn't want to leave her," I explained to Blue, my face streaked with tears. "She made him go. That's why he was so sad all those years. How could he leave her like that?"

"He left her in order to take care of you, Mai."

He left her by the wall, and though she had pushed him to leave and save himself, she felt so alone in her desiccation, the only place she could live out her coma was on the railroad bridge.

That Saturday afternoon, I prepared for dinner guests. I stood alone at the grill in our back yard, slowly poking metal tongs at burgers and portabella mushrooms as an excuse to turn my back on company. Michael was half of her, half of me. What did he take from her? What did he leave behind? Why was he a boy?

I pushed the spatula under a shrunken meat patty and lifted it onto an upper rack away from direct gas heat, its edges cracked and oozing juices, with bits of onion threatening to fall away, singed *black*.

Flash. Her burned body. Flash. Her body against the plaster, the small of her back arching away, her eyes traveling from her toes, up her legs, to....

I turned the flame down low and closed the grill. I brushed past a cluster of friends on the steps to get inside the house. While the meat sweltered, I closed the bathroom door, sat on the toilet cover, and loosed my feet from my flip flops. My eyes traveled from *my* toes up the curves of *my* shins and past the hem of *my* shorts. Of course. He was a boy ... so he wouldn't have a vagina. It was for his own protection.

Preparation

In my fifth year with Blue, I dreamt the longest dream ever....
I'm on the first floor of a stone house with several children and a woman. We sit on a sofa. The woman wears a black Morgan le Fay dress with long sleeves and a train trailing behind. Suddenly, a man shouts from upstairs that it's time to see something. The woman leads the children into the foyer where they each put on a helmet, then climb to the man.

Above him, hovering and shrouded in a halo of light, is a little girl. She appears to be made of fire, but cool flames, not hot. She projects images that the helmets receive. They stare at images on the fringes of her halo but can't look at one in the center because to view her head-on would burn their eyes.

Trailing behind, I put on my helmet and then reaching into my pocket, I find a yellow strip that feels like a fruit roll. It's two inches wide and six inches long. I stick it on my forehead then, fully protected, begin climbing to meet the burning girl.

Flash.

I'm in an alley. Children come running. I don't know any of them. They swarm over me in play. I feel a hand slip into my pocket and shake them off. I hold out my hand without understanding why. One of the boys pulls from his pocket a yellow strip that looks like a fruit roll. I take it back as the children run off and wave for me to follow inside a stone house.

Flash. More cycles follow, each starting a little earlier in the dream narrative, until I have thoroughly rehearsed confronting the burning girl and preparing to receive her truth.

The alarm clock sounded. Climbing stairs to Blue's office, my arms and legs felt light and distant, like after a hard mile run.

"My people are preparing me," I said to Blue.

"And who is the burning girl?"

The one who knows everything? "She's ... me."

He nodded; there wasn't much else to say.

A yellow strip across my forehead is grief, meditation, a third eye to the wisdom of the lost and departed, because Vietnamese wear mourning headbands when loved ones die. At my grandmother's funeral, and again for my aunt just a few months later, my mother and her siblings wore yellow cloth across our foreheads, which seemed almost necessary to bind together the structure of their tired, tear-blotched faces, as if their the flesh might fall off without support. The rest of the family wore white bands. They were as wide as half the height of the kids' faces. On me, the fabric cinched tightly; it concentrated everything to do with the dead into a thick, sludgy reduction that filled behind my eyes.

Tiger

Over the following year as Michael and Eight gradually reintegrated with one another, tigers appeared to me in a series of dreams.

I'm outside in a wild place where orange dust covers the ground. It could be a canyon, or a quarry. I notice two large, orange-on-white tigers stalking me on opposite ledges high above. They circle, shoulders undulating with each stride. I scan the canyon surface for an escape route and realize the quarry has filled with rainwater. I glide in and tread water, hoping to hide long enough for them to lose interest, but they also slip into the water. These cats can swim! I can't stay ahead of them; I'm a mediocre swimmer. I will hold my breath and stay underwater as long as I can. Cats don't dive, do they?

Flash

I'm standing in a village on flat terrain the same rusty orange color as the quarry. People mill about, tending children and making food. Out of the corner of my eye, I spot a white and orange Tiger approaching the village. People scatter in alarm and scramble into huts.

I run inside my hut and heave my weight against the door to slam it shut, just as the thud of Tiger's face pounds the outside. Tiger penetrates my door, punching one large white paw through. My door doesn't break or splinter because it isn't rigid. Tiger's paw juts through between the torn panels like through the seam of a cardboard box where flaps fold on top of one another; like through leather, through skin. I put both hands on the paw and try to push it back out of my house, but Tiger is stronger than me. Its front quarter comes through, then a shoulder, a large white head, a second leg. It drops its paws to the floor and I shift my hands to its face. I ring my fingers around its muzzle to keep it shut, not quite covering the circumference, and again push with all my weight. But Tiger keeps advancing, sliding me backwards on my bare feet. I'm a child and it's much heavier than I am. The opening in my door has stretched far and wide but without tearing, to the width of Tiger's torso.

Now Tiger stands its entire body in my living space, tail elegantly switching. Overpowered and cornered, I call out to someone in the kitchen to bring a dish of food. If I give Tiger something to please it, maybe it won't hurt me. When the dish appears, Tiger hunches its shoulders, lowers its head without a single growl and patiently laps up the kibbles.

David touched the small of my back and I woke up.

Still fuzzy-headed and on my way to Blue's office that morning, my foot touched on a cross walk as the symbolic meaning of a Tiger pushing its way through my door seeped in. Benjamin had had a harder time getting through my birth canal than Tiger did. I realized I knew who Tiger was, and that he had a human form.... I paused mid-step and a taxi honked.

"It must have been frightening for a little girl to be invaded like that," Blue said in a way that left off the question mark at the end of a query.

He waited just a little too long for a response, then pivoted. "How does thinking that you know who the Tiger was make you feel?"

There was a wall of space between him and me where empathy had been just a few moments before—a shield or a prison, I couldn't tell.

It was a relief to know Tiger's identity; one less mystery to consume my energy, but which particular person Tiger was didn't matter. Blue was after what mattered.

"It separates me from other people, because I'm the type of person it would happen to and other people aren't."

On my side of the separation from Blue, I felt numb. He didn't try to challenge my use of a hypothetical rather than a past tense.

"It also separates you from yourself, Mai," he said for me, leaning forward into the divide then sitting back again when my back stiffened at his physical invasion of my space, "although I do think that is improving. Getting to know the Eight-year-old helps with that."

Lioness

By the time Tiger appeared, Eight was well enough to sit in my lap, though she flew down to the well at night to rest with Michael. Fingertips still attached to him at times, she grew stronger every day from the inflow of his life force. I wrapped my arms around her lightly as I coasted in rush-hour traffic to work. She felt as heavy as Alexander, which was a good sign.

After a couple weeks of this, just as I felt compelled to lift her and uncross my legs from numbness, she flew out of the well one last time. Maybe she smelled early summer, maybe it just felt too humid down there with the change in season. Most likely, she didn't fit there anymore. She had enough muscle tone now to stretch her limbs and move about.

The Little Girls and Michael went to the pool David and I took our kids to. Teen held Baby's hands as she toddled around in water at the level of her chest, while Four and Seven chased each other around the fountain.

Eight sat by herself in shallows wearing a white swim suit. Waves from the others' activity lapped past her feet and extended legs, up to her middle. She closed her eyes and leaned back on her hands. With sunglasses, she would have passed for a little heiress on the French Riviera.

"She likes how the water feels when it reaches her crotch," I explained to Blue.

"Why?"

"It's soothing. Her crotch is irritated and the water is cool."

"What happened to her crotch?"

I looked at him a while before remembering he didn't know what it was like to have a vulva. It just gets irritated sometimes.

"The thing is, I don't see Michael anywhere. I don't think he's still in the well, but he's not in the pool either. And Eight doesn't seem worried that he's not there. I don't understand that; they were so clingy with one another."

Eight knew exactly where he was. She could feel his limbs unfurling to fill up her own, inside, like a foot in a sock. She stood and waded into the pool until water reached her waist. She stood there, arms outstretched into an "A" along her sides and fingertips resting on the water's surface, soaking in the sun.

* * *

I quit my job at the end of my fourth year with Blue. Because it was my first "grown-up" job after more than a decade of schooling and training, it took some time for me to build up to the decision, but when it came, I was excited to segue into more responsibility for making policy decisions.

I landed at the federal agency responsible for running Medicare and Medicaid, in a new unit established by the Affordable Care Act as the research and development arm of the agency. Tasked with rapidly testing and spreading novel ways of paying for and delivering health care that could improve health and lower spending, the Innovation Center was a generously funded government start-up guaranteed to be burdened with high expectations and tremendous scrutiny—from the industry, lawmakers, and the media.

This meant it was *the* "room where it happened" for the issues I cared about most in health care. The center director looked around at the half dozen employees at his disposal in October of 2010, a bare six months after the law passed, and assigned to me the stand-up of what would become one of our flagship programs.

My first week on the job, I settled into a new routine. Rise at 6:15 a.m. and grope in the dark to make school lunches, shower, wake up the eleven-year-old and send him out the door to the bus stop, hop in the car and navigate my highway route. David would take care of Alexander.

On the eve of day six, my parents came for their weekly visit. My mother fed us full of steamed dumplings and warm phở soup, until there was nothing left to do but fall into bed.

Near morning, before my waking, the Lioness appeared. She was tawny and sleek, barely an adolescent, the new hormone surge making each muscle swell beneath her coat. She paced in front of a door. It was her door and she was on the inside. When she turned, I saw a large wound on her flank. Its neat edges formed a rectangle, as if a flap had been cut off her surface. In the opening, parallel pink-red muscle fibers ran over her hip. The wound was old; she didn't bleed. But it still pulsed, reddening then paling with each heartbeat.

A sound from outside the door made Lioness pause mid-stride. She gazed unblinkingly at the knob, knowing there was no way to lock it, no point in a barricade. Rather than running or hiding, she dug each paw into the ground and girded herself. The door swung in.

Tiger stood there in his human form. She wasn't afraid; he was familiar and his face was calm. He even smiled faintly. A flicker passed over her face as the wound throbbed. She readied herself and Tiger crossed the threshold.

That morning, I searched for Eight while driving to work.

She was in the diving well of the pool and was underwater, legs and torso undulating mermaid style, propelling her across the tiled bottom. I watched in awe, dazzled by her ease in the deep. She had gone where none of us dared, and she would stay down there as long as necessary. Who could have guessed she would grow to be the fiercest of them all?

Storm

My girlfriends fall into two camps—those claiming to have always known good sex, no matter their life stage or the caliber of man they landed, and those claiming it is always disappointing. In middle age, I broke from the second camp by finding a new freedom and complexity of pleasures that seemed to appear from nowhere.

"What's different? What's changed?" Blue asked.

"I don't know. I'm sure David and I have each gotten better at it."

He stared at me noncommittally. "What did you *feel* during sex in the beginning?"

…nothing. Each time, after the initial dread, tunnel vision set in. I could see David, his neck, the folds of his eyelids, the underside of his chin down to the pore, but from very far away, like through the long eyepiece of a telescope.

"And where were *you*?" Blue persisted.

I was in a warm place moving my limbs freely, so far from David I couldn't feel his weight pressing on my flesh. Sometimes I felt Michael's arm falling around my shoulders.

Suddenly, while Blue waited for my response, Eight started stomping around the pool's perimeter. She had climbed out of the diving well in a rage, water flooding off her shoulders to bleed in a circle on the scorching concrete. She marched with jaw and fists clenched. She marched five, six, seven times around, glaring at me each time she passed. Her bare feet were blistered from heat and friction. Teen dragged a lounge chair into the shade of a tree with a sympathetic look, and laid a towel on it where Eight finally collapsed to fall asleep.

"Why is she so angry?" Blue asked.

"I think she's angry at me." I was sure of it. "She's angry that I didn't say 'No!'…I should've said, 'NO!'" I screeched it at him then, a pent-up screech.

"'No' to what, Mai? To whom?"

No! Don't touch me! Stay out there.

Blue watched me shrink on the edge of the sofa, the tears dripping onto my lap.

He leaned forward to say in his most matter-of-fact tone, how one explains to a child that sky is blue and grass is green because that is the nature of them, "How could you have said, 'No'? What in your experience up until that point could have possibly prepared you to say 'No'? Could you have said 'No' to leaving Việt Nam? Could you have said 'No' to learning English? To your parents?"

The stronger Eight grew over the following days, the weaker Tiger became. In the periphery of my vision, a sleekness of fur walked in an arc, crisscrossing its paws to keep eyes on me. Tiger was now white with thin gray stripes and had shrunk to the height of my hip. Shaggy skin draped over his ribs. He was meek and hungry. I felt a pang of pity.

"Was that the end of his story?" Blue asked.

"Yes," I said flatly, tears flowing. It was November, a year into my new job. The windows of Blue's office magnified atomized sunlight, sending small puffs of warmth flowing left to right over my face. I turned away from it, toward the chill of the opposite wall.

It isn't my job to feed Tiger, but he's hungry. His energy is sapped and he can't decide where to turn, whether to pace or stand or sit.

I wept silently at my helplessness and his.

The place we are in is barren, chalk dry. I'm a grown woman, not a child anymore. There must be something I can do for him. Look how thin he is.

"What *could* you do for him?" Blue asked.

"All I know to do is to let him rip into me. Is that what I should do?"

"What would that feel like, Mai?"

"Nothing. It would feel like nothing." Suddenly, the room's air was autumn crisp again and I was no longer paralyzed on the sofa. My back straightened and the tears dried, shriveling up like a throttled stream bed.

"Off like a spigot," Blue said snidely. Scanning my blank face, he sighed to himself. "It doesn't feel like nothing, Mai. It *hurts* to be ripped into."

Six months later on a quiet weekend morning, I found Eight sitting by herself. She was down by Wissahickon Creek, sitting on the bank, hands wrapped around her knees. She was still in her white swimsuit. Michael was with her.

"She doesn't want to talk to me."

"Why?" Blue asked.

I searched for a bit. "Maybe she's still angry at me?" If she were afraid, she would worry about who else was there in the woods. But she just looked out over spilling water.

I hadn't had time to wonder about her for months, too preoccupied with dramas in my new job, the serial legal, data, and political issues that threatened my program and caused my physiology to go haywire. My stress-induced hives broke out each day at dusk, the early warning of bristles under my skin creating an aura of impending doom. Blue and I spaced my sessions to every other week to make the scheduling more manageable. He hadn't resisted the logic of slowing therapy down to make room for the rest of my life.

But now his gaze intensified into something slightly unfriendly.

"You're avoiding her. You're afraid of what Eight has to say."

I frowned. I really didn't understand why he thought that.

"I'm sorry I didn't see it before," he went on. "I'm sorry I didn't realize sooner that you chose to pull back on this work just as she was recovering and able to talk…. The new job was a convenient foil."

I redirected him. "I—don't—know—what—to—do—for—her," I said through clenched teeth. I didn't like this role reversal; usually I was the one pushing us to speed up and he was trying to slow us down.

"You could just hold her," he suggested in a softer tone.

Late that night, she finally stood to turn toward me. She climbed up the slope on all fours, pitting the mossy loam with imprints from her hands and feet, leaving a zig-zag of tiny trenches and sending bits of dirt flying that made shit-colored pocks on her white suit.

She lifted her face and opened her mouth in a wide grin, showing heavy, monstrously oversized copper jaws where her tongue and teeth should have been. They were like crude implants from some medieval dungeon. She drooled from the metallic weight. I pulled her tight to my chest, stroking her hair until her lips closed softly and she drifted off to sleep.

Part Four—Harvest

Thrill

Near the end of my second year in government, my center director emailed me the article with the clipped preface—"This is bad."

It was in a trade paper, a blow-by-blow account of a too-frank discussion I had with what I thought were just economists at a think tank. Instead, a reporter had slipped into the room unannounced with a smirk and a laptop. Minus context from the overall conversation, the quotes from me read like spectacular bombs strewn across the browser page.

I said it would be much harder for our programs to save money than to just improve the quality of care; we were understaffed while battling bureaucracy and deep-seeded agency habits; hospitals and physicians might not be ready for things we were designing. A new center some considered the crown jewel of the Affordable Care Act, facing high expectations that it would solve the problem of runaway health care spending while trying to settle inside an established agency, simply couldn't afford this kind of publicity.

"I'm sorry." I emailed back. It was Thursday. He called me over the weekend. Higher-ups were furious. He warned me to lie low, and to document precisely how the speaking invitation came about and whether there were any inaccuracies in the news account. There weren't; just misrepresentations.

"You can't speak your mind that freely, Mai. You have too high a profile. People care what you say and you just said a lot."

On Friday my immediate supervisor called to check in on some outstanding documents, and I breezed through the conversation hoping he wouldn't bring up the incident. He didn't.

On Tuesday, I showed up in the office for the first time since the press story ran. The center's second-in-command, a friend, appeared at my cubicle, our press person at his side.

"Don't come to the leadership meeting today," they warned in soft tones. "This will take a while. We don't know what's going to happen yet. Don't respond to any outside inquiries."

Their faces reflected knowledge of processes I couldn't see, and a protectiveness bordering on pity.

After the leadership meeting, my immediate supervisor took me into a room and said incredulously, "You didn't tell me on Friday???"

"....I thought they already told you," I said meekly, not really believing it.

Over the rest of the week, I had occasional visits from one well-meaning colleague or another—with advice to not use my computer for unofficial purposes, to not do anything that would bring more scrutiny. On Friday, the center director called again.

"What's on your blog?" he asked. I had casually mentioned that I was blogging my memoir in an earlier conversation.

"Personal stuff," I replied, taken aback.

He told me to send him the link. He called back after a quick scan. "It says on there where you work. Take it off. Make sure you scour out anything that mentions your work."

"Why?" I asked, "I'm pretty sure I'm allowed to do this."

He persisted, "Do me a favor and check with the ethics office. Then scour the blog. If people come looking for other things to hang on you, I don't want them finding it."

"What people? Why would they come looking? You know how important this blog is to me; if I can't do this and work here, I'm not sure I can work here."

"Do like I ask," he pleaded, and I snapped back into our familiar dynamic of a teenage daughter with her new driver's license in hand, watching her father trying to anticipate her next move. I obediently called the ethics lawyer, who reassured me that if I removed any references to my work now, I wouldn't have to fill out any extra paperwork and the historical pages with those original details would disappear too. The blog platform was accommodating that way.

On Sunday I single-parented. I tried to find a distraction and wondered about a journal manuscript of mine meandering through the approval process for some months. I emailed our communications person to ask about it and he wrote back snidely—"Think about whether you really want to push this now?"

The palpitations began and I could feel my pupils dilating, red and white scotomas flitting across my field of vision. I was walking back from the Metro after dropping Benjamin off at a field trip. I punched David's number into my phone and got no response. I tried two friends without luck. November dusk set in. I called my supervisor.

"Hi, it's Mai. I'm sorry to bother you at home."

"No, no, this is a good time." I could picture him in his study, closing the door, bracing for a long conversation. He was a physician of the Marcus Wellby mold, a weather-worn practitioner who had built a small private practice and floated into national prominence because of a gift for translating those front-line experiences into policy insights that were intuitive and compelling. He was used to confessions.

"I'm in a very bad place," I told him. "What happened in that presentation was me being passionate and compelling, inspiring the audience, moving them along by being honest about our work. I'm not sure I'm a good fit for this place. I'm not sure I can rein this part of me in and even if I could, it would feel like a mortal threat to my sense of self."

"You're not any less a good fit now than you were two weeks ago," he said. "You live right on the edge. You always have, whether you knew it or not. It's where you make the magic happen. You can't see the box where other people have to talk themselves into stepping out of it. That's your superpower and your greatest liability, because if you constantly live on the edge, sometimes you're gonna go over. That's just how it is. Not much you could do about it if you tried."

"I'm not confident I can control this," I said, and the dam broke. I sobbed in desperation in the shadow of willow oaks as the park emptied out.

"It's got to hurt," he went on calmly. "It's got to hurt to give of yourself that much, that authentically, and have this one episode be judged as something so negative. But that's all it is, just one episode." He slipped into his physician mode, systematically walking through the list of diagnostic assessments.

"Are you sleeping?"

"Not really."

"Can David help?"

"He's been abroad for three weeks this month; it's hard for him to be helpful before I can debrief him on everything that's happened."

"So you've been single-parenting during all of this, too, since that part of your life doesn't just stop. What about your therapist?"

"I cut back to every other week."

He offered to translate the conversation for the center director, and we hung up. He called back a half hour later.

"Listen, I've gotten confirmation that everybody in your chain of command wants you to stay. Everybody from me way up to the head of the agency. So go to sleep, amp up the therapy, come find me tomorrow."

Monday afternoon, my supervisor hovered while I straightened papers on my desk. He eased into the chair opposite and waited.

"I'm not panicking anymore," I said, "I just feel bad."

He raised his eyebrows expectantly.

"I screwed up."

He nodded knowingly. "Shame and guilt…" He shared that some years before, he had screwed up badly enough to cost a patient's life and trigger a lawsuit.

"Was it public?" I asked.

"It's always public." He arched his head to the ceiling. "Depositions, people talking about you. I consider that the most courageous thing I've ever done was to keep coming to work throughout that time."

"How do you get over it?"

"You find people who care about you and unpack those feelings. And you keep coming to work."

So I did. I adjusted to a new routine, reinserting Blue back into my weekly life. He watched me rubbing the spasms in my neck.

"What you did doesn't really compare to causing someone to die, does it? Why so much shame, Mai?"

My shame wasn't relative to anyone else's shame. I lost sight of the actual misdeed I had done, and became preoccupied instead with the tightness in my chest that came at any mention of the incident, the warmth on my face that slid down around my shoulders, down to my hips and groin, and when it sank there, it dragged blood away from my torso, leaving the chilly vacuum that comes at the bottom of a roller coaster's swoop.

The warmth was familiar, addictive, and it anchored me to wherever I happened to be sitting. I couldn't stay standing with it in my groin or the vacuum in my chest. I had to sit.

"I know this sensation," I whispered to Blue. He watched the slight scowl forming on my brow and tensed expectantly. But no trance came. Whatever my new awareness was, it didn't declare itself that day, and we said our goodbyes.

Outside Blue's office, on my way to the car, my cell phone rang. My supervisor asked if I would be in the office the next day.

"Listen very carefully," he said. "There is an investigation. Tomorrow a woman is going to come to the office to interview you. As your immediate supervisor, I will be in the room. Answer her questions truthfully. Don't be defensive; remember she's just doing her job. Don't elaborate on any point she doesn't ask about. Look at me for cues. You understand?"

"I didn't know this was a step."

"I didn't either," he said. "Apparently the process is that they don't tell anyone until 24 hours beforehand. I'm trying to communicate the most critical points to you as efficiently as possible."

David was unfazed when I told him. "What are they going to do, fire you?" He knew it would never come to that.

The next day, I sat across from the middle-aged woman with a kind voice and a notepad, my supervisor between us. She explained the process.

Someone filed a complaint against me that triggered an internal agency investigation. She already completed interviews with other relevant people. Mine would be the last interview. She would type up a summary, and I would review it for completeness and accuracy. Then she would submit it and unnamed decision makers would review the investigation and determine if the organization should take any course of action against me.

"What actions would those be?" I asked.

She said they could determine that no action was required, or a censure, or something more drastic.

The warming sensation began to settle in when we sat down. It intensified as she spoke, until I emitted a violet-red glow. I slowed my breathing, wondering when the heat would reach their faces and make them flush. Then her questions began and she took down my responses in long hand on a yellow notepad.

"How did you come to be presenting at that gathering on that day? Did you receive permission to attend? From whom? Did you know who would be in attendance? What was the presentation supposed to be about? Who was in the room? How many people? Did you know a reporter was there? She read out aloud from the article each line quoting me. Do you remember saying this? What did you mean by it? Did you think it was appropriate to say that in public? Did you say that these were your personal opinions?"

I answered them each slowly in a thin voice.

My supervisor thanked her and showed her into the hallway, gesturing with his left hand for me to stay put. I couldn't feel my legs and couldn't have moved. He returned, closed the door gently. "I want to apologize to you on behalf of the entire agency. I am deeply impressed at how calmly you managed that interview."

We walked silently back to our section of the building, then parted ways. I couldn't go back to my desk. The weight in my groin was starting to slip downward, oozing an oily heat down the insides of my thighs, taking oxygen with it. I felt lightheaded and my teeth ached from cold. I didn't think I'd be able to sustain balance in a sitting position. I counted the steps to a hidden pleather sofa at the end of the aisle of workstations, tucked in a shadow between two windows, its seat blocked from view by a high seat back.

I lay down on my side, knees and thighs clasped together to hold the oily weight in place, drawing deep long breaths, and waited the half hour for the heat to dissipate. I knew if this had come when I was home—when I could be in my own bed behind a closed door, alone, when I could bring myself to an orgasm—that my release would have come sooner.

Over the following two weeks, I lurched between near paralysis from this heated weight, and rage. Red rage. Roaring rage. Rage that drove eviscerating fantasies of revenge and redemption, that generated white noise between my ears and glowing scotomas in front of my eyes. Each oscillation between shame and rage could pass within as little time as an hour, making each day and night a long emotional slalom.

I glared at Blue when we both returned from holiday.

"You could have called me," he said. "I told you I was checking messages."

"I was too dissociated to bother," I hurled back.

"Actually—shame and rage and back again—it sounds pretty integrated to me, Mai…."

I stared at him, incredulous. There was no snark in his voice. He didn't offer any explanation.

"What does it make you think of?" he asked more quietly.

Michael in a red room, by himself, naked on his knees on the wood floor. Michael in warm red light.

My breathing grew heavy and the sobbing began.

"He was raped … this is his feeling, this heat…….." I started.

But not the rage. Michael never felt rage.

"The rage doesn't belong to him," I explained to Blue. "It's Eight's…."

She was raped. At age eight.

"I was raped."

"That's the first time you've said that, Mai."

The rage was mine. It didn't matter that I had no concrete memory of the event. Neither Eight nor Michael would let me scrub their stain away. The shame and the rage were indelible, melded to each of their frames, bound under their skins, the blood color as true as when he and she were born of me.

Trace

The last time Eight shared something important with me, I was sitting with Blue and thinking of a map, a long tri-fold glossy of center city in Philadelphia. During the early 1990s when I was in medical school, the city health department produced these heat maps of public health priorities, on which the grid of William Penn's town was etched in pale gray, with a wide, bright red arrow shooting straight up its spine along North Broad Street through my campus in the ghetto, marking the epicenter of the HIV, measles, and drug-resistant tuberculosis epidemics.

I stared down at the arrow from the northern perspective, its head menacing upward at my torso, my body cleaved in two on either side of the avenue.

"Someone had to be there for Tiger. I had to give him what he needed, even if it literally tore me into pieces."

Blue watched me cry. "That was a terrible burden for a child to take on, for you and for him."

But Eight chose that moment to distract me. She climbed into my lap and sank into my chest and belly. Her hair was freshly shampooed and cool, the peach fuzz on her plump cheeks just visible beyond my chin. Then her frame shuddered with a giggle at something funny, and she buried her forehead in my chest to control it.

"I've never felt her so soft," I wondered out loud to Blue. "She seems … happy."

"She's come a really long way." He agreed. She had her story heard.

Within a year, Blue and I agreed to wind down our sessions. We sat one last time to celebrate our journey and mourn.

"You've been in my life, too, Mai," Blue said quietly. He meant, I could always come back if I needed, but he wouldn't be able to reach out to me. We held hands for a long minute. I felt an echo of leaving Carpenter after high school. He sat still and let me plant a kiss on his forehead.

"Hên gặp lại," (Until we meet again) I said on my way to the door.

Michael and the Little Girls settled. Now, when I'm curious about what they're up to, I conjure their scenes of mischief in a quiet moment. I might smile and say, "That's just the four-year-old in me," to explain some goofy thing I do, or feel Eight at my side when my temper flares up.

But most of the time, they all just float somewhere inside my limbs and behind my eyes, safe in the vault of my clear-eyed understanding of how much we need each other, and how strong we are.

Bah...Bah...BS

Passing for normal is like all other lies. It only works if you can keep it simple and limited to the singular falsehood. It takes a different level of commitment to sustain different lies to different audiences ... unless they aren't actually lies so much as how one serves up the same reality in different accents and cultural allusions to help them land with different people. Then, passing gradually becomes a pass-through, and the resulting chameleon serves as an ambassador to bridge and translate between tribes.

Ambassadorship like that leaves marks over time. To engage in it stretches your understanding of what is normal and your tolerance for the unfamiliar. It forces you to hold multiple and sometimes conflicting truths, and forbids black-and-white judgments. It leaves you feeling at once homeless and at home everywhere. It takes many years of uncomfortable, lonely practice to get to some semblance of acceptance of this role.

What began for me as small experiments to adapt to the different realities I grew up in—slight changes in diction and sense of humor for different groups of school friends, how often I nodded modestly for my parents' American versus Vietnamese guests—became a more permanently distorting habit. If I could mimic the Highlands' clothing styles, why not also play on flute the Scottish jigs and reels Jenny played on her bagpipes? Then why not try Scottish country dancing in college even if I was the only colored face in the crowd? Once competent at those formal Scottish traditions, it wasn't much a bridge farther to tolerate the goofy English Morris dancing that David introduced me to, then get pulled into the broader Anglo American folk music and dance scene.

I carried my formative clinical years as a doctor caring for poor communities into more sterile settings where I did research, analyzing the role of money in health care while nagged by vivid memories of how distortions in those money flows left chaos and unmet needs in the lives of the most defenseless people. Leaving research to enter government, I found myself at times caught between leaders who had to make many consequential decisions a day, and analysts who pleaded with me as a kindred spirit to slow things down just long enough to allow science and evidence some play. And as I went from government into the private sector with its anti-regulatory reflexes, my corporate and former government colleagues both joked about whether I had just left or joined the dark side.

The bridges I live on are multi-lateral. I muse at my array of allegiances—art leagues, physicians, policy wonks, Jews by choice and of color, immigrants, Vietnamese Americans, folk community, family. If I am a black sheep in any, I'm a black sheep in all of them.

Chosen

Of all the Little Girls, only Four knew she was a Princess. You could tell by how she plumped out her belly and radiated glee, and was never surprised that someone wanted to play with her or give her a choice morsel to eat. Seven was preoccupied with her scientific tinkering and figuring out how the world works. Teen had to grind day to day, trying to fix things. And Eight ... would have spat at the word Princess.

But Michael was always a Prince. He didn't need to know it; he lived it. He deserved to have Rich travel around the world to save him. Important people trusted him with secret diplomatic assignments of one kind or another. He worked hard, but the talent would've oozed out anyway. He strode across a lawn at Harvard in an anonymous graduation gown feeling no need to announce himself. His world was simply structured to acknowledge all his potential.

No matter what Blue believed, I was not six feet tall. My edges felt rougher than Michael's. Success took effort and persistence. I wasn't comfortable flattering up, as I saw some people do. And I often felt, despite degrees from elite universities, that I somehow never received that secret handbook I was convinced other people had on how to hopscotch to high professional appointments without putting in the time. I made choices that threw me back to relying on work and grit, betraying my mistrust that anyone would simply choose me the way they chose Michael.

Despite a long trail of achievements, of not only being in many rooms where it happened but having had the humbling privilege of making decisions affecting tens of millions of lives and billions of health care dollars, of earning a national profile that allowed me to change hearts and minds through writing, speeches, and debates—despite all the personal and professional milestones, the distances I had covered—I stared at a widening chasm between where I was and where Michael stood, and knew I would never catch up. I felt depleted after six years in government, but only partly from the work itself.

By the time I quit my job, it had been several years since my last session with Blue. I dialed the familiar office number.

"Some part of you feels invisible," he said, "and we know how important it is to you to be seen."

I didn't find that a compelling explanation anymore. My new skepticism that anything I could do next professionally would be meaningful was a new, and deeper doubt.

All my negative reflexes felt irrationally amped up—anger at people who couldn't keep appointments, drivers making turns without flashing signal lights, customers at checkout lines who cost me an extra fifteen minutes because they wouldn't bag their own items. Rage at some unnamed loss. But this time, it wasn't emanating from Eight. It belonged wholly to me. I knew I needed to get into a different head space before I started any new job.

I called my rabbi next. I had stopped going to Danny's temple when I began my government job; the long daily commute left me little energy for another crosstown drive each week. This rabbi led a Renewal mynian in borrowed church space, but conveniently also offered digital discussions on Wednesdays, and was married to one of my closest friends. For this conversation, we sat in his study, overlooking his garden.

"What does it mean to be chosen?" I asked.

"That's usually an easy one, Mai, but tell me, why do you ask?"

In as few words as possible, I explained to him my history of dissociation and Michael—his ease navigating the world, so enticingly lingering just ahead of me at every stage of life, waiting for me to catch up.

"If I'm not chosen," I paused momentarily as it sank in, "...Believing Michael was chosen is what kept me alive all those years. If he wasn't—if I'm not chosen, then I don't see a path forward." It was raining softly outside.

Rabbi wasn't too fazed. He knew this wasn't the usual convert's insecurity about not being a hereditary Jew.

"I usually respond to that question the way my Rebbi explained it to me … We aren't *the* chosen people, Mai. We are *a* chosen people. *Everyone* is chosen for something."

He gave that a moment.

"But for you, a crisis of faith in your own chosen-ness is maybe more about … misunderstanding." He had a way of lightly releasing the most important word in a phrase, to let it hover. "Recalibration is the path," he said, "and that'll require emptying the mind, the reflexes, the consciousness of time; anything to allow you to just experience the moment and divination of what it is you *are* chosen for."

Or what it is I choose for myself. I drove home and wandered through the next few days trying not to think, in an amateurish attempt at mindfulness. I watched Benjamin unicycle a little too fast down the sidewalk, and Alexander spend an hour using a stick to scrape away dirt around a flagstone in the back yard so he could lift it and view the busy maze of ant tunnels underneath.

I reached for Michael with one hand, checking his face to see whether he was disappointed in me, and listened for whispers from my grandparents. But Michael was as calm as ever, smiling knowingly at me over his left shoulder before turning back to whatever he was reading, and the ancestors were watchfully content. Maybe I had already done what they needed me to do and the rest was for me to choose.

Offering

He died fifty years almost to the day after he named me.

Tuấn and I brought our families to my parents' townhouse that morning to celebrate the lunar new year. Our kids were teenagers by then, too old to easily delight, but my father still made a show of giving each a bright red envelope holding a crisp fifty-dollar bill for good luck. Had my mother not been watching, he might've given twice as much. We ate red sweet rice, asparagus crab soup, spring rolls, and grilled lemongrass pork she spent all week preparing, then lazed over board games, Godiva chocolates, and cut fruit for dessert—his idea of bliss. The gathering was so routine, for once he didn't insist on group photos.

That night after we drove off, he stood up from their dinner table and crumpled heavily to the floor, eyes closed and gurgling from vomit. By the time we met my mother in the emergency room, his brain had herniated downward from the pressure of a massive thalamic hemorrhage, his limbs warm but inert except for occasional, macabre posturing indicative of brain stem failure.

Tuấn and I sent tandem texts throughout the night to Ân and Chương, our spouses, cousins, aunts and uncles; nearly all my mother's relatives were in town for the Tết holiday. It took a day for her to consent to removing life support, once she was spent from crying with her siblings in the waiting room, and another half day for him to pass. That was the ellipsis at the end of an epic existence.

I took the first watch after they removed the ventilator, trailing as nurses wheeled his bed from the ICU to a private room. Under the amber light, I massaged his limbs, still toned through no special effort other than the pace of his life. I caressed his forehead and cheekbones, recalling that same generous contour in photographs of Ông Nội and on my aunts in Việt Nam. I smiled when he snored in a familiar, obnoxious rumble, held his hand and pressed my thumb over the rounded heave of his pulse.

In retirement, he self-published another bilingual collection of short stories first printed in magazines by his friends in the local Vietnamese literary society, became a popular partner at the ballroom dance classes he dragged my mother to, survived prostate cancer, rounded the world on vacations, swam or walked miles each week, indulged in season tickets to the Kennedy Center, racked up outrageous luxury purchases, and reveled in and spoiled his grandchildren.

Going through his closet, my mother found two boxes each housing a handmade cashmere sweater he had bought for Tuấn and David, waiting for their birthdays. The receipt in one read $500. "Is it made of gold?" Tuấn asked me. And our financial forensics revealed that he had set up a small bank account kept secret from my mother, not for a mistress or to gamble with, but so he could write bigger checks for his grandkids than she would approve. Those were the only withdrawals he made from the account.

Although several of his sisters lived to their nineties and one past a hundred, he could hear the insistent whistle of time. He was determined to both avoid regrets and hungrily feast on his hạnh phúc (blessed happiness), to cancel out the weight of sadnesses from long ago.

My father and I stood opposed in basic life decisions. I'm an urban warrior who composts and lives under solar panels, married to a man who chose working for nonprofits over Microsoft, while Bố went on petrol-guzzling cruises and dreamt of his children living in McMansions. I worked in the Obama administration while he went to an inaugural ball for George Bush. He had a commendation from Pope Benedict; I was a Jew by choice.

Yet of his four children, I, the odd one and the only girl, was the one who inherited most of his impulses. We all live his work ethic and devotion to family, but I shared his discontented drive to leave some broader mark on the world, to wrestle with the question of balance between ambition and "good enough," of the stories we tell versus the truths we embody, of standing looking both backward and forward. Our mutual perplexity at how the other could arrive at such different choices, our mutual pride in one another, and cautious empathy for the other's opaque sources of pain, was the fulcrum that long held us in tension, a silent query of what might have been for either of us had all gone well.

Bố alienated a number of relatives and friends through the years over imagined slights. His paranoia over being cheated seemed to trigger more quickly and violently as he aged.

Attempting to broker a truce with one uncle, I quietly asked my father, "Do you think it's possible that when you feel this way you are really thinking about times you were cheated a long time ago? Maybe it's about the college exam in Sài Gòn? Maybe you had to fight back harder then because the stakes were higher—those were dangerous times. This is not a dangerous time, and no one is trying to cheat you now."

I did my best impersonation of Blue's steady gaze and slow speaking rhythm, to give him a beacon to present day reality. I saw a brief flash of understanding on his face, but the anchoring pull of the past was too strong for him. He calmed down, but refused to apologize to my uncle, and I let it go for the same reason I never forcefully pushed him to find a therapist; I didn't have the heart to inflict on either of my parents the pain of fully debriding so many deep wounds. Never did I believe Việt Nam would survive a true embrace of Freud. That country couldn't cry enough tears in anyone's lifetime. I thought it better to just dump Zoloft in the water supply, a mild anesthetic washing over the landscape, just until the war generations found their rest.

In one last interview a few months before he died, I asked Bố what he would most want his grandchildren to know about him. He stretched the pause over a whole minute, gazing into a corner of the dining room ceiling, mentally scanning the longitudinal file of his life rather than reaching for intuition.

"You know, I had many, many lucks," he finally said, then ran through a long list of examples, from escaping Japanese bombs when some friends did not, to getting that break-through job as an interpreter for the U.S. Army, to professors who became his boosters at Teachers' College, to having Dan Ross as a friend. My eyebrow arched higher and higher at this preposterous theory.

"Don't you think it's possible, Bố, that you made your own luck? Isn't *that* what your grandchildren should understand?"

He fell silent, neither willing to admit nor deny that truth. Chosen indeed.

We buried him in the dual plot my parents pre-selected for themselves, a few dozen paces from Bà Ngoại and my aunt, atop a sloping hill in a vast Catholic cemetery. I was responsible for orchestrating the gray day—brain whirring in both languages to manage the funeral home staff and guests, one eye on cousins from my father's side who were grossly outnumbered by my mother's more Americanized relatives, another eye on my mother, who was small, frail, and made of tears.

I remembered that we are Việt kiều—sojourners—as if exile and internment by the Washington, D.C., beltway were mere spiritual pit stops back to our ancestral rice fields and riverbank, where anxious forebearers waited with hopes and judgments so different from ours.

He was far from done with life. The asymmetry of sixty-five years of hardship and loss traded for fewer than twenty of an easier retirement stokes my deep grudge against whatever cosmic authority manages that accounting. The suddenness of his loss robbed us of that last chance to reconcile the fragmented parts of me he never knew, the remaining secrets in his psychic dungeon, and my claiming all I might inherit from the village chief, just as unreconciled national traumas float untended down the Mekong and Red Rivers.

Several years before, I felt compelled to make my own ancestor worship table in a metal sculpture class. For the legs, I bent square steel rods into long letters spelling the four last names in my and David's families. Slimmer rods formed smaller letters for names of our ancestral villages and countries, the Vietnamese, Polish, and Lithuanian syllables horizontally chasing each other around the rim to support two layers of glass on top. Photos of the dead float between the glass. Bố's slightly too-large portrait hung on the wall above.

For every civilized advance that offered my ancestors greater physical safety, longevity, or fulfillment, they had to fend off human-made scourges that threatened to shred their sense of wholeness. Influence in the court of medieval kings led them to flee in panic to Hải Dương. Long range sailing ships brought French slave masters, poverty, and rebellion. Foreign philosophies and alphabets brought Hồ Chí Minh and Catholicism, the oppositional vision of socialism to Việt Nam's native feudal Confucianism, and the psychic cleavage of civil war. Iron, steel, and America's elbowing on the world stage offered my family a frantic escape to the other side of the world. But the opportunity to begin anew one last time in one last place also swallowed, for a time, our sense of belonging in a village, of safety, worth, and empowerment. Along the way, we lost untold numbers of names, tombs, and memories.

Thus trauma bleeds. It seeps from one generation to the next in the dark of secrets, numbness and denial, staining and fraying our sense of self until its threads separate under the sticky weight of congealed blood. I could not transcend my traumas without understanding theirs and acknowledging that their breathtaking losses fueled my very existence, just as unearthing my own numerous losses fueled my eventual wholeness.

My ancestors and parents did what they had to do. And here in America a century after Bà Ngoại's story began, their insistent life force gave me the security, Internet search tools, and the luxury of access to a kind man in blue to help hunt for the many pieces lost. I hoard our gathered stories in the vault where Michael and my Little Girls sleep. I offer them up, with this book, at the altar. The gesture settled, to some degree, the persistent anxiety I've had since childhood that I was responsible for healing my ancestors.

Legacy

When I reached out to Blue for support after Bô died, he reminded me about the biology of grief—that the reason Jews practice structured mourning for a year is because humans need at least that much time, and there was no way for me to get through it any faster. But I never had the peace to focus on just letting go of my father.

Just a few months after the funeral, Alex had their first mental health crisis in school. The demands of escalating writing assignments in tenth grade collided with the unique way their autistic brain analyzed and generated concepts, and the strain of communicating those subtle ideas. The resulting stress compounded their anxiety and "stuckness" in not being able to ask for help or even responding verbally. We watched our brilliant, confident kid tighten into a coil of depression and frustration, even gestures of self-harm. Having been lulled into complacency because Alex had seemed happy and thriving in younger years, we had to scramble to find a new psychiatrist and a counselor to help us understand what was happening. I was tight with fear and helplessness. We were unbelievably lucky to get referred to a former educator I call our "autism coach," who explained to Alex this was the high price they were paying for their extreme talents, that it was all one complicated and wondrous package, and to their parents and teachers strategies that might help them. Monica also referred us to an understated psychiatrist who had trained at a center with expertise in autism and could gain Alex's trust.

In a moment of equilibrium later that year, I finally had enough peace to wonder how we had gotten to this point, about why Alex's diagnosis came so late at age nine, why finding clinicians who understood developmental disabilities like autism felt like panning for gold, and how families with fewer resources and connections than we have could possibly navigate and conquer the casually cruel system of dispersed services their disabled loved ones need. I started conversations with policy and clinical experts in our orbit, asking questions until I had affirmed my theories about why all these gaps persisted. That exploration seeded the conception of a new organization that could marry expertise in making big changes in healthcare, with authentic respect for people with intellectual and/or developmental disabilities as partners in making change.

Blue was delighted when I tentatively told him about the idea, and eager for me to take the leap long before I felt ready. He had clear vision beyond the horizon of my grief, and my hesitation at abandoning the national profile and expertise I had built in payment policy.

"I've been telling you for ten years, Mai: You'll be much happier building your own thing than working for someone else."

I had read about a sociological theory that people typically spend 10–20 years climbing in a given profession, before their growth curve and influence plateau (I was already doing my corporate job with my left hand), and thereafter they either spend the rest of their years struggling to remain relevant, or jump to a new field and new learning. I felt both that shove from behind and a wall of doubts in front of me. We had taken the kids on their first trip to Việt Nam that summer and spent a few days on a hiking and spelunking eco tour in rain forests and limestone caves. We watched as they scampered and leapt up and down craggy, slippery rocks, light and surefooted on their spindly legs like gangly grasshoppers. We struggled to keep up. Age had dulled our perception of depth and sharpened our perception of risk.

In retrospect, I was mourning my old professional life along with my father and Alex's happy childhood, all of which stretched my grieving period and made it difficult to disentangle what was feeding my paralysis. Then COVID arrived, and for a few months I found it hard to walk away from the fascinating intensity of activity at an insurance company during the start of a pandemic. I waited for signs from the universe. Then David made it clear he was supportive of my making this pivot despite the likely dramatic drop in my income. And I successfully recruited five prominent healthcare leaders to join me as founders of this new organization. Blue sarcastically asked how many signs I needed.

I quit my job in spring of 2020 and pulled together a small band of passionate volunteers and advisors. We birthed IEC (Institute for Exceptional Care), a nonprofit committed to making healthcare better and safer for people with intellectual and/or developmental disabilities so they and their families can lead their best lives. Our growth trajectory was breathtaking. We started projects to improve care in hospital emergency departments, to measure what is most important to the community about their health, to change clinical culture from one of bias and fear to one where clinicians are prepared, confident, and committed to serve this marginalized population. We built a reputation as a trusted partner who could bridge the gulf of mistrust between disability and healthcare communities. My fingertips tingled as they soaked in the newness of it all—disability history and politics, the revved up metabolic rate of a small start-up and the dark art of private fundraising, horrifying clinical stories and inspiring ones, a slew of disability acronyms, a startlingly kind and welcoming community of advocates. And the bridging reflexes I developed over a lifetime of belonging nowhere and everywhere kicked in; I discovered that, instead of leaving behind my payment policy relationships and healthcare industry street cred, I could both leverage them for IEC and bring insights from our disability work to shape broader healthcare conversations. I could sit in the middle of a virtual meeting room with insurance executives, government leaders, adults with disability, and clinicians of many stripes, and practice multi-lateral empathy for their respective desires and anxieties. The joy lay in witnessing how coaxing our diverse partners into that mindset resulted in creative, meaningful solutions that we were confident had purchase because they integrated everyone's perspectives. My missions and worlds collided in the best possible way. I have never felt so actualized in my professional life.

I imagined my father would have flashed his familiar mix of pride at my agency and bewilderment at my ditching stock options for a nonprofit venture. But I'm crafting my story now, building legacy for my children, in my country.

Immigration stretches far beyond the journeying. It is generative, feeding layers of creole narratives in the new land, until our feet anchor in its depths as if we had always stood there, and we've metabolized our trauma into something sweeter, to help build a better version of the country that everyone wants to come to.

Beloved

For all the stories uncovered and questions answered, all the documents catalogued and translated, the pointillistic portraits I generated of family history over thirty years, something truer still felt elusive. Something remained out of reach about what it was the ancestors needed me to know or give back to them. If I was responsible for healing them, what wound had I not addressed?

Like everyone else, I discovered rarefied corners of Netflix and other streaming services during the Covid-19 pandemic. One day, I came across *Fantastic Fungi,* a documentary about the remarkable biology and medicinal power of mushrooms. Near the end, the film turned toward psylocibin. I learned about its use in shamanistic traditions as a method to unblock paths to enlightenment, and evidence of its potency in relieving anxiety and fear of death in terminally ill patients. Coincidentally, the kids and I also began watching an animated series called *Undone,* that began as a sci-fi novella about time travel and mental illness in a Mexican American family but ended with a wide-eyed dive into mystical forces that shape generational trauma and healing. Benjamin and Alex enjoyed both shows and moved on, but I found something permissive and alluring there, and I couldn't let go of them.

I started telling anyone who would listen about wanting to try psilocybin, which is legal in Washington, D.C., Maryland, and Virginia. I was convinced that plant medicine was the portal to more direct communion with my ancestors. This is how I learned that among our friends I was slow to come to psychedelics. Some months later, one friend who supported "guided journeys" offered me a slot to join a group session.

This was a welcome distraction from David's most recent polyamorous episode, the first time he claimed that label. I found nothing unappealing about the young woman, who was bright and funny, kind and incredibly considerate of my feelings. But it still mystified me in a way just to the left of outright jealousy. I felt secure in the solidity of our marriage, but what could he or I have done to prevent this from happening over and over? Because this was the first time we put a name to what was happening, we went through cycles of awkward and angry conversations, trying to negotiate guardrails for complicated emotional configurations.

The morning I was to leave for the psilocybin journey, I was alone at home. David was flying back from a work trip in California. It was my grandmother's yartzeit (death anniversary), so I hastily lit incense and placed filled tea cups, fruits, and rice cakes on the alter. Then I grabbed the portrait I had painted of her, some family photos, and an overnight bag before hopping in the car for the drive to a discreet suburban location.

Over dinner, I learned that nearly all my journey-mates were women who had survived traumatic and abusive relationships. Realizing that plant medicine held therapeutic appeal for them, I remembered the caution that such journeys don't always follow a person's intentions but felt confident in my openness to whatever might come.

Our group of seven and the guides did some bonding exercises the following morning, before we each got comfortable on our air mattress with blankets, eye shades, and water bottles at the ready. I was the novice in the group, so it took the lead guide several tries to get an effective dose of macerated psilocybin and lemon juice into me. That's when they appeared.

On an open grassy plain, golden and just turning warm in mid-morning sun, Bà Ngoại came forward as the majestic and quietly commanding matriarch I remembered from Sài Gòn. Behind her I could see faint shadows of my father, my grandfathers, and dead aunties I never met. I was ready. *I have so much to share with you, I told her. I want to tell you about Alexander and my book and....*

In my mind's eye, she raised one arm and used that hand to silence me and brush aside my offerings. *We already know all that, she said. You are not taking care of what is most important right now. Focus on what's important.*

As she melted into the background, David's face then appeared. He beamed in sunglow, and I began weeping in love and joy—not sobbing, just a flood of release tears. Waves of understanding swept over and around me. Of course I loved him, which explained why, not only that he loved other women, but that they loved him—because he was lovable. I soaked a box worth of tissues, beaming.

The guides told me afterwards that at this point in my journey, I sat upright and, still blindfolded, began using uplifted hands and outstretched fingers to sense the wind. I was trying to locate where he would be returning to our house. I let my left fingers feel for direction in the air and gestured with my right hand in repeated sweeps inward, powerful arm motions and a commanding spread of my fingers in come-hither gestures to help David overcome inertia and reunite with me. Then once I was convinced he had heard my calling in the wind and was on his way, I changed my posture to use both arms in broad inward harvesting motions, to pull and guide him toward me. I danced this way, sitting on the mattress, for almost an hour. The guides told me that they and some of the other journeyers stopped to watch the theater and beauty of it all. For the first time ever, the guides considered videotaping my dancing to show me afterwards, but they didn't out of privacy concerns. It made them weep too.

And in that time, all my resistance and anxiety and mistrust of David's polyamory dissolved. All I needed to embrace was the whole of who he was.

Near the end of the journey, I wanted to see his young face from when we first met, just for fun, so I used both my thumbs to gently smooth away his face of today to uncover the layers underneath. Over my hands, I suddenly felt the gentle weight of Chương's expert sculptor hands guiding me. Then above his, those of my paternal grandfather's. Three pairs of Phạm hands helping me find my way back to my husband.

This, said Bà Ngoại, *is what we always wanted for you. This is the most important thing.*

To not just have, but treasure my beloved, as she treasured the beloved torn from her. The beloved so many of the people in the room around me did not have.

It was always about more than just survival, she explained calmly, signaling the end of her seeking and my Việt kiều sojourneying.

She left me spent and sleepy. When I finally took off the eyeshades and could refocus my eyes, the first object they lit upon was her framed portrait. Waves of remembrance washed over me of the years since I had painted it, of the many wormholes David and I had passed through with each other—his openness to and embrace of living in Việt Nam, his dogged pursuit of written history of my grandfather and other relatives, the space he made for me during years of therapy, our fluid sharing of birthing and parenting, the buffering he did between me and my mother, and his frugality and disciplined management of our family finances that allowed me to take the plunge and found a nonprofit. As he matter-of-factly reminded me each time I considered leaving a high-paying job for lesser income, "I've arranged our lives so you should never have to think about money when making career decisions."

Of course my psilocibin journey happened the weekend of Bà Ngoại's yartzeit. It was *beshert,* Yiddish for "destiny," something meant to be. She had anointed David as my beloved because she saw in him my path to making the life choices that would justify my ancestors' sacrifices, heal their losses with my happiness, and tether my sense of self to the mass of our inherited stories. I am a ghost no more.

Index

Bảo Đại (Emporer) 133

Center for Medicare and Medicaid Innovation (Innovation Center) 207

dissociated stories (my internal narratives) 34–6, 39–42, 48–52, 75, 77–8, 90, 93, 111, 160–8, 174–80, 188–93, 198–211, 219–20, 225
Dissociative Identity Disorder (explained) 157–8, 164, 183
Đổi Mới (and other newspapers edited by my grandfather) 112–4

Groves, James 124, 142

Hải Dương Province 124, 130–1, 134, 152–3, 229
Hồ Chí Minh 64, 98, 112, 115, 117, 124, 129, 229
Hồ Chí Minh City *see* Sài Gòn
Huế 114, 124

Institute for Exceptional Care 231

Jamison, Neil 104
Judaism 36, 84–5, 110, 194–8, 224–5

Lê Lợi (King) 123–4
Lê Thị Cạnh (maternal grandmother) 12–3, 15, 17, 59–61, 63–5, 81, 86–7, 93–4, 113–8, 139–42, 144, 154–6, 170, 195, 203, 234–5

Nguyễn Đức Chính (great uncle) 112–3
Nguyễn Đức Kính (maternal grandfather) 60, 63–5, 98, 111–6
Nguyễn Thị Đoan (maternal grandmother) 128–9, 151
Nguyễn Trãi 123–4

Phạm Hữu Sán (paternal grandfather) 60, 98, 125, 128–32, 153, 226, 235
Philadelphia 17, 22–4, 29–30, 66, 68–9, 73, 75, 84–6, 119, 127, 136–7, 139, 142–5, 151, 154–6, 160, 195, 219

Rosses (Faye and Dan) 10, 17, 20–1, 23, 29–30, 45–7, 60, 72, 137, 142, 144, 160, 177, 228

Sài Gòn (Ho Chi Minh City) 7–19, 59, 68, 72, 81, 92–3, 98, 104, 115, 118–9, 123, 130, 133–6, 137–48, 160, 167, 181, 194, 227

Trần Huy Liệu 64, 112–115

Understanding Vietnam (book) 124

Việt Cộng 3, 17, 89, 118
Võ Nguyên Giáp 113, 115

Zemel, Danny (rabbi) 196–7, 224

www.ingramcontent.com/pod-product-compliance
Lightning Source LLC
Chambersburg PA
CBHW070345240426
43671CB00013BA/2407